Art Smart!

Ready-to-Use Slides and Activities for Teaching Art History and Appreciation

Susan Rodriguez

photographs by Paul Blumenthal
illustrations by Cathy McNeil

FAMILY EDUCATION NETWORK
Pearson
Boston, Massachusetts 02116

Library of Congress Cataloging-in-Publication Data

Rodriguez, Susan, date.
 Art smart!
   p. cm.
  ISBN 0-13-208408-2
   1. Art appreciation—Study and teaching (Elementary)—
United States.   2. Activity programs in education—
United States.   I. Title.
N362.R63   2007   87-19133
701'.1   CIP

Printed in the United States of America

10 9 8 7 6 5 4 3 2 1

We thank the following for permitting us to use their artwork:

The Metropolitan Museum of Art in New York

Majas on Balcony, Goya; *View of Toledo*, El Greco

The National Gallery of Art in Washington, D.C.

The Swing, Fragonard; *Seascape at Port-En-Bessin*, Normandy, Seurat; *The Equatorial Jungle*, Rousseau; *Beasts of the Sea*, Matisse

The Museum of Modern Art in New York

The Starry Night, Van Gogh

Art Resource in New York

Bison; Mummy Case; Hieroglyphs with Egyptian Wall Painting; The Parthenon; Olive Gathering; Victory; Paeonius; Rose Window; Gargoyles; The Lady and the Unicorn; November; Mona Lisa, da Vinci; *Ranuccio Farnese*, Titian; *Marriage of the Virgin*, Raphael; *A Princess of the d'Este Family (Ginevra d'Este)*, Pisanello; *Sistine Chapel Ceiling*, Michelangelo; *Portrait of the Artist at His Easel*, Rembrandt; *Lady Reading at an Open Window*, Vermeer; *Still Life with Crabs and Fruit*, Van Beyeren; *The Artist and His Family*, Jordaens; *Back from the Market (or The Provider)*, Chardin; *The Ford (or Il Guado)*, Lorrain; *Keelmen Heaving in Coals by Moonlight*, Turner; *The Gleaners*, Millet; *Georges Clémenceau*, Manet; *The Cathedral of Rouen in Full Sunlight*, Monet; *At the Grenouillère*, Renoir; *Moulin Rouge*, Toulouse-Lautrec; *Still Life with Peppermint Bottle*, Cézanne; *Women of Tahiti (or On the Beach)*, Gauguin; *Still Life Chair Caning*, Picasso; *New York City*, Mondrian; *Japanese Ukiyo-e Woodblock Print; Africa Mask*

Deepest appreciation and thanks to the following people and institutions for their assistance:

Ira Bartfield, National Gallery of Art, Washington, D.C.; Deanna Cross, The Metropolitan Museum of Art: bequest of Mrs. H. O. Havemeyer; Gina Guy and Thomas Grischkowsky, The Museum of Modern Art; Irine Kim, Art Resource; Felicia Pickering, Smithsonian Institute; Marjorie K. Sieger, Division of Education, Philadelphia Museum of Art; David Silverman, University of Pennsylvania Museum; Marianne Promos, the Free Library of Philadelphia; The Luber Gallery, Philadelphia, Pennsylvania; Judith Stein, The Pennsylvania Academy of Fine Arts; Hiroshi Harada and Family, Tsuyoshi Takemori, Kampo Cultural Center, New York; the Musée D'Orsay, Paris; and Arnie Ahrenberg, Color Film Corp., Stamford, CT.

ISBN 0-13-208408-2

FAMILY EDUCATION NETWORK
Pearson
Boston, Massachusetts 02116

ABOUT THE AUTHOR

Susan Rodriguez teaches art in the Philadelphia Public Schools. She is a veteran of 18 years' experience with both regular and special needs classes, and has taught students of all ages. She has also held teaching posts at the Philadelphia Museum of Art, Temple University, and the Philadelphia Colleges of the Arts, where she remains on the faculty today.

An exhibiting artist as well as art educator, Susan Rodriguez earned her B.F.A. and M.Ed. from The Tyler School of Art. She completed the art appreciation and philosophy program at the Barnes Foundation in Merion, Pennsylvania, and also holds a Doctorate of Fine Arts from the Moore College of Art.

Susan Rodriguez is a member of the Author's Guild in New York and the National Art Education Association. She is the author of *The Special Artist's Handbook: Art Activities and Adaptive Aids for Handicapped Children* (Prentice-Hall, 1984).

to

my mother, Toby
my husband, Costa
my son, Rennie
my daughter, Nicole
...all my own true caryatids

ABOUT THIS BOOK

"Can you draw it for me?"

What art teacher hasn't been asked this tricky question! My own response? "Sure. But then, whose art would it be—yours or mine?"

The student gets the point. Not wishing to surrender ownership, a bargain is usually struck. Another way of solving the problem is sought. And, in the end, everyone is usually satisfied.

So, it *does* matter. You invested a part of yourself in your art, and you're not so eager to give it up. It is, after all, yours. For what you have made belongs to you. It is your experience.

The Chinese proverb takes this premise further:

"I hear, and I forget;
I see, and I remember;
I do, and I understand."

It is the act of *doing*—in this case, *making art*—that yields what we commonly call experience. The byproduct of an interactive process, experience is the strongest possible basis for full understanding. Clearly, this applies not only to the act of making art, but to appreciating it as well.

To teach children appreciation and history has been something of a *bête noire* in art education. Many of us have our own unspectacular, cloudy memories of college art history survey courses. The recollection is too often one of a monotonous voice in a dark room, mercilessly recounting names and dates to the drone of a projector. Perish the thought of inflicting this on our own students! As educators, we know just how disastrous such an introduction to art history and appreciation can be—particularly for young learners. We would do anything to avoid it, yet problems remain.

How can art appreciation be fully integrated into our curriculum effectively? How will it have the greatest impact? Giving information about art and artists is fine, but is it enough? How, in fact, can we bring art history to life—and make it stick?

The method that addresses all of these concerns is surprisingly simple. It permits discovery and leaves room for individual interpretation. It is also a way to recreate great works and periods of art, while learning all about artists and their times. The means by which this can be accomplished is the most convincing, readily available, and personally meaningful—and it's none other than the student's own art! It is to this principle that *Art Smart* wholly dedicates its task.

Exposure to slides and reproductions of major periods of art and artists is coupled with lively discussion and often includes visual or movement exercises. But most important, an art activity that encapsulates the style and characteristic quality of the artist or art period follows. This activity by no means suggests mimicry, such as the repeated copying of artists' works from reproductions. On the contrary, learning art history and appreciation through the process of *doing* invites active involvement and invention.

Art Smart! lessons are designed to teach students about the particular influences and forces that have acted upon major artists. Students will respond to these influences by drawing upon their own base of experience—an indispensable part of both the creative and educational processes. We tend to integrate information that is received in this vital way, for it becomes part of us. The artwork that results from such a course of action is original—and is far more memorable to the student who makes it. It is one thing to be told about an Egyptian wall painting, another thing to examine an ancient clay wall covered with powerful images—and quite another thing to paint the wall yourself! In *Art Smart!*, we try to get as close to painting that ancient Egyptian wall as we possibly can, given the circumstances of classroom presentation.

There is nothing passive about *Art Smart!*, but then, there is nothing passive about art. When we internalize art and art history—in the words of the wise Chinese sage, only when we "do"—then do we truly understand. And in so doing, we come to know art history and the artists who have shaped the way we see our world. They no longer remain hard-to-pronounce names in some book, alien and foreign, with no association to us at all—*Art Smart!* activities acquaint us in a way that will make the art and artists more real to us. In effect, we will make friends with art history. The natural outcome of such a relationship is appreciation.

The benefits of appreciation are plentiful. Appreciation comes to us by way of understanding and familiarity. That with which we've become familiar has new meaning and implication. We can be comfortable with our knowledge, for we've earned it through our own art.

As we travel through art history, we just might find that we want to learn more. Familiarity has, again, given us the needed confidence for honest appreciation. Entering a museum will be like catching up with dear old friends. Students will recognize and enjoy what they see, and bring to the art an intimate, working awareness. They will not be intimidated by the art on the walls, as are many adults, who defensively cry, "I may not know much about art, but I know what I like!"

After we've become "art smart," we'll know quite a bit about art, firsthand, and we can say with assurance, "We like what we know!" With this comes the invitation to a lifelong membership in the appreciation and enjoyment of art.

What more could any art teacher want?

Susan Rodriguez

HOW TO USE THIS BOOK

Art Smart! is specifically designed to introduce children to art history and appreciation in the most engaging manner possible. Clearly, we would be delighted for our students to become "art smart." But we'd be even more gratified if their interest extends into an ongoing involvement with art. History, and the appreciation of art, is the source to which all great art works have a debt. Every artist is indeed the sum of past experience and certain influence. Nowhere is this reality more identifiable and better illustrated than in the history of art.

Art history is the lineage that links time and cultures. From the compelling art of the Stone Age cave to the wooden Polynesian icons that so affected the artist Gauguin, from the exquisitely detailed Persian miniatures to the striking patterns of Henri Matisse—influences reach out and cross over generations. East to West, Cro-Magnon to Computer Art, the past is there. There is a logical sequence, a cause and effect—and we are the products of it. It is, in fact, our heritage. As promising young artists, the more we find out about our history, the greater our chances for contributing to it.

THE LANGUAGE OF ART

Art Smart! begins with the belief that the most simple and direct means for learning art history and appreciation are the most effective, particularly for children. You will, therefore, find a general absence of vocabulary words that might otherwise proliferate in college art history texts. Words like "chiaroscuro" and "sfumato" may be of some interest to older students, but tend to confuse younger ones. Often, they are beside the point and distract rather than describe. Therefore, the students' own vocabulary will serve as a basis for discussing works of art.

This will fulfill a definite purpose. Students will not be discouraged by words they don't understand, and they can feel comfortable with their own vocabulary. Art history itself becomes more accessible when put in clear, everyday language. It starts students off on a sure footing.

This is, of course, not to imply that you should avoid introducing new words when appropriate. Opportunities can be seized for building descriptive vocabulary skills. Merely watch out for use of terms that obscure meanings.

There are, however, four uncomplicated but very important words that students should know. They are

- Light
- Line
- Color
- Space

These represent *the four elements of art.* They are present, to a greater or lesser degree, *in every single painting.* When considering works of art, a question that addresses these elements can lead to comprehensive discussion. Use them to open up dialogue on the paintings you see in slides, reproductions, or on museum walls. Students should become familiar with these elements when they talk about art.

Another art vocabulary "must" is the terminology for identification of art subjects. Students should be aware of the differences between and the meanings of

- Still Life
- Landscape
- Portraiture

These categories can be further defined ("landscape," for example, can be splintered into "cityscape," "seascape," etc.) depending on the age level of your students. Nonetheless, these three items are the solid building blocks which will help students to recognize subject matter. It is necessary for students to learn them. Specific lessons will reinforce this knowledge and widen its application.

Other art vocabulary terms will surface in the process of presenting *Art Smart!* lessons. You may want students to keep their own vocabulary lists while you build an accompanying art glossary. But many of the lessons will in themselves introduce words to students, such as "mobile," "perspective," and so on. The natural way to become aware of the new word is to understand it as the concept it represents unfolds.

Names of artists and periods of art will also be learned as part of the *Art Smart!* program. Encourage students to use them when discussing and identifying works of art.

LEARNING BY DOING: AT THE HEART OF *ART SMART!*

The art activities are the very fibers from which *Art Smart!* is made. They comprise the art history and appreciation program that the book supports. Nonetheless, the activities are constructed to be used in a variety of ways. Depending on your own school schedule, your curriculum and programmatic needs, consider the following suggestions for implementing the activities.

A Complete Chronological Course of Study

Select one or more activities from each period, going from the book's beginning to end. The manner in which you integrate the program into your own curriculum will depend on your schedule. Perhaps you will present one activity a week—or select a more suitable time frame for yourself. You may also want to present an art appreciation program to selected classes, while offering single lessons to others.

Independent Lesson Presentation

The book will lend itself just as easily to single or "fast" lesson presentation as it will to using it as a full program. Single lessons may be couched in numerous ways and may, in fact, be inserted into any ongoing art curriculum.

Lesson Clusters

You may want to group lessons together to teach a specific period or style of art. Activities may also be joined together to introduce (or round off) the media-based components of your art program, such as painting, 3-D construction, etc.

Holiday Tie-Ins

Certain activities are ideal companions for holidays, while also lending an additional historical significance. For example, stained glass (Activity 22, "Rose Roundels") is a fine Christmas activity, and masks (Activity 34) can't miss for Halloween!

Meet the Artists

Perhaps your interest lies in teaching children about specific artists and their art and times. Activities that follow "The Middle Ages" are best for this, since it wasn't really until the Renaissance period that individual artists emerged as such. Other than in their chronological order, the "All-Year 'Art Smarty' Calendars" are one way to celebrate particular artists on (or around) their birthdays! The calendar can be used as a novel way to introduce children to artists, such as "Happy Birthday, Toulouse!" On that date, Activity 62 on posters can take place in honor of the famous poster-maker. Calendar months may also be designated to the periods of art that they each illustrate.

Museum Visits and Field Trips

There is nothing like a museum for appreciating art! Slides and reproductions are the next best thing but can never replace the real article. Use the *Art Smart* activities as a direct follow-up to museum visits, selecting lessons on the basis of the art exhibits you experienced. Nature walks, zoo visits, and trips to the planetarium can also be hooked into specific lessons.

Interdisciplinary Activities

Classroom and art teachers may form ready partnerships with *Art Smart!* activities, especially in areas of social study and cultural units. Opportunities may be most prevalent in the activities dealing with "Art of the Americas," "Art of the Middle and Far East," and "Art of Africa."

Clubs and Workshops

If you teach in a school that offers extracurricular activities, many of these art appreciation activities can be used. Some of the sewing or fabric lessons, such as Activity 26 ("Unicorns Unlimited"), may be well-suited for club projects.

THE ANATOMY OF AN *ART SMART!* ACTIVITY

All *Art Smart!* activities are in a unified format. The elements of the format would appear to be self-explanatory which, to an extent, they are. Yet it is equally important for you to be informed of their intended purposes.

Slides and Reproductions

Ideally, activities should be introduced with a presentation of slides. There is a handy identification sheet that accompanies the slides. The slide script may provide you with basic information and facts, as well as schools of art, traditions and "isms." Slides are keyed to specific activities as indicated, but may be used with any lesson teachers find suitable.

Carousel projectors are most convenient, generally, for slide presentation and storage. But other methods, as well as the less-than-modern projector models, can also be used. Slide viewers of various sizes and costs may be investigated by you in photographic supply and camera stores and catalogs. Even little hand-held slide viewers might be considered if budgets are extremely tight. On the other side, a liberal budget (if you are so fortunate) might suggest the expansion of your audio-visual equipment.

What if you are unable, for some reason, to introduce the lesson with a slide presentation? Should you then cancel the activity? Certainly not! Again, *Art Smart!* activities are written with such possibilities in mind. The brief descriptions that lead into the activities should provide a basis for understanding the lesson, along with the photos of finished products, the supportive material, and the plan itself. Nevertheless, it is advisable to have a good back-up system, which brings us to the next point.

Postcards of paintings from museum bookstores, all sorts of reproductions (from art magazines and elsewhere), and art history reference books should be in permanent residence in your art room. The more art history reference material you have on hand, the more convenient your activity presentations will be!

If you have not yet started a reference shelf of painting reproductions (and other art reproductions), now is your chance. You'll find tear-out posters in teacher magazines, and calendars and datebooks will often use art reproductions, too. Save the greeting cards you receive that have them—collect all you can.

When lessons refer to the use of reference materials, your stock will be assumed. In addition, the library will provide what you need. Don't overlook the children's section; there's plenty there, also.

Slides and reproductions can do more than motivate students and offer ready reference. They may be used to compare one artist to another. Contrast will immediately dramatize a point you might want to make. It is also a surefire method to stimulate debate. Further, slides and reproductions clearly show the influence of one artist and period upon another. They can be most convincing! Try to amass a full range of artists in your postcards and reproductions in general, and for your *Art Smart!* activities in particular. Also, remember that *Art Smart!* activities are made to quickly adapt to your existing art appreciation materials. Feel free to match activities up with your audio-visual and reference library items.

Preparing for the Presentation

It's a good idea to read the activity you want to present well in advance of class. For one thing, it may require supplies you don't have on hand. For another, it may ask that you rearrange your room a bit. However, these activities will not generally send you off in search of exotic materials. Usually, you will already have what you will need. If you look over the supplies that activities require in advance, you'll probably find that they are common materials. The "unusual" has been purposely avoided for your convenience; it's also unnecessary for producing perfectly good art.

There are some items that might grab your attention. One is acrylic paint in gold and other metallic shades. This paint is called for in a number of activities. Do *not* substitute with anything other than waterbased paint.

The following are a few pointers on safety in the art class.

SAFETY CHECKLIST

1. *Use only waterbased paints and markers!* No solvent-based markers, no oil paints, no turpentine, no dry pigments, no spray paint, and no aerosol sprays (such as fixatives) are to be used.

2. *White glue and library paste are fine!* No rubber cement, no resins, and no solvents are to be used.

3. *Use wet clay and modeling clay.* No dry clay mixes, no powders, and no clay flours are to be used. Exercise extreme caution with kilns. Do not let children handle unmarked glazes or do glazing without teacher supervision. Most glazing and firing techniques should be done by the teacher—not by young children. *Never* use lead glazes or unvented kilns.

These safety rules strictly apply throughout the book and throughout your art program as well. An excellent text on art room and studio safety is *Artist Beware!* by Michael McCann (New York: Watson–Guptill, 1979).

The supplies we'll use for "studio" activities are of the soap-and-water cleanup variety. Instructions for distributing paint on palettes, for preparing room setups, and so on, are detailed in Section One. You'll also find suggestions for the presentation of other mediums and the techniques to be employed in a number of *Art Smart!* activities.

Step by Step

The activity plan will alert you to several aspects of the lesson presentation. Under "Teacher Preparation," the length of time you can expect to set aside for the lesson will be indicated, if it is likely to run beyond a regular class period. Of course, everyone is on a different schedule, so this is hardly an exact science. Some lessons will be sectioned into "parts" where a natural break occurs; but other extended lessons may not lend themselves to such divisions. In any event, you will be able to get some sense of the activity time frame by first reviewing the "Teacher Preparation" and reading the lesson.

After you have previewed the lesson, you will likely have a sense of how to use it— and to which classes you will present it. Since the lessons span grades 3–9, you may indeed find that some activities are entirely inappropriate for the younger children, and vice-versa. However, the bulk of the activities can go either way if you make minor adjustments. You know your students. Certain activities that might otherwise be suggested for one level could be perfectly suited to another. You are in the best position to decide the age-appropriateness of the activities.

Finally, you will notice that the activities include not only the usual directions, but that almost all of them will suggest means for beginning motivational discussions as well. These have been intentionally included in the steps of the plan (usually steps 1 or 2) because they are considered an integral part of the presentation process.

What Else Is There?

What's the most important element of *Art Smart?* You! Because you, the teacher, will bring the experience of art history and appreciation to your students. And you will do it in your own unique way. You are the essential ingredient that will make it all happen dynamically.

The *Art Smart!* activities are not inscribed in granite; they ask for your interpretation and special touch. Certainly, you may take the lessons for what they are, or you can use them as points of departure and springboards for other ideas. One idea begets another, then another, and another. You and your students will set off this explosion of creativity— the best chain reaction of all!

And students! Where would we be without them? How many innocent remarks and well-placed observations have guided us into some of our most persuasive lessons ever? Clearly, my own students are written into every line of this book. As teachers, we remain on the lookout for our students' clues—and, together, we can all become "art smarter."

ACKNOWLEDGMENTS

There are many caring people who helped in the production of *Art Smart!* For the high quality of student work submitted, I'd like to thank: Chris Houston, Stan Lilly, Amy Jared, Megan Steinmetz, Marsha Schamber, and Anita Halpern. These talented art educators richly deserve acknowledgment for their contributions of student art to *Art Smart!*

For the "architectural element" of *Art Smart,* the Foundation for Architecture's Education program, and its excellent director, Rolaine Copeland, are credited and thanked. Also, Greta Greenberger, Marci Abau, Oscar Harris, and Michael Selditch have the author's appreciation.

Arlene Gostin, of the Philadelphia Colleges of the Arts Education Department, has been indispensable to the making of *Art Smart!* Debbie Pollack, Jamie Newstat, Susan Myers, Mary Sweeney, Omar Jimenez, Lisa Petitt, and Richard Metz are also thanked for their assistance. And, of course, Wendy Leuchter!

Cathy McNeil has been more than an illustrator—Paul Blumenthal, more than a photographer. I thank them for their extra help. And to Diana Hess, my magical typist, who turns word collages into typed pages—a large measure of gratitude!

Evelyn Fazio, my editor at Prentice Hall, is the force behind the flame. She is further appreciated for her encouragement and friendship.

More thanks than I could rightly offer go to the principal of the Philadelphia School District's Overbrook Educational Center, Marilyn A. Moller. Without her belief in art education and her constant support, *Art Smart!* could not have become a reality.

My friends, family, colleagues have indeed made it possible. But it is the students of the Overbrook Educational Center who must be credited with a capital C! It is their talent, enthusiasm, and love of art that keeps this author going. They are the reason for *Art Smart!*

CONTENTS

SLIDE PRESENTATION

SUGGESTIONS FOR USE OF SLIDES

What is a slide? It seems like a silly question, but it is *very* important that students understand the difference between slides and original paintings before you engage them in a presentation. A slide is a photograph of a painting or a work of art, printed on color-slide film. It is a reproduction, animated by light. It is not the real thing.

No matter how good or faithful slides are, they can never truly replicate an original work of art. For one thing, slides will consistently conform to the size you project on the wall. Therefore, the actual dimensions of the painting will not be represented. Another point to make with students is that the color and texture of paint, when compared with slides, is never the same, either. The time has not yet arrived when we can scientifically reproduce a slide to the exact color and texture of an original canvas. Slides may even make some art appear so vivid that when it is actually seen, the viewer might be disappointed! It's a good idea to explain that painted canvas and color slide do vary from one another significantly.

There are other "ice breakers" you may want to use when discussing slides or reproductions in general:

- Is it a portrait, landscape, or still life? Figure group? Design? Can you identify any other subcategory—seascapes, for instance?
- Discuss light, line, color, and space. For instance, are the colors warm or cool (or both)? Describe the space inside the picture—is it crowded or empty? Flat or deep? Use your own words.
- The artist has created a reality in the painting. What would it be like to visit the world inside the canvas? Describe....

Remember that slides are gateways to museums and learning. They are points of departure—they should invite students into the appreciation and creation of art. As the Japanese *Soshi,* Calligraphy Master Kampo Harada points out...

"Just to hear...is less than nothing.
Walk the path,
Experience...!

To this we add...*enjoy!*

SLIDE IDENTIFICATION SCRIPT

SLIDE #1. *Bison.* Altamira Grotto in Northern Spain. Cave Wall Art. 15,000–10,000 B.C. Drawings were found deep in the rock shelters where cave dwellers lived thousands of years ago. Animals were most commonly pictured running, leaping, standing, or wounded. Was the art pure hunting magic or art solely for its own merit? We can't be sure of the reasons. We do know that this powerful yet graceful work survived time—and began our own art history! (*Activity 1*)

SLIDE #2. *Mummy Case.* Decorative wooden coffin. 12th Dynasty. Middle Kingdom. Egypt. Cases that housed mummies were filled with colorful patterns, as well as hieroglyphs and striking motifs. Mummy cases were used to preserve the body and soul for the afterlife— or "forever"—as is consistent with ancient Egyptian art and belief. (*Activity 5*)

SLIDE #3. *Hieroglyphs with Egyptian Wall Painting.* Tomb. Ancient Egypt. Egyptians were a practical people who viewed their life on earth as a short transition to the "forever." Their art chiefly concerns the daily activities and exchanges with the gods that would best serve them for eternity. Painting was not separate from the scribal arts. Hieroglyphs consisted of *phonograms* (the combination of sounds), *ideograms* (pictures of actual things), and *determinatives* (to show the meaning of the words they follow). (*Activity 7*)

SLIDE #4. *The Parthenon.* Acropolis East. Athens, Greece. c.450 B.C. The ancient Greeks built the Parthenon entirely of marble as a shrine to Athena, the goddess of wisdom. This monumental classical temple of the Doric order stood 65 feet tall; a 40-foot high statue of Athena, made of ivory and gold, was placed inside! The Parthenon did indeed achieve the Greek ideal of perfection in its grand scale proportional harmony. (*Activity 12*)

SLIDE #5. *Olive Gathering.* Black figure ware. By the Antimenes painter c.520 B.C. British Museum, London. The *amphora*, a jar used to carry oil or wine, provided the contoured surface for this lively slice of ancient Greek life. The line quality of pottery drawings, which was incised by a sharp tool, is still respected as skillful and sensitive today. Decorative Greek vases in a variety of shapes depict many subjects—mythological legends, feasts for the gods, animals, warriors, athletic contests, and so on. What other action scenes would lend to the rounded surface of the vase? (*Activity 13*)

SLIDE #6. *Victory.* Female Greek Statue. By Paeonius. 425 B.C. Olympia Museum. The years have destroyed the classical features of this goddess' face, as well as portions of her limbs and flowing robe. Her wings are gone, too, for "Victory" originally represented flight. But her strong posture and solid volume remain intact. What particular feature of this sculpture still suggests movement? How? (*Activity 16*)

SLIDE #7. *Rose Window Stained Glass.* Notre Dame, Paris. c.1200. The extraordinary rose window, like similar stained glass windows built during the Gothic period, was constructed of hundreds of pieces of colored glass. The glass shapes that fit within the greater medallion framework would allow diffused colored light to enter the cathedral. An intended effect of this visual spectacle was to enlighten and uplift the spirit. Where have you seen stained glass within the walls of architecture—or hanging independently? (*Activity 22*)

SLIDE #8. *Gargoyles.* South side. North tower. Notre Dame, Paris. Did you know that gargoyles are not merely ornamental or decorative figures but may serve as rainspouts, too? Fantastic monsters that project from cathedral exteriors seem awfully well suited to guard the building from any unwanted guests! (*Activity 24*)

SLIDE #9. *The Lady and the Unicorn.* Tapestry 3.78m high × 4.66m wide. End of the 15th Century. Cluny Museum, Paris. Large, intricate medieval tapestries required the teamwork of artisans who wove them to completion. The unicorn tapestries were part of a series of six and are regarded foremost among great works of textile art. Here, as in other unicorn pieces, *mille fleurs* surround heraldic beasts and assorted small animals. How many creatures can you find in these enchanted woods? Name them, too! (*Activity 26*)

SLIDE #10. *November* (Acorn Harvest) from Les Très Riches Heures du Duc de Berry. Limbourg Brothers. c.1400. Condé Museum, Chantilly. The miniature painting of devotional books—and painting on panels—was the popular art form of this period. The Limbourg brothers illustrated these exquisite calendar pages that show the toils of labor cast against courtly castle life. There is a love of fine detail shown, which is characteristic of Northern art. Space is better understood in depth, along with a realism as clear as each little hair on the hog's back! (*Activity 29*)

SLIDE #11. *Mona Lisa.* Leonardo da Vinci. 1503–1505. Oil on panel. 30¼ × 21″. Louvre, Paris. In this most famous painting, you'll find that light and shadow are used to model the figure's volume, and to create a harmonious relationship between foreground and background. The artist moves the viewer's eye from the folds on Mona Lisa's sleeve to the ribbonlike water that flows behind her. This unifies the composition and draws attention to the sitter's face, while topping it all off with a halo of hazy light. There is, after all, more to Mona than her mysterious smile! (*Activity 32*)

SLIDE #12. *Ranuccio Farnese.* Titian. 1542. Canvas. 35¼ × 29″. National Gallery of Art, Washington, D.C. Titian was a major Renaissance artist who seemed able to turn paint into gold with his brush. As in this portrait of a boy, Titian described fabric and texture eloquently. Interest in material goods, along with the suggestion of a sort of fuzzy softness—particularly around edges and contours—was typical of Venetian painting generally. The Venetian "glow," a warm light that imbued paintings of this period, can be seen in the portraiture of Titian. What fabrics or materials can you identify in this painting? (*Activity 35*)

SLIDE #13. *Marriage of the Virgin.* Raphael. 1504. Oil on panel. 67″ × 46½″. Brena Gallery, Milan. A panel is no more than a flat, one-dimensional surface until a painter manipulates the planes with the illusion we call a picture. Raphael created a dramatic perspective in this painting. He also connected a foreground to a strongly contrasted background by placing subsequent figures deep into recessed space. Where is the "vanishing point" in this painting? What other optical devices has Raphael used here? (*Activity 36*)

SLIDE #14. *A Princess of the d'Este Family (Ginerva d'Este).* Pisanello. c.1440. Tempera on panel. 16⅞″ × 11¾″. Louvre, Paris. Clearcut, linear profiles and a pleasing, flat decorative quality are synonymous with the Florentine school—a Northern Italian painting style. The charming pattern behind the girl is repeated on her clothing. Does this remind you of another overall treatment of floral motif seen in these slides? (See Slide #9.) (*Activity 37*)

SLIDE #15. *Sistine Chapel Ceiling.* Michelangelo. 1508–1512. Fresco. The Vatican, Rome. To create a unified painted surface out of the many compartments of the Sistine ceiling presented a challenge to Michelangelo, both artistically and physically! He solved the problem by working within the constraints of the job—he painted frescoes of numerous biblical scenes onto the ceiling's framework, which included *The Creation of Adam*. The robust, vigorous treatment of subject clearly revealed the sculptor within the painter called Michelangelo. (*Activity 38*)

SLIDE #16. *Portrait of the Artist at His Easel.* Rembrandt. 1660. Canvas. 111 cm × 90 cm. Louvre, Paris. Much of portrait painting is concerned with covering blemishes, removing moles and wrinkles, and flattering the sitter. Not so with Rembrandt, whose portraits are among the most honest ever painted. He penetrated the surface to examine the character of the sitter. And he was never more frank nor candid than when he turned his brush to his own self-portraits. What does this painting tell you about the artist who painted it? (*Activity 40*)

SLIDE #17. *Lady Reading at an Open Window.* Vermeer. c.1658. Canvas. 33¾″ × 25⅜″. Louvre, Paris. Vermeer's output of paintings during his lifetime was modest, and the scale of his work small. But the jewel-like quality of his paint consistently sparkled! Vermeer imparted a dignity and elegance to simple, everyday events of Dutch life—called *Genre*—of which he was a master. His interiors had a mood of complete serenity. Can't you just feel the gentle flutter of breeze? (*Activity 41*)

SLIDE #18. *Still Life with Crabs and Fruit.* Van Beyeren. c.1655. Canvas. 98 cm × 76 cm. The Hague, Mauritshuis. Still life became a subject of abundance during the golden age of Dutch painting. The canvases often overflowed with banquet-sized offerings of food and worldly goods. Eye-fooling realism, along with objects highlighted against dark backgrounds, were the mark of the Dutch still life. What might this still life suggest about the household from which it was gathered? (*Activity 43*)

SLIDE #19. *The Artist and His Family.* Jordaens. Oil on canvas. 1593. 71¼ × 72¾″. Prado, Madrid. Any family that is about to have a portrait painted will dress in their finest clothing and look for an attractive spot, such as a garden, in which to sit for the occasion. The preparation for a formal group portrait was much the same then as it is now. Notice the way the group has been arranged and the details of their costumes. Who do you think is who? (Clue: One person is a servant.) What other hints about them can you find? (*Activity 44*)

SLIDE #20. *Back from the Market (or The Provider).* Chardin. 1793. Oil on canvas. 18½ × 14¾″ Louvre, Paris. Chardin was a French painter whose interest in daily chores placed him high into the ranks of Dutch genre. His French interpretation of Dutch genre was original and outstanding. Chardin's paint quality had a grainy, pitted texture that was perfect for the rustic scenes and household objects he so enjoyed. No one's copper kettle gleamed brighter than Chardin's! (*Activity 45*)

SLIDE #21. *The Swing.* Fragonard. c.1765. Canvas. 85″ × 73″. National Gallery of Art, Washington, D.C. The art of Fragonard is as light and as charming as a romantic comedy. The subject was usually the pastimes of the French aristocracy, whose carefree games ask to be taken no more seriously than a lawn party. Fragonard painted their escapades in candy colors, with pastel blue and frothy pinks typical of French Rococo. (*Activity 48*)

SLIDE #22. *The Ford (Il Guado).* Lorrain. Louvre, Paris. It has been said that Claude Lorrain was truly the first landscape painter. He did, in fact, place the entire importance of his paintings on the landscape itself. His small, classical figure groups, animals, and other compositional elements were only incidental to vast sweeps of space. Lorrain's warm, poetic vistas, his sunrises and sunsets, strongly recall the Venetian "glow." Describe what it might be like to take a stroll in this painting. (*Activity 49*)

SLIDE #23. *Majas on a Balcony.* Goya. c.1810. Oil on canvas. 76¾″ × 49½″. The Metropolitan Museum of Art, Bequest of Mrs. H. O. Havemeyer, 1929. The H. O. Havemeyer Collection. Goya was the official court painter, yet he continued to keep his passionate political views. He also managed to slip a good dose of social commentary past his royal portrait sitters. The balance of artistic interest divided somewhere between reporting the heinous crimes of war and, on the other side of it, displaying the colorfully costumed beauties of his native Spain. What has Goya done in this painting to accentuate the lovely Majas on this balcony? Do they have a foil? A contrast? Where? (*Activity 50*)

SLIDE #24. *View of Toledo.* El Greco. c.1597. Oil on canvas. 47¾″. The Metropolitan Museum of Art, Bequest of Mrs. H. O. Havemeyer, 1929. The H. O. Havemeyer Collection. El Greco was a genius of lighting effects, which he used to enhance the mystical theme of his work. Although much of his art included portraits and scenes of religious devotion, his treatment was always one of creative distortion. People were stretched and elongated, compositions were multilayered, and the mood was "other worldly." He gave an emotional identity to this electrically charged landscape of Toledo, which was treated with the lightning line and biting acid color that is one with El Greco. Compare this slide to Slide #22. Discuss the differences. (*Activity 51*)

SLIDE #25. *Keelmen Heaving in Coals by Moonlight.* Turner, c.1835. Canvas. 36½ × 48¼″. National Gallery of Art, Washington, D.C. The romance of the high seas attracted Turner's attention, as evidenced in his many seascapes. He imparted a misty atmosphere to these works, which, it has been said, "…painted with tinted steam." What do you think this means? Compare this slide to Slide #30. Discuss uses of technique, color, and their effects on picture solidity. (*Activity 53*)

SLIDE #26. *The Gleaners.* Millet. 1857. 33″ × 44″. Louvre, Paris. The noble chores of peasants and the undisturbed, rugged beauty of nature were the ideals to which "Barbizon" painters subscribed. Millet chose to illustrate farmers in their fields, which connected him to another closely associated painting notion—Realism. Both painting philosophies asked that artists work directly from their subjects, which were usually quite down-to-earth, and to describe them without exaggeration. Compare this slide to Slide #19. (*Activity 54*)

SLIDE #27. *Georges Clémenceau.* Manet. 1879–1880. Oil on canvas. 37″ × 29¼″. Jeu de Paume, Paris. Manet invented a kind of shorthand with paint. A little spot of color here, another there, and you have a very believable portrait! This original method of terse paint application, and an ability to move shadows around to suggest solidity—plus a way to stretch a modicum of color into broad, sheetlike planes—all placed Manet as a forerunner to modern art. His own palette grew from the economical darks of the Realists, to the sunny pastels of the new movement which he indeed led—Impressionism! (*Activity 55*)

SLIDE #28. *The Cathedral of Rouen in Full Sunlight.* Monet. 1894. Canvas. 107 cm × 73 cm. Jeu de Paume, Paris. Monet's dedication to painting outdoors has become the trademark of Impressionists. No artist has likely been more persistent in the pursuit of sunlight than Claude Monet. He studied it, timed it, and painted it. His canvases caught the light as it reflected on frog ponds, bounced from cathedrals, danced around the lily pads, and was absorbed in the flowers of his gardens at Giverny. What time of day might it be in this painting? (*Activity 58*)

SLIDE #29. *At the Grenouillère.* Renoir. 1879. 73 cm × 93 cm. Jeu de Paume, Paris. Renoir's lustrous painting communicated a clear and profound delight with the natural world. His canvases convince us of the delicate beauty in a child's face and the juicy deliciousness of a ripe plum. Color was used to describe volume structurally from the inside-out. The result was solid mass—yet still a feeling of air and light remained! Renoir's mastery of paint elevated Impressionism to its highest and fullest form. (*Activity 60*)

SLIDE #30. *Seascape at Port-En-Bessin, Normandy.* Seurat. 1888. Canvas. 25⅝″ × 31⅞″. National Gallery of Art, Washington, D.C. Gift of the W. Averell Harriman Foundation in memory of Marie N. Harriman. Seurat is best known for his achievement with a technique known as Pointillism. Also referred to as Divisionism, or Neo-Impressionism, this method essentially organized a picture surface from particles of paint. Dots compose the color fields and build the volumes. But it's more than a cold, scientific theory in the hands of Seurat, whose quietly moving paintings express the many moods of life. What other pictures can you think of that use a system of dots to form an image? (*Activity 61*)

SLIDE #31. *Moulin Rouge.* Toulouse-Lautrec. 1891. Poster. 67″ × 47¼″. Lautrec's fascination with Parisian night life is documented in his paintings, drawings, and prints. Characters and performers—can-can dancer June Avril and the infamous La Golue—continue to make their appearances in Lautrec's art to this very day. His sense of design, advertising graphics, and fine draftsmanship converged to form Toulouse-Lautrec's witty and unforgettable posters. (*Activity 62*)

SLIDE #32. *The Starry Night.* Van Gogh. 1889. Oil on canvas. 29″ × 36¼″. Collection, The Museum of Modern Art, New York. Acquired through the Lillie P. Bliss bequest. Vincent Van Gogh's application of paint was indisputably direct, for he often squeezed paint straight from the tube onto the canvas! His restlessness registered in his art, animating skies and trees into a swirling embroidery of line and color. There is an emotional quality in Van Gogh's art that seems to always evoke response. Compare Slide #24 for possible similarities. Discuss. (*Activity 63*)

SLIDE #33. *Still Life with Peppermint Bottle.* Cézanne. 1890-1894. Oil. 25⅞″ × 32¼″. Would you want to take a bite from Cézanne's apple? Of course not—all the fruits are rock hard! Cézanne cared little about realism, for this artistic giant was interested in the architecture of nature. He sought structural planes in mass—an analytical view that predicted Cubism. Compare this slide to Slide #18. (*Activity 64*)

SLIDE #34. *The Equatorial Jungle.* Rousseau. 1909. Canvas. 54¼″ × 51″. National Gallery of Art, Washington, D.C. Rousseau, who did not start his painting career until age forty, was a government clerk—*Le Douanier* in French, which became his artistic nickname. He painted many little village scenes and officers in uniforms, whom he seemed to admire. Yet it is the snake charmers, the sleeping gypsies, and fantastic dreams that have distinguished Rousseau's work. The charming world he forged from his imagination may seem naive, but it has been vividly crafted with considerable skill! (*Activity 65*)

SLIDE #35. *Beasts of the Sea.* Matisse. 1850. Paper on canvas (collage). 116⅜″ × 60⅝″. National Gallery of Art, Washington, D.C. Bold shapes, assertive line, and dynamic patterns. Power equals simplicity in the work of Matisse. His influences have assisted him—motifs from Islamic tiles and Persian rugs, oriental design elements—and now more than ever in the papercut-natural organic shapes. Matisse redefined collage with his innovative papercut, and his sense of design revolutionized textile arts. Many variations and imitations of these powerful papercuts can still be seen in designs arts and fabrics today! (*Activity 66*)

SLIDE #36 *Women of Tahiti (or On the Beach).* Gauguin. 1891. 27″ × 35½″. Jeu de Paume, Paris. If a place has a spirit, Tahiti's soul has been forever cast into the art of Gauguin. He has arrested the bright tropical colors in his exotic beaches, filled with splashy sarong patterns and powerful carvings. But Gauguin went beyond the decorative charm of the island to reflect on the character of the people who so intrigued him. What expressions do you read in the faces of the women in the slide? (*Activity 67*)

SLIDE #37. *Still Life with Chair Caning.* Picasso. 1911–12. 10½″ × 13¾″. Private Collection. Picasso made the leap to cubism from classical roots. His early work, the Blue and Rose periods, consisted chiefly of sensitively portrayed figures and haunting portraits. Cubism represented a radical departure from the past. Instead of using line to explore shape, Picasso broke volumes apart and examined them from many angles at once. Cubism also invited the participation of real items from the everyday world—or "found objects"—into the art itself. What objects can you recognize in this slide? (*Activity 68*)

SLIDE #38. *New York City.* Mondrian. 1940–41. 57″ × 45″. Lyme, Connecticut. Harry Holtzman Collection. Is it a street map? Is it a floor plan? Or is it simply a design? This modern work was linked with a group of artists, architects and designers, the name of which was collectively De Stijl. Here, principles were strong and all these arts overlapped into life. Houses and furniture were built on the lively geometry of Mondrian—so perhaps his painting is indeed "all of the above"! (*Activity 69*)

SLIDE #39 *Women Washing and Starching Linen.* Kiyonaga. c.1785. Edo Era. Woodblock print. 30″ × 15″. Ōban triptych. The subject of this delightful print—women stretching kimono fabric—is Japanese genre. Ukiyo-e (oo-key-oh-eh), or *the floating world,* features scenes of "the transient life"—many city vignettes, while nature and landscape are included in the general group. Ukiyo-e might picture actors of the Japanese stage, or wrestlers, with the same matter-of-fact ease that children are shown playing games on the street. The open and expressive quality of the Japanese print, the remarkable division of picture space, along with delicate linear drawing, had a sizable effect on many Impressionists and Post-Impressionists. Can you think of any? (See Slide #31.) (*Activity 91*)

SLIDE #40. *African Mask.* Mossi plank mask. It is important to remember that African art has many styles, and varies dramatically from region to region. Varieties of the African mask—whether in the form of a headdress, headpiece, or face covering—are among the most compelling. Masks bring with them a sense of magic, ceremony, tribal history, and art. Strong African design often claims ordinary, available materials to further dramatize the impact of masks. What materials may have been used to make the mask in this slide? (*Activity 93*)

Section One

STUDIO METHODS FOR THE CLASSROOM

What do you picture when you hear the word *studio*? A large, airy room with skylights, containing at least one easel, a drawing table (maybe), a model, and a podium?

And, of course, there is the artist or sculptor who works within the studio. It is a place to go that is special—almost sacred. A place where great art is made!

This perception is fairly accurate. Artists do require studios, as much as palettes need paint! But not all studios are situated in garrets or lofts. The term *studio* also refers to the methods and techniques that artists use. Studios are not necessarily defined by a specific, formal spatial arrangement—they are, to an extent, a state of mind.

Your classroom is the ideal place to introduce the concept of studios, and the respectful attitudes that artists have toward art. This doesn't imply that you must immediately stock your closets with all sorts of professional-quality materials and haul in a podium. On the contrary, most professional materials—such as oil paints and turpentine—are entirely inappropriate for use with children. There are alternatives to these supplies that are every bit as effective.

STUDIO PAINTING IN THE CLASSROOM

Acrylic Paint

In the area of painting, acrylics are generally considered far safer than oil-based paints and require only a soap-and-water cleanup. (NOTE: Some students may have allergic sensitivity to the preservatives in acrylic paint. Be aware of this. Should any such reactions occur, discontinue use. More severe reactions, although rare, would require that you contact the school nurse.) Acrylics may be purchased in jars, which are more economical than paint tubes. However, acrylics have a fixed shelf life so discard any that have developed a rancid smell or evidence of mold. They also air dry quickly, so be sure the lids are on tightly!

You may use acrylics with regular paper or lightweight board, for they are thinned by adding water—thus, you may do acrylic wash painting. But the manner in which studio methods utilize acrylics will be introduced through palette application.

Palettes and Mixing

There are a number of ways in which you may use palettes in the classroom. The first choice is, of course, the genuine article, wood palettes. The next choice? Paper palettes, made for just this purpose. One palette contains several sheets, which will easily be removed to serve a number of students. The shape of the purchased palette will also suggest the real thing for students, who will then probably feel more "professional."

There are other alternatives for palettes. Sheets of hard acrylic, such as rigid plastic, in suitable sizes can be convenient if you have access to them. But probably more practical are simply *boards*—either masonite remnants or heavy paper boards. Paper plates can be used in a pinch, as can styrofoam meat trays. Both are good as mixing surfaces.

Setting Up the Palette

For every book you read on artists' techniques, that is how many different recommendations you're likely to find on the right way to set up a palette. If you've ever seen more than one artist's working palette, you'll quickly note that one does *not* resemble another. The arrangement of the palette seems to be a fairly personal thing.

Nonetheless, there are some rules that will start you off on the right foot, particularly in the grouping of colors. It's a good idea to provide children with a model for a basic arrangement—one from which they may depart at a later point, if so desired.

It's suggested that palettes follow a distribution of paint that goes from warm to cool colors clockwise, with white on the "warm" side and black on the "cool" side. Glazing mediums are not necessary for classroom use.

The center of the palette is, as you know, primarily for the mixing and blending of colors. This will need to be pointed out to students—just as the setting up of the palette will have to be demonstrated. You can opt to have palettes ready for students in advance of class when time constraints are a problem. However, students really do enjoy doing the setup part themselves! The paint may also be saved (for a little while) without drying out by wrapping the palette in plastic food wrap.

Brushes

The long-handled brushes that are used for oil painting are fine, as long as students are careful not to poke themselves—or their neighbors—in the eye! Other brushes, such as the soft hair type, may be used but stiff brushes are best for painting on boards.

Painting Surfaces

It is wonderful if you have stretched canvases at your disposal but since this is unlikely, canvas boards are a fine initiation into the world of professional studio painting for the classroom. Failing that, resort to illustration boards. Canvas paper from a pad is also a possibility you might explore.

Easels are indeed desirable, but not required, for classroom painting. Should you happen to have one or two, you might certainly work out an arrangement where students could take turns painting at the easel. But your best bet is to have a supply of drawing boards, made either from wood or heavy cardboard, on which students may place their paintings for work on hard-to-reach angles.

Studio Attire and Etiquette

Rule number one: Roll up the sleeves! Smocks or men's old shirts are a necessity. These may be provided by the students themselves, or kept for the students by the teacher.

Rule number two: Absolutely no eating in the studio! This means you, too! Professional artists forget this rule, only to end up endangering their health by ingesting quantities of their materials. It adds up! Students must be aware that while the media they use are fairly safe, they are *only as safe as directed!* Paints *are* chemicals and must be treated as such. Make sure cleanup is thorough, and hands are paint-free at end of lesson.

Other Painting Methods

Tempera and poster paint are common to most art classrooms. Art teachers are familiar with their use, but might enjoy other methods of distribution for them. Some recommendations for "repackaging" your paints are using styrofoam egg cartons and muffin pans. The egg carton lids allow space for mixing colors.

Watercolor boxes are so much a part of artroom inventories that their proper usage is often taken for granted. However, many students do not seem to know how to keep their paints fresh. It's a good idea to remind students of the following:

1. Plenty of water on your brush makes paint flow more easily.
2. Mix paints *only* in the lid—not *on top* of one another!
3. Wipe your brush off on the paper towel, which becomes your "paint rag," *every time you change colors.* This keeps colors, as well as water, fresher.
4. Do not *grind* brushes into the paint! It ruins both paint *and* brush. Use a light touch.
5. Do experiment! Try drybrush and other brush-stroke techniques.
6. Leave the paint box in the shape that you would want to receive it.

Sound too simplistic? It's really very easy to overlook or forget the methods for school watercolor painting. Reminders, as well as demonstrations, can't hurt. Your students' art will reflect it!

Tip: Coffee cans and plastic containers provide a nice change from "school regulation size" watercolor cups.

THE CLAY STUDIO

We haven't forgotten the potter or the sculptor! On the professional level, these artists have their own special studio needs. The potter usually needs a wheel, glazing materials, and a kiln—at least! The sculptor needs an armature and casting materials. Both need lots of clay, plaster bats for preparing it, and tools for manipulation.

In the classroom, we can do just fine with the clay itself. Wet, prepackaged clay is recommended. Clay has a way of changing into various states—very wet clay needs drying out, very dry clay requires water. Hence, plastic containers, such as rubber garbage pails with tight fitting lids, will aid in clay cycling.

To prepare clay for modeling activities (and firing), it should be wedged. (See Figure 1.) This means aspirating the air bubbles which weaken clay. Pounding out clay is best accomplished on wooden boards or plastic bats. (See Figure 2.) Piano wire, passed through a hunk of clay, will reveal whether or not air bubbles are present—you can see

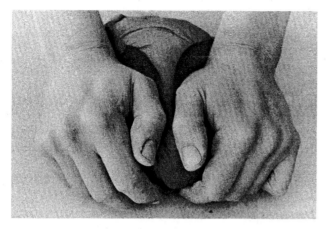

FIGURE 1. To wedge clay, simply press down upon it, then roll back. Repeat several times.

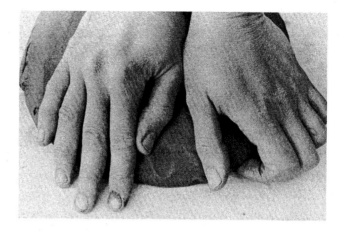

FIGURE 2. Watch out for air pockets. These can occur when clay is rolled out too flatly and air gets trapped inside.

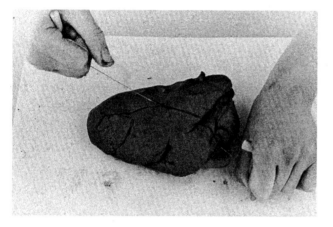

FIGURE 3. Use a length of wire to slice clay.

FIGURE 4. Air bubbles will be revealed if you have them. They appear as little holes in the clay. Go back to wedging if they occur; otherwise, proceed with clay activity.

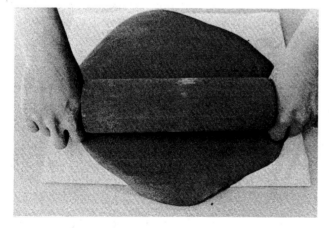

FIGURE 5. A rolling pin is a clay studio "must." In a pinch, coffee cans may suffice. This method is recommended for slab construction as well as the production of tiles.

FIGURE 6. Roll clay into a wooden frame for tile making. The frame shown here is excellent, but you may substitute it with wooden strips.

FIGURE 7. Try for an even thickness. This rule applies to all clay construction generally.

FIGURE 8. Remove the tile by easing it away from the frame.

FIGURE 9. Here's the finished tile. Clay tools may be used to smooth edges if desired. Note the way in which the wooden frame has been constructed; perhaps a friendly industrial arts teacher could be enlisted for this handy clay aid.

them if they are there. (See Figures 3 and 4.) More important, wedging will create an even moisture content throughout the clay.

There are tools that make clay lessons brighter: rolling pins, toothbrushes (for "scoring," or joining clay parts), natural sponges, revolving clay stands (e.g., Lazy Susans), containers for water, manicure sticks and, of course, tools that are made expressly for clay use. Other objects may be gathered for the purpose of creating interesting textures, such as a meat mallet and various household (particularly kitchen) items. The garlic press, as shown in Activity 24, Figure 67, can't be beat for the results it produces!

Each clay technique may have its own guidelines. For example, Activity 42, "Miles of Tiles," will require a slab method. Roll clay out evenly with a rolling pin or an empty can on its side. (See Figure 5.) Use a ruler (or wood strip) to level off edge, and cut with clay tool into a square. An alternative is to make a frame from four wood strips into which clay will be rolled. (See Figure 6.) Clay thickness of the finished tile should be consistent throughout. (See Figures 7 through 9.)

Clay may be wrapped in sheets of plastic, with a moist paper towel next to its surface to keep it malleable between lessons. If you are working on a sculptural form, such as the gargoyles in Activity 24, you may want to hollow out your piece with the proper clay tool (or with a tablespoon) and stuff it with crushed newspaper for drying purposes. Later, remove the newspaper carefully. (NOTE: Well-wedged clay doesn't necessarily require scooping; it may be pierced through the center with a pencil. The thicker the body of clay, the more pencil holes you'll pierce, as in Activity 24, Figure 68.)

Glazing and kiln firing will vary from school to school. It is important that you know what you are doing, for example, what glazes you're using and the firing temperatures for them, etc. Your kiln, too, should have a set of instructions to assist you. *Never* use lead glazes or operate unvented kilns!

Because of the technical nature of this phase of the procedure, it is best that you refer to manuals applying to your own situation. However, precaution should be taken with all of these processes. Unvented kilns, for example, can be hazardous, as can unmarked glazes. This entire area is best handled by the teacher—not the student!

It is *not* necessary to have glazing or firing procedures available to work with clay. Clay will air-harden. Just be sure that the clay walls are not too thick. Wrapping the clay in plastic between work times will also prevent premature cracking. Clay is more fragile with this method, so treat accordingly.

SETTING UP THE ROOM

Any studio workshop, whether it is for painting or clay, will require movement and activity—and the attendant cleanup concerns. To avoid elaborate cleanups at the end of each lesson, it's advisable to cover desks with brown butcher paper, plastic throws, newspaper, or similar material at the outset. It's a general rule, but one that saves work in the end.

Other Materials and Techniques

If your art room is fairly standard, you will have the necessary supplies to carry out the activities in this book. As for the "extras"—if you have not lately visited a home decorating center for discontinued wallpaper books or a lumberyard for wood remnants—then maybe it's a good time to do so! These materials will be called for in the activities, and they are handy just the same!

A box of fabric scraps, buttons, and trimmings should also be developed if it is not already in place. This is another useful addition to classroom stock. Attractive giftwrap paper scraps, old greeting cards and, of course, magazines, are also helpful for *Art Smart!* lessons. Cardboard, the sort from which boxes are made, will be needed from time to time as well.

The Prop Box—A Studio Must!

No respectable studio would be caught short without a prop box or costume trunk! Building up a collection is easier than you can ever imagine, and will lead you into some wonderful adventures—rummage sales, thrift shop hopping, collecting from friends and relatives who are glad to part with old wardrobe items. Students can certainly contribute too!

Hats, scarves, and other accessories are just as important as full costume regalia. One of the author's personal favorite props is a paper Oriental oiled umbrella—it can really do so much for a composition—and a lesson!

Old jackets, fans, military gear, and uniforms are great! Even a single glove, used as part of a gesture, can be quite expressive. If you haven't yet done so, get started on your treasure chest right away!

The Finishing Touch

Display, as we all know, is of utmost importance. It gives the students the means by which to communicate through their art—not to speak of the pride of recognition!

You may want to set aside a little "gallery space" in your own room, in addition to any hall display you might already have at your disposal. A predetermined wall, a small easel, a portable bulletin board—any of these will accomplish the idea—particularly with identifying graphics, such as "Masterpieces of P.S. 101" or "Artist(s) of the Week."

You might also want to enlist the support of a friendly shop teacher if you need some help in display assemblage and framing the works as well as hanging them. In addition, you might keep a cache of hardware, such as braided picture wire, mounting hooks, and so forth—for "advanced" hanging requirements.

A FINAL NOTE

We've said it before, and we'll say it again—reproductions are essential to art appreciation. Postcards of art works are ideal—they even lend themselves to impromptu matching games, such as "Which artists are Impressionists…" or "…Pick two paintings from the same period"…"Find one landscape, one seascape, one cityscape." Truly the variations and benefits are endless for simply keeping art reproductions handy, especially postcards from museum bookstores! Posters of artists' works should also be on the classroom walls. They have a definite impact on students.

Perhaps the most important of all your backup material is a comprehensive art history survey book. While *Art Smart!* does provide basic information about art history, chronology, periods, and styles of art, as well as individual artists, its uniqueness lies in the fact that it is primarily an art appreciation activities book. Therefore, it is suggested that the teacher have an art history textbook on hand for further reference. The following is recommended as a general art history reference book:

History of Art, third edition, by H. Janson and A. Janson (Englewood Cliffs, NJ: Prentice Hall, 1986)

Finally, enjoy your own students' interpretations of *all Art Smart!* activities. Every lesson has been tested and produced in art classrooms, forged by the hearts and imaginations of many young artists. However, outcomes of lessons may vary sharply from student to student. Keep this in mind, particularly if the results you expect in your own artroom appear different from those shown in the book. This can often be an unpredictable business, even when plans and directions are provided. Yet that's the nature of art...and the source of much of our creativity.

Section Two

ART SMARTY!
AN ALL-YEAR CALENDAR
OF PERIODS OF ART
AND ARTISTS' BIRTHDAYS

The next twelve months are filled with artistic possibilities! Some suggestions for appreciation include the following:

1. Each month represents a period of art chronologically. (For example, the art of the East and Africa is on the December page.) You might plan to spend a month on a given period(s) as shown on the calendar.

2. Celebrate an artist's birthday by studying the artist's works—and, of course, by doing the related art activity. (NOTE: Many artists do not appear in the calendar. Unfortunately, not all birth dates are available, and calendar space is limited as well. However, you might refer to the "Art Smart Chart" at the back of the book to gather artists within a particular period.)

3. Experiment with different approaches. See what works best in your own situation.

The calendar will require filling in of dates, for it is not designed for any single year. Therefore, you may want to make several photocopies before you put dates in place. This way, you may reuse it many times— and try many ideas.

CAVE ART

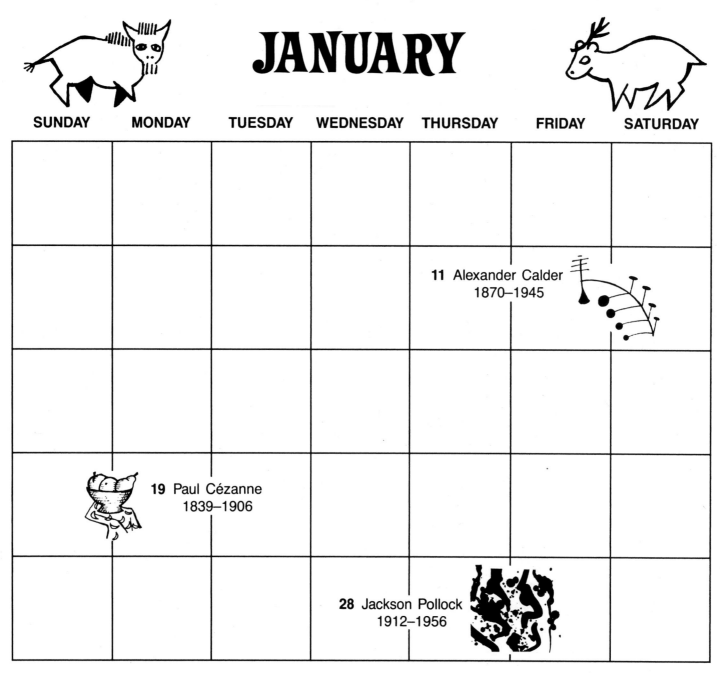

JANUARY

SUNDAY	MONDAY	TUESDAY	WEDNESDAY	THURSDAY	FRIDAY	SATURDAY
				11 Alexander Calder 1870–1945		
19 Paul Cézanne 1839–1906						
			28 Jackson Pollock 1912–1956			

STUDENT BIRTHDAYS AND MEMOS:

FEBRUARY

SUNDAY	MONDAY	TUESDAY	WEDNESDAY	THURSDAY	FRIDAY	SATURDAY

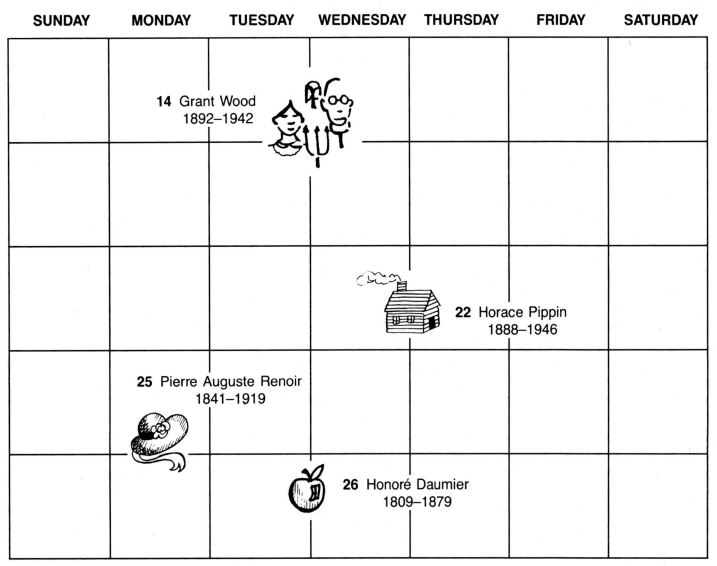

14 Grant Wood 1892–1942

22 Horace Pippin 1888–1946

25 Pierre Auguste Renoir 1841–1919

26 Honoré Daumier 1809–1879

STUDENT BIRTHDAYS AND MEMOS:

GREEK AND ROMAN

MARCH

| SUNDAY | MONDAY | TUESDAY | WEDNESDAY | THURSDAY | FRIDAY | SATURDAY |

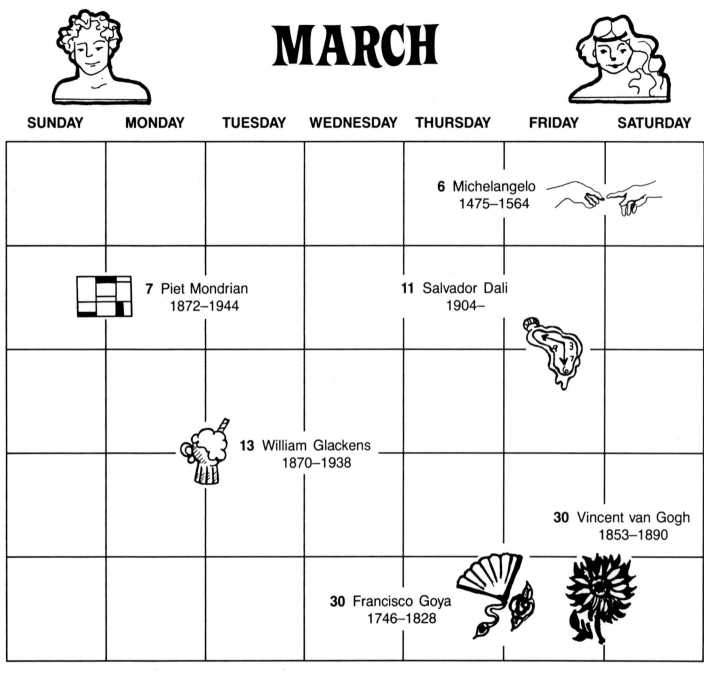

6 Michelangelo 1475–1564

7 Piet Mondrian 1872–1944

11 Salvador Dali 1904–

13 William Glackens 1870–1938

30 Vincent van Gogh 1853–1890

30 Francisco Goya 1746–1828

STUDENT BIRTHDAYS AND MEMOS:

APRIL

SUNDAY	MONDAY	TUESDAY	WEDNESDAY	THURSDAY	FRIDAY	SATURDAY

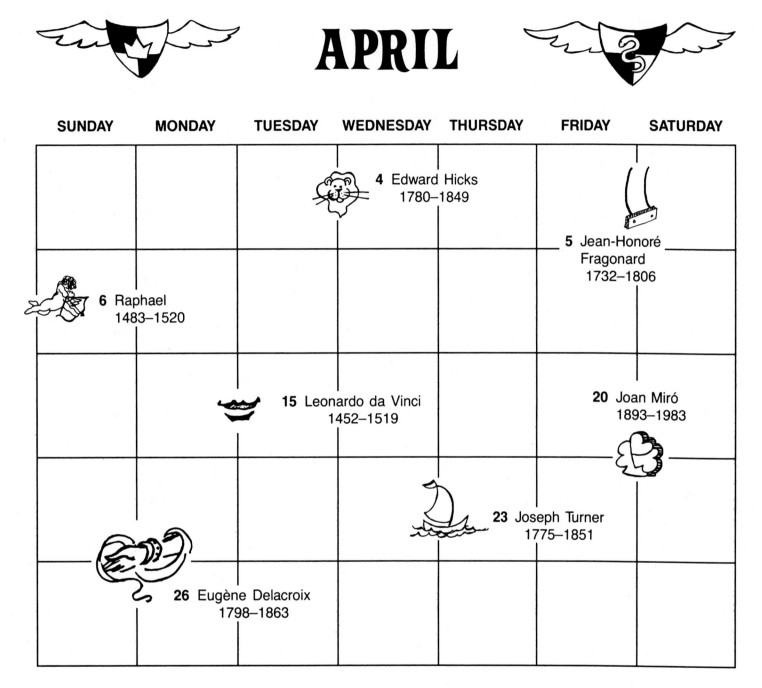

4 Edward Hicks 1780–1849

5 Jean-Honoré Fragonard 1732–1806

6 Raphael 1483–1520

15 Leonardo da Vinci 1452–1519

20 Joan Miró 1893–1983

23 Joseph Turner 1775–1851

26 Eugène Delacroix 1798–1863

STUDENT BIRTHDAYS AND MEMOS:

THE RENAISSANCE

MAY

SUNDAY	MONDAY	TUESDAY	WEDNESDAY	THURSDAY	FRIDAY	SATURDAY
				14 Thomas Gainsborough 1727–1788		
				21 Albrecht Dürer 1471–1528		
 **22** Mary Cassatt 1845–1926					**21** Henri Rousseau 1844–1910	
			 **27** Georges Rouault 1871–1958			

STUDENT BIRTHDAYS AND MEMOS:

JUNE

SUNDAY	MONDAY	TUESDAY	WEDNESDAY	THURSDAY	FRIDAY	SATURDAY

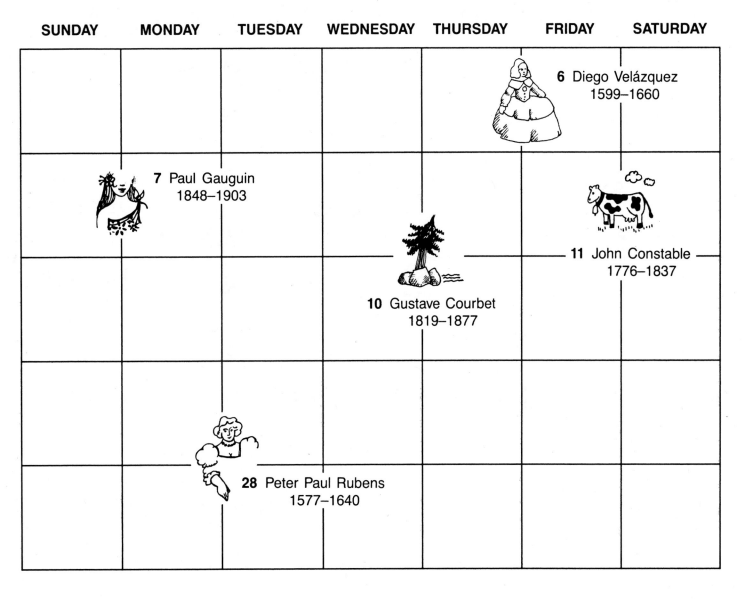

6 Diego Velázquez 1599–1660

7 Paul Gauguin 1848–1903

10 Gustave Courbet 1819–1877

11 John Constable 1776–1837

28 Peter Paul Rubens 1577–1640

STUDENT BIRTHDAYS AND MEMOS:

JULY

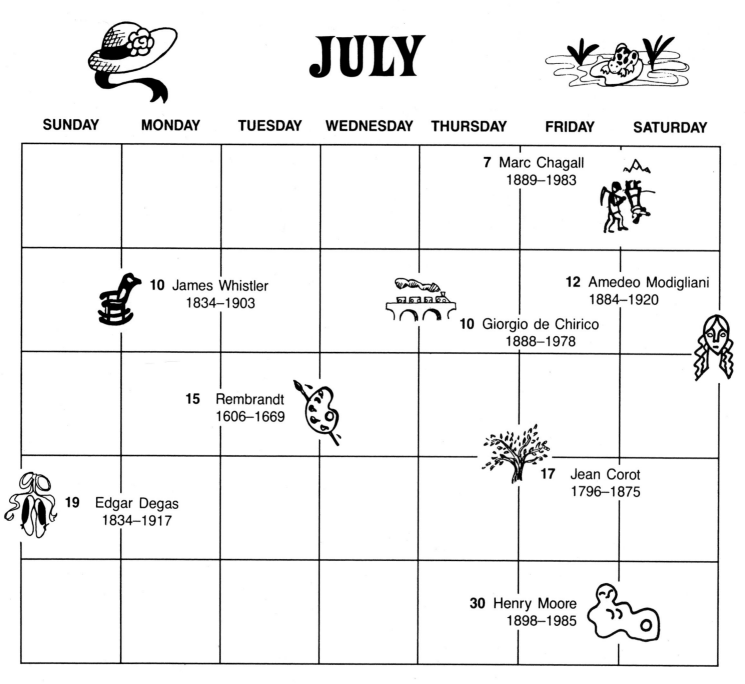

SUNDAY	MONDAY	TUESDAY	WEDNESDAY	THURSDAY	FRIDAY	SATURDAY
				7 Marc Chagall 1889–1983		
	10 James Whistler 1834–1903			**10** Giorgio de Chirico 1888–1978	**12** Amedeo Modigliani 1884–1920	
		15 Rembrandt 1606–1669			**17** Jean Corot 1796–1875	
19 Edgar Degas 1834–1917					**30** Henry Moore 1898–1985	

STUDENT BIRTHDAYS AND MEMOS:

AUGUST

SUNDAY	MONDAY	TUESDAY	WEDNESDAY	THURSDAY	FRIDAY	SATURDAY

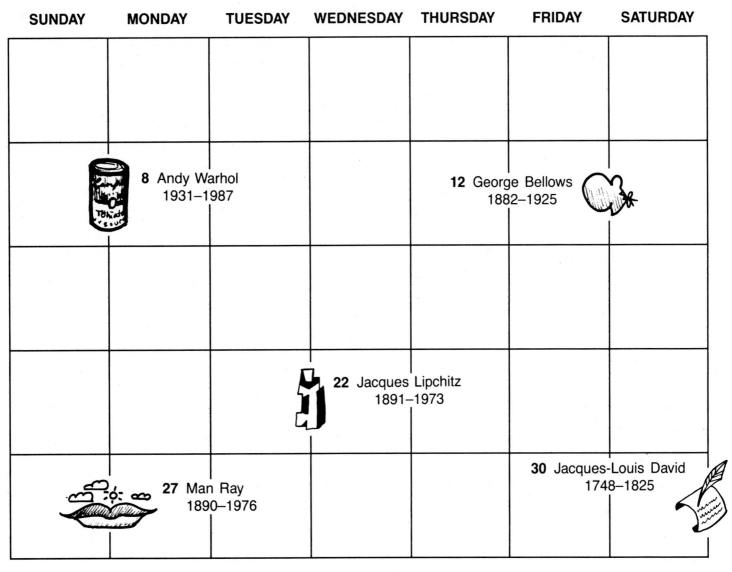

8 Andy Warhol
1931–1987

12 George Bellows
1882–1925

22 Jacques Lipchitz
1891–1973

27 Man Ray
1890–1976

30 Jacques-Louis David
1748–1825

STUDENT BIRTHDAYS AND MEMOS:

MODERN ART

 **SEPTEMBER**

SUNDAY	MONDAY	TUESDAY	WEDNESDAY	THURSDAY	FRIDAY	SATURDAY
		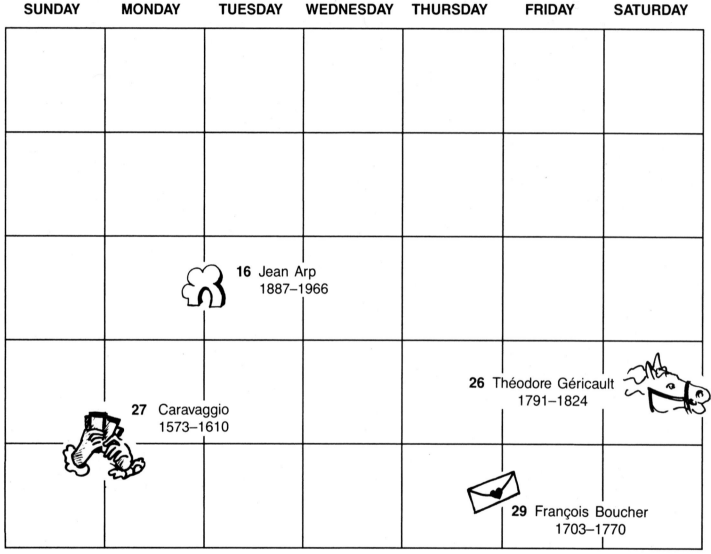 **16** Jean Arp 1887–1966				
		27 Caravaggio 1573–1610			**26** Théodore Géricault 1791–1824	
					29 François Boucher 1703–1770	

STUDENT BIRTHDAYS AND MEMOS:

OCTOBER

SUNDAY	MONDAY	TUESDAY	WEDNESDAY	THURSDAY	FRIDAY	SATURDAY

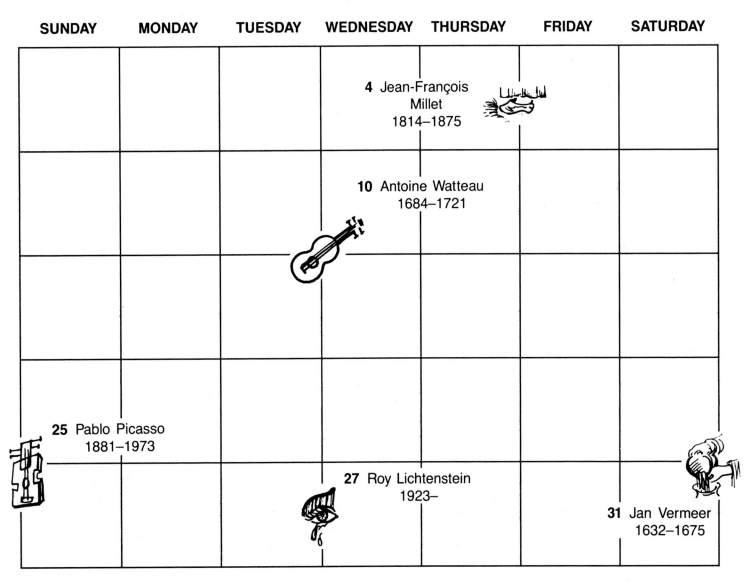

4 Jean-François Millet 1814–1875

10 Antoine Watteau 1684–1721

25 Pablo Picasso 1881–1973

27 Roy Lichtenstein 1923–

31 Jan Vermeer 1632–1675

STUDENT BIRTHDAYS AND MEMOS:

ART OF THE AMERICAS

NOVEMBER

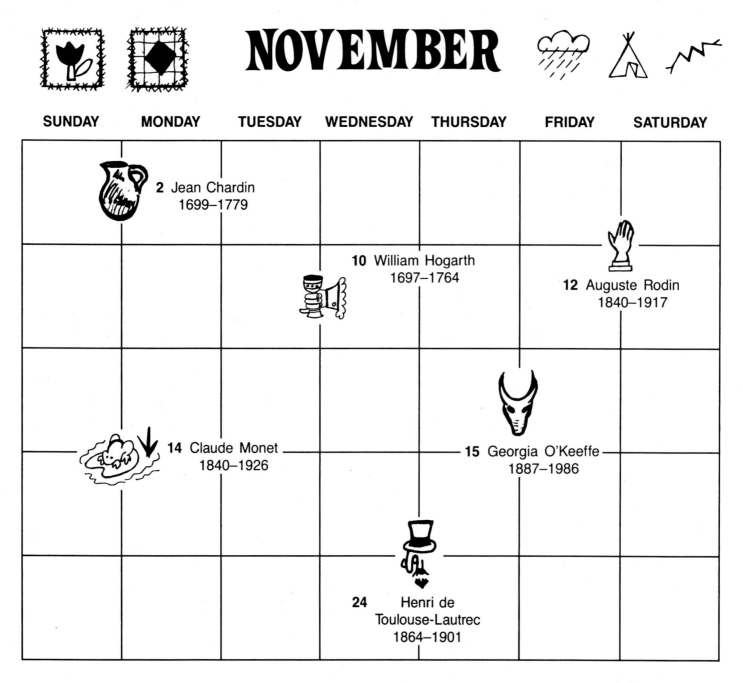

SUNDAY	MONDAY	TUESDAY	WEDNESDAY	THURSDAY	FRIDAY	SATURDAY
	2 Jean Chardin 1699–1779					
			10 William Hogarth 1697–1764		**12** Auguste Rodin 1840–1917	
			14 Claude Monet 1840–1926		**15** Georgia O'Keeffe 1887–1986	
			24 Henri de Toulouse-Lautrec 1864–1901			

STUDENT BIRTHDAYS AND MEMOS:

DECEMBER

SUNDAY	MONDAY	TUESDAY	WEDNESDAY	THURSDAY	FRIDAY	SATURDAY

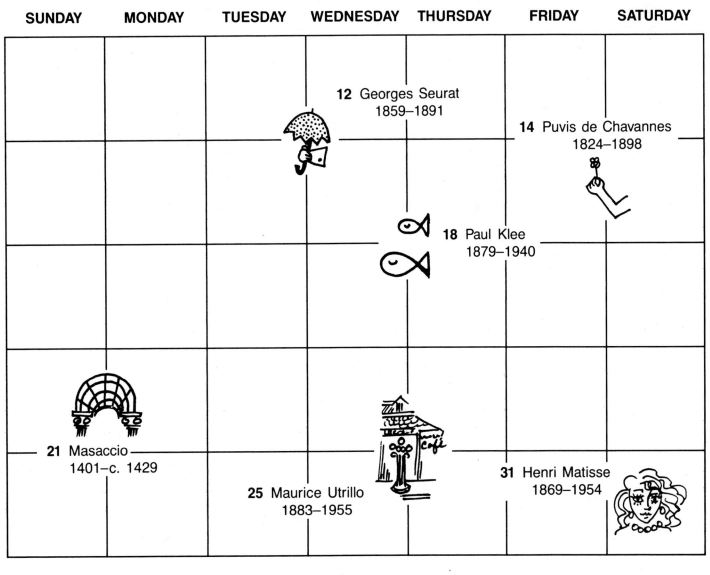

12 Georges Seurat
1859–1891

14 Puvis de Chavannes
1824–1898

18 Paul Klee
1879–1940

21 Masaccio
1401–c. 1429

25 Maurice Utrillo
1883–1955

31 Henri Matisse
1869–1954

STUDENT BIRTHDAYS AND MEMOS:

Section Three

ART ACTIVITIES FOR BECOMING ART SMART

THE STONE AGE

32,000 B.C.	15,000 B.C.	8000 B.C.	3500 B.C.
Upper Paleolithic ....Mesolithic ....Neolithic			

It is a popular belief that the cave dwellers made art to perform magic. If the Stone Age artist could first "capture" the animal he wanted for food or clothing in a drawing on the wall, success would likely follow in the hunt. Drawing the animal's image was a way to possess its spirit and gain control over it in real life.

No one can argue that art gives the artist a sense of power! This was an early discovery in our history, as the cave art attests. As to whether or not the animals were drawn for purely ritualistic purposes, well, that is another matter for our speculation.

Just as people today paint and sculpt for many different reasons, we can assume the same held true for the Stone Age artist. Art is created for the enjoyment and pleasure it brings and to allow us to express our ideas. Our early ancestors, with their often-elegant images on rocky walls, did indeed begin this process we call Art History. And you may be sure it will continue—whether we draw with plant roots, paint brushes, or computer keys. Our need to communicate is as old as the cave art itself, and just as basic and compelling.

ACTIVITY 1
Art of the Cave Dwellers

MURALS: Drawing, Rubbing

Animals are the most common image found in Stone Age art. To the Cro-Magnon, they represented life itself! They were the primary source for food and clothing, so it is easy to understand why cave dwellers had animals on their minds.

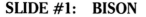

FIGURE 10. "Mother and Daughter" by Carlton, age 10.

SLIDE #1:   BISON

MATERIALS

- Twigs (see Teacher Preparation)
- India ink or black poster paint
- Butcher wrap paper
- Masking tape
- Paper towels

- Broken crayons (wide type preferred) —black and brown
- Watercolor paint and brushes
- Watercups or containers

TEACHER PREPARATION

An effective way to gather primitive drawing tools is to go on a "twig hunt." This can be accomplished on a class nature walk, a field trip, or by searching out twigs on school grounds. However, if none of these suggestions is feasible for your school, then you may want to provide twigs and sticks for the class. Should all else fail, visit the lumberyard (watch for splinters, please) or buy manicure sticks at the dime store. (See Activity 3.)

Butcher wrap paper should be precut into mural sections of approximately one yard in length. Find a wall, preferably on the outside of the building, that has a rough texture. Depending on your group and schedule, either tape the paper onto the wall prior to class or have the students tape their own panels when the lesson begins. Students may want to work together on a panel.

HINT: Portion the India ink into well-balanced containers to prevent spills in the classroom. You may want to use black poster paint instead of India ink with younger children.

DIRECTIONS

1. Discuss the subject matter most often seen in cave paintings. Some examples are bisons, buffalos, bulls, wooly mammoths, and other large mammals. Before making the images, students should create a surface on the brown paper that resembles the cave's texture.

2. Tape brown paper to the wall. Students may work in small groups, using the sides of the crayons to create a rough textural effect on paper. Once the paper surface is fairly well rubbed by the broad side of the crayon, remove the mural paper from the wall and return to the classroom to work on table surfaces.

3. Distribute ink (or poster paint) in containers. Students will be using twigs (see Teacher Preparation) as drawing tools. Create animal imagery on paper with linear drawings.

4. After ink outlines dry sufficiently, bring out the watercolors. Talk about *earth colors:* brown, orange, yellow, red, tan. Students should be selecting earth colors from the watercolor box to paint their animals. Ask students to think about adjusting the amount of water in their brush, by using the paper towel to absorb the excess, to achieve light and dark shading effects. Subtle variety of color tone can be observed in original cave paintings of animals.

5. Display completed works together on a suitable wall. Paintings placed side-by-side can give the impression of a real cave.

ACTIVITY 2
The World's First Art Gallery

3-D CONSTRUCTION: Charcoal, Chalk Drawings

When we want to find out what artists of the past and present hope to communicate to us, we visit an art gallery or museum. To better understand the art of our earliest ancestors, we refer to the pictures they left for us on their cave walls some 20,000 years ago.

MATERIALS

- Manila paper (or substitute brown shopping bags—you will need *half* the number of your class size)
- Charcoal sticks (chamois cloth)
- Conte crayons (if available)
- Colored chalk (optional)
- Empty refrigerator carton (see Teacher Preparation)
- White glue
- Masking tape (optional)

FIGURE 11. In a former life, this "cave" was a refrigerator carton. The transformation is impressive, isn't it?

TEACHER PREPARATION

Your "World's First Art Gallery" is an empty refrigerator carton turned upside down. The cave entrance will be cut out by the teacher using heavy shears or a mat knife. Should you have difficulty locating an oversized appliance box, you may want to experiment with several smaller cardboard cartons by cutting and taping them together. You will also need to decide if *one* refrigerator carton is suitable for your class size. (One can accommodate about fifteen drawings.) Should you decide on more than one "cave," they can be displayed side by side. Another choice is to rotate the "show," changing the exhibit as required.

You might want to purchase or collect inexpensive linoleum floor tiles that have pebbly surfaces to use for your cave (a.k.a. art gallery) exterior. (See Figure 11.) Nonetheless, you'll want to paint the outside with a neutral color (gray, brown, etc.). This is a job for a few students to do.

Further realism may be gained on the cave's inside art exhibit by *tearing* the edge of your manila paper first (tear brown shopping bags into drawing paper size), imparting a more natural look to the artwork.

DIRECTIONS

1. Encourage each student to pick a partner (or assign partners), thus cutting in half the number of artworks to be displayed inside the cave gallery.
2. Discuss the concept of *action* between the beasts (wooly mammoths, bisons, etc.) to include hunting as well (try to avoid too much aggression here!). Animals should be imagined in various postures, such as running, leaping, and chasing each other.
3. Draw animals with charcoal, *shading* with the little finger or chamois cloth. Indicate animals' fur patterns. If colored chalk is used, select *earth* colors.
4. Upon completion of drawing, both of the Stone Age artist partners should sign their names in the true manner of that period—with the sign of a *handprint*. They may trace their hand's outline for it.
5. You might want to experiment with the finished drawings by crumpling the paper, thereby lending further resemblance to an actual cave wall.

**FIGURE 12. The view inside the
"world's first art gallery."**

6. Students (or teacher) will mount their Stone Age art inside the wall and ceiling of the cave (with rolled masking tape if you are changing exhibits). Perhaps you will want to have a Stone Age art opening? If so, here's a recipe for a time-honored beverage, *Pebble Punch:*

   1 bag of miniature marshmallows

   1 gallon of fruit juice

   paper cups

   Float the marshmallow "pebbles" in the cups of punch. Invite artists to discuss their work. Mingle. And don't forget a flashlight!

   NOTE: Charcoal *does* smear and "gallery" visitors should be apprised of this fact! Fixatives and other aerosol sprays are *not* recommended because they are irritating to the respiratory system and are generally *not* safe for classroom use. Simply exercise a little care in handling and viewing the art.

ACTIVITY 3
Art Hunt

HANDMADE ART TOOLS:
Experimental Painting

Dinner had to be hunted in the Stone Age, and the same held true for art supplies. Primitive people hunted and gathered fur, bones, horns, and many other materials to produce their own art tools. Some implements were made to incise or carve rock; others were for the application of plant dyes, animal blood, and earth pigments. Since there were no art supply stores or hobby shops back then, the materials were sure to be as inventive as the cave art itself.

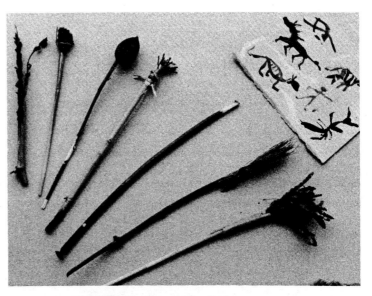

FIGURE 13. Elegant in their simplicity, these student-made tools are ready for the jobs at hand!

MATERIALS

- Branches; also reeds, bamboo (see Teacher Preparation)
- Pine needles
- Embroidery weight thread, or lightweight string (grass may also be used)
- Poster or acrylic paint (see Teacher Preparation)
- Manila paper
- Scissors

TEACHER PREPARATION

The most effective and meaningful presentation of the activity will follow our own "hunting and gathering" of materials. This will require scheduling an appropriate time for students to go on a nature walk. Should this not be possible, teacher and students will bring natural materials to class (unassembled) which they've collected on their own. Use imagination in your selections, but watch out for irritating poisonous plants, such as sumac and poison ivy! You may want to identify these sorts of plants beforehand.

The ingredients you use for the lesson may be entirely composed of natural substances. The brush hairs can be fashioned from pine needles and of other various small leaves; the handles made of branches, bamboo, reeds, and so forth. Tools may be bound with grasses, but you could substitute with heavy thread if you're not concerned with being a purist!

Students will work best as partners during the nature walk and for the duration of this activity. Paint will provide the test for the tools. If there is a desire to extend the activity beyond tool construction, see "Suggestions for Further Development."

DIRECTIONS

1. Search for your art tools! Be open minded—some objects that appear to be unlikely candidates work out quite well! Pods, for example, as well as small pine cones, are surprisingly effective drawing implements. Do not overlook the simple and obvious choices, such as sticks for "pencils." Remember, you'll need handles, brushes, and binding materials.

2. In the classroom students will assist each other as partners while constructing tools. One student may hold materials in place, the other can wrap and tie parts together. Scissors should be nearby.

3. The class will trade "parts," completing tool tops and bottoms. Adjust lengths.

4. The students' own hands are "tools" too! Fingers should tie, twist, tighten, etc.

5. When art tools are complete, distribute paint and paper. You may tear edges of paper and crumple it a bit to make it appear more naturalistic.

6. Try out your handwrought brushes and pen. Thin your paint if necessary. Experiment!

7. Save art tools for suitable activities. (See Activities 1, 2, and 4.) They are, after all, working tools of the trade, and as time-tested as can possibly be!

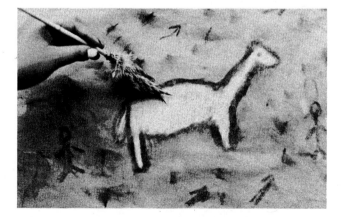

FIGURE 14. Experiment! The cave drawing shown here is dusted with a dry brush.

SUGGESTIONS FOR FURTHER DEVELOPMENT

If this sort of activity intrigues you and your students, you may wish to extend it to the creation of natural paints and dyes. Again, safety precautions must be used against poisonous plants, but a lesson in *plant dyes* will take you into the field for research once again! Should you pursue it, such substances would be the perfect companions for your handmade art tools.

There are books available on the subject of plant and vegetable dyes that can be used in the classroom by students and teachers. Consult your librarian for suggestions.

Who knows? Next, you might even want to make your own paper—thus making this lesson into an entire study unit that is 100 percent pure!

ACTIVITY 4
Rock Masterpieces

ROCK PAINTING: Paperweights

FIGURE 15. Some rocks just ask to be painted!

Each rock wears its own history, shaped by the rain, sand, and wind it may have known. All rocks are not alike. They are unique natural sculptures—some smooth and shiny, others craggy, rough, and wrinkled. As in all areas of nature you'll find both the plain and the fancy. Many a rocky wall has exerted its appeal to artists, who were compelled to leave their marks upon it for posterity!

MATERIALS

- Rocks (see Teacher Preparation)
- Acrylic paints
- Brushes (assorted)
- Practice paper

TEACHER PREPARATION

Clearly there are certain rocks that lend themselves to painting upon, while others are more difficult to use for this purpose. If you or your students have saved rocks, either for reasons of pleasure or for serious rock collection, you may already possess a few possibilities for our rock paperweights. You'll want smooth, flat rocks over bumpy ones; size is discretionary.

Other means for finding the "right rock" include a field trip or a visit to a gardening supply center where the more comely rocks may be purchased. Also, check out sources used by landscape architects, such as construction suppliers to that trade.

You may want to seize this opportunity to learn more about the rocks that are indigenous to your region, as well as the comparative qualities of rocks and stones in general. Books on geology and fossils can be engaging and are closely aligned to this activity. Reference books on Paleolithic art and cave art are recommended for their pictorial imagery.

DIRECTIONS

1. Consider the characteristics of rocks. Students will describe rocks, either on nature walks or in the classroom. Try to anticipate the receptivity of the surface to the brush. Distribute all materials.

2. Test your brush on the face of the rock by painting your initials or a small mark. This will give you some idea of what to expect. Go to the practice paper and try some images based on reference materials and your own ideas.

3. Paint both sides of the rock using analogous ideas, such as fish and water, birds and clouds, a leaf and tree. Keep it simple, like the original cave art (or fossils) you'll observe in the illustrated books.

4. One side of the rock will have to dry before you paint the other side unless you manage to prop up your rock firmly. Painting in small strokes may work better than continuous flowing lines if the surface is porous. Darker rocks, like Japanese river rocks, will look best when painted in white line.

5. You may want to experiment with the tools constructed in Activity 3 first on practice paper and then on your rocks for various effects.

6. Finished rocks will hold down paper and your interest! They're reversible, too.

FIGURE 16. On the flip side of the fish—the analogous wave.

SUGGESTIONS FOR FURTHER DEVELOPMENT

There are other ways to turn rocks into art activities. One of these is the combining of small rocks and stones with other natural materials, such as twigs and pinecones, to assemble little sculptures. Animals' heads, such as a deer with antlers (even miniature figures), may be fashioned from stones and wood with glue.

EGYPTIAN

3000 B.C.	2000 B.C.	1500 B.C.	1000 B.C.
Old Kingdom . . . . Middle Kingdom . . . . New Kingdom . . . . Late Period			

There is no denying that the religious customs of the ancient Egyptians figured deeply in their society and, consequently, in their art. The tombs with their elaborate paintings, the mummies' sarcophagi, the jewelry, and other artifacts strongly reflected their beliefs. Yet, the art of ancient Egypt—although influenced by the theories of afterlife—was anything but somber!

The decorative, flattened images were stylized, but they also managed to be quite expressive. There seemed to be much joy—singing, dancing, playing musical instruments—and, of course, they depicted the daily business of life along the Nile.

The pharoahs and their dynasties were ever-present as well. The great pyramids that rose from the desert sand were the monuments built by them and for them. It is remarkable that these colossal structures were brought up without any benefit of modern technology. Every bit as impressive are the statuaries and the hieroglyphic messages contained inside.

Mixed in with the painting of figures, animals, and plant forms were symbols and hieroglyph. Pictures, words, and signs blended harmoniously together, reminding us that at one time, art and writing were one. These pictorial compositions had a poetry of their own and are at the roots of our language. In a very real sense they translate into powerful statements. Egyptian art does indeed have a story to tell!

ACTIVITY 5
The Case of the Mummies

LIFE-SIZED DRAWING: Body Tracing

The art of the ancient Egyptians is filled with symbols and decorative designs. As the archaeologists uncover more tombs, the world of Egypt is revealed to us. Of all the Egyptian art objects and paintings, it is hard to find anything more fascinating than mummies!

SLIDE #2:   MUMMY CASE

MATERIALS

- Butcher wrap paper
- Oil pastels (substitute with crayons or poster paint)
- Thick black crayon or dark waterbased marker
- Scissors
- Gold acrylic paint (optional)

FIGURE 17. "Mummy" by Kentrell, age 8.

TEACHER PREPARATION

You might want to cut lengths of butcher wrap paper ahead of time to accommodate students' heights. This is recommended when time and space are limited—and when you want to avoid excessive movement in the classroom.

DIRECTIONS

1. You may want to introduce the lesson by discussing the meaning of mummies to ancient Egyptian life. Talk about the elements used to decorate mummies—birds, serpents, stylized eyes, creatures that are half-man, half-beast, etc. Some mention should be made of the way that Egyptians communicated through pictures and signs, as in the art of hieroglyphs.
2. Next, fold butcher paper down the center lengthwise.
3. Place open paper *flat* on the floor where students will be traced either by you or by each other, depending on the ability of students. Use thick crayon or marker for outlines.
4. The student will lie down in the middle of the paper, on the center line. *Trace around only one side of student,* using a "mummy-shaped" outline.

5. Have student get up; fold paper in half again. Place paper on appropriate surface and cut out mummy shape on the outline. Open and you will have a perfectly symmetrical mummy case.

6. Design your mummy. White is effective for the face, although in ancient Egypt, men were often depicted as brown, and women as yellow. Be sure to talk about the use of black lines around the eyes, the shape of the headdress, the decorative "beard," and the facial expression.

7. For the mummy's overall look, you will want to decide on the design of the case. Students may want to start with bands of dark outlines into which design elements are arranged. Here is where symbols, hieroglyphs, stylized animals, and people can dynamically combine with the student's own imagination.

8. When the surface appears rich with color and imagery, your Egyptian mummy is complete. Mummies displayed side-by-side make an awesome sight!

NOTE: "The Case of the Mummies" is an ideal partnership project. Students can double up to work on one mummy, cooperate in making design decisions, and share the pride of the finished product.

ACTIVITY 6
Carved in Stone

SCRIBAL ARTS: Styrofoam "Tablets"

To be a scribe in ancient Egypt was no small matter. It was a prestigious job that required a specialized talent. Scribes were, after all, the recorders of history! The ancient Pharoahs were indebted to their royal scribes. Without them, how could hieroglyphs have ever carried forth their dynastic legacies?

MATERIALS

- Styrofoam meat trays
  (See Teacher Preparation)
- Stylus pens
- Cardboard
- Gold acrylic paint
- Scissors
- Glue
- Labels (self-stick)
- Practice papers
- Pencils

FIGURE 18. Carved in styrofoam, the message reads, "Her magic scares the king..." (The thoughtful words of a 12-year-old scribe.) Yet another message suggests "Rich men weep too." Students display both artistic and literary talent in this activity.

TEACHER PREPARATION

You'll need to ask your butcher or friendly supermarket counter person for styrofoam trays, or ask students to wash and save them. Yellow or gold trays will put you one step ahead—they're "golden" before paint application begins!

Reference materials may include Egyptian design elements, such as lotus leaves, scarabs, birds, and so forth. Reproductions of Egyptian wall paintings may suggest further ideas, particularly those combining pictures with glyphs.

Stylus pens work best to inscribe styrofoam, but ballpoint pens may be substituted. Cardboard may be cut ahead of time into manageable pieces.

DIRECTIONS

1. Study the reference material. What do you think the pictograms might mean? Guess! Distribute materials.

2. Paint your styrofoam tray in gold. Let dry.

3. Use practice paper to try out your own inscriptions. Be imaginative—a secret message, clues to a buried treasure, an original quotation, even a birthday wish list—are all worth trying.

4. Inscribe ideas into the dry tablets when you're ready. Cardboard cut into relevant shapes may be glued into the tablet. Paint them also and let dry again.

5. Write the meaning of your tablet on the self-stick label in pencil. Peel and afix to the back of the tablet.

6. Can your message be decoded? Try to understand each other's intended communication. "Scribes" may tell all after guessing has taken place.

7. Golden tablets may be propped up against a suitable ledge or mounted for display.

SUGGESTIONS FOR FURTHER DEVELOPMENT

For the tablets that incorporate cardboard reliefs: a sheet of tracing paper placed on top, along with the application of the broad side of a crayon, will produce original temple rubbings!

 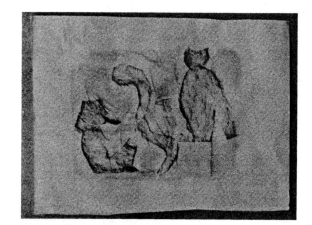

FIGURE 19. A "tomb" rubbing.
(Examples of hieroglyphs may be
found on the February calendar.)

ACTIVITY 7
Hieroglyph-O-Grams

HIEROGLYPHS: Scribal Arts

Hieroglyphs are composed of written language, drawings, and symbols. Much like a rebus, the combination of pictures and words tell a story. We will deliver our messages via our own unique communiqué—the hieroglyph-o-gram!

SLIDE #3:   HIEROGLYPHS WITH EGYPTIAN WALL PAINTING

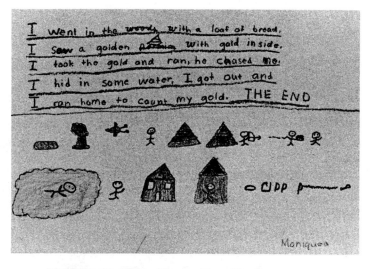

FIGURE 20. Write like an Egyptian!
Moniquea's pithy story is told with pictograms.

MATERIALS

- Pencils
- Crayons or markers
- Manila drawing paper
- Butcher wrap paper (optional)

TEACHER PREPARATION

Students will benefit from looking over various examples of ancient written languages before originating their own hybrid forms. Reference materials on Sumerian and Egyptian scribal arts would be helpful for this and other art activities on Egypt.

DIRECTIONS

1. Discuss possibilities for page arrangements. Messages can read horizontally or vertically! What are some topics to use for your hieroglyphs?
2. Encourage students to select events that may be reported in a simple, straightforward manner. Subjects may include student "news"—a recent experience, or even a bit of fantasy!
3. As in any good story, this message must have a beginning, middle, and end. One action should follow another in logical order, no matter how the page is organized. Teacher will support student invention, of course. The students' pictorial languages will be essentially their own.
4. Finished products may be rolled into scrolls and "sealed" (with a self-stick circle or a bit of decorated masking tape). Exchange heiroglyph-o-grams or appoint a "messenger" to deliver them at random and read them aloud.
5. For an effective display cut brown butcher paper into large triangular shapes to resemble pyramids, folding in half before cutting. Affix students' hieroglyphs to "tomb" walls.

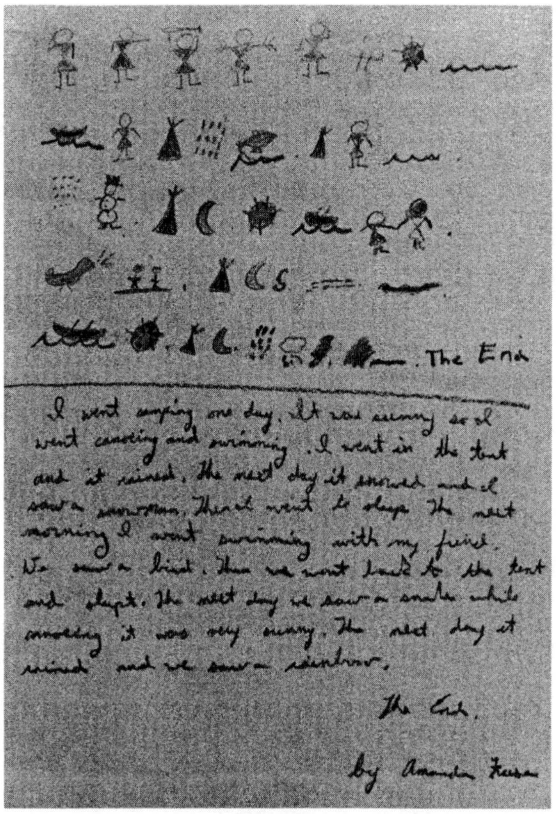

FIGURE 21. Students may well end up inventing their own personal picture language.

ACTIVITY 8
The Writing on the Wall

WALL ART: Painting

Egyptian painting is a language of pictures and words. Together, these powerful forms produce the evocative images we know as Egyptian art. Highly stylized figures, animals, and plants effectively communicate a real sense of life! You can almost feel the busy moments and small pleasures of this ancient world by observing the severely designed, but oddly moving, painting that is tomb wall art.

FIGURE 22. Boys fishing. Wall sized.
Based on an original Egyptian tomb painting.

MATERIALS

- Butcher wrap paper
  (see Teacher Preparation)
- Acrylic or poster paint
- Gold acrylic paint (optional)
- Assorted brushes (wide to small)
- Gesso (see Teacher Preparation)
- Markers (optional)
- Tape (optional; see Teacher Preparation)
- Yardsticks
- Pencils

TEACHER PREPARATION

Precut lengths of butcher wrap into mural-size panels. Next, paint with gesso. Allow it time to dry before "wall" painting begins. Gesso is best applied with wide, flat brushes. Drying time of one coat is fairly quick, depending on the humidity. Gesso will simulate the chalky tomb wall where ancient paintings and hieroglyphs were found. Students can participate in gesso application if desired.

Butcher paper may be taped against classroom walls for the effect of real wall painting, but can be removed at any point and placed on flat work surface until completion. NOTE: thinner paint tends to drip.

This lesson may require several sessions. Set up for a full-scale painting activity.

Reference materials including illustration of Egyptian wall art are recommended.

DIRECTIONS

1. Observe your reference materials. Notice the posture of the figures? Ask students to stand up and assume the classic Egyptian poses! Sit down again.
2. Once understanding is reached about the wafer-thin nature of silhouetted Egyptian figures with their full eyes shown in unfailing profile, turn attention to overall composition. Notice the lining up of pictorial images and hieroglyphs, and how space is divided. Also observe the wall's texture.

3. All materials should be made available with gessoed panel "walls" in place. Students will work in groups. They should agree upon subjects and decide who will paint the determined areas.

4. Outline figures and objects in pencil. Yardsticks may be called upon to regulate the glyphs in columns.

5. Choose earth colors and other selections that best express the Egyptian originals. Turquoise and yellow, burnt orange and ochre are excellent! Don't be afraid to outline with markers, which can also be helpful for drawing hieroglyphs. Gold acrylic may also be applied as desired.

6. Some indication of wall surface may be attempted by replicating cracks and rough areas. Carry out the composition to its fullest degree! Work all students' names into the hieroglyphs.

7. Mounting paintings directly on the classroom walls will recreate the splendor of an ancient Egyptian temple. The effects are powerful, indeed.

SUGGESTIONS FOR FURTHER DEVELOPMENT

There is another direction toward which you can take this lesson, which will teach students about archaeology and restoration. To do so, follow the directions as indicated previously. You should then ask students if they are willing to submit their work to an "excavation." Explain that this will mean their work must be altered, but will be restored in the end. If they are willing, proceed as follows:

1. Remove sections of the painting in advance of the class with a mat knife, keeping them intact. Hold these "fragments" aside. Distribute "excavated" murals at class time (less the missing parts) to groups that did *not* originate them. In short, switch groups. Distribute the materials listed, plus some sections of brown wrap, preferably gessoed, for patching the paintings.

2. The object is to anticipate the missing parts and reconstruct them. It will be important to match colors and stylistic elements. This is the challenge of the archaeologist on the dig—to uncover and preserve the remains of civilizations. New sections will have to be glued or taped in place from the back of the panel.

3. When the conservation has been completed, you should bring out the "fragments" removed earlier. How well did the students do? The "missing links" will tell!

4. You might want the students to tag the "fragments." Reference books on archaeology will provide pointers. In the end, you will have an activity that combined art, archaeology, and the restoration of ancient ruins.

ACTIVITY 9
Under the Papyrus

GRAPHIC DESIGN: Notepapers

Egyptians invented several forms of pictorial language, known generally as hieroglyphs. The Egyptians have long been regarded as the all-time great communicators. So, it is quite fitting that we design original notebook paper in their honor.

FIGURE 23. Notable notepaper, fit for the Queen of the Nile.

FIGURE 24. More notepaper for the Queen and the Pharaoh.

MATERIALS

- Pencils with erasers
- 9″ × 12″ practice paper
- Typewriter or tracing paper
- Black felt-tipped pens

TEACHER PREPARATION

Examples of Egyptian design motifs should be made available to students for reference. Should the teacher have samples of stationery using strong graphic borders (such as Art Nouveau), these may be used as samples for page design.

DIRECTIONS

1. Practice different themes for borders based on Egyptian-style decorative elements. *Remember to leave center blank for writing space!*
2. Once a border is chosen, transfer the design directly to typewriter or tracing paper. Try to leave some "extra" space around edges for leeway in copying later.
3. Develop strong design contrasts by selectively darkening areas, as well as blocking in shapes, with black felt-tipped pen.
4. Give an artistic signature to the artwork, respecting the flow of the design.
5. Finished products will be considered as "originals," from which other prints or copies will be made. (See "Suggestions for Replication.")
6. Should further development of design be desired, hand-color with markers or colored pencils. Note papers will make wonderful gifts when wrapped in ribbons or presented in decorated cigar or shoe boxes!

SUGGESTIONS FOR REPLICATION

If there is a financially feasible way to do it, the best way to make copies is to take the originals to an instant copy center. The desired number of copies may then be made on white or on any colored paper suitable—goldenrod, bright yellow, buff, and orange are perfect.

Other possibilities for reproducing stationery include transfer of the image onto a ditto master or stencil and then running off copies, if such methods are readily available. When all else fails, consider layers of carbon paper as an alternative.

ACTIVITY 10
The Powerful Pyramid: Inside and Out!

ARCHITECTURE: Paper Construction

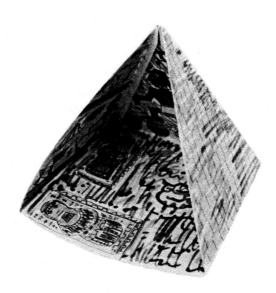

FIGURE 25. The pyramid holds many mysteries.

The spectacular Egyptian pyramids have continued to amaze us throughout the centuries. Their monumental size alone is breathtaking. But when you consider that these colossal structures were brought up in the middle of the desert, without a single advantage of modern technology, it becomes even more astonishing! Inside the pyramids exist the remarkable hieroglyphs, art, and artifacts—all of this to serve as tombs for the mighty pharoahs. It is no surprise that the great pyramids, alongside the Sphinx, are foremost among the Seven Wonders of the World.

MATERIALS

- Oaktag (see Teacher Preparation)
- Pencils
- Scissors
- Markers (fine tip)
- Glue
- Rulers
- Masking tape

TEACHER PREPARATION

Figures 26 through 28 will be your guides for pyramid construction. You may want to cut the oaktag ahead of time to match the recommended scale, or first experiment with other sizes for student assemblage. Creating templates for tracing the pyramid shapes is strongly recommended. Should you want students to produce their own patterns, provide plenty of time for trial and error. Be prepared to offer assistance in either case.

Materials that clearly illustrate pyramids—their shape, surface, construction, relative size—as well as reproductions of the interiors are recommended. Books on artifacts, such as King Tut's treasures, will further stimulate interest.

You may want to use this activity as a gateway into the origins and history of architecture. (See "Suggestions for Further Development.") If so, books on the subject, such as *Pyramid* by David Macauley (Boston: Houghton Mifflin, 1975), will be helpful.

DIRECTIONS

1. Study the reference material. Remind yourselves that these structures were designed as tombs—and you'll be recreating miniature versions of the inside and outside. Describe what you'd expect both to look like or to contain.

2. Distribute all materials. Students may begin with either the outside wall or start inside the tomb—it's a matter of personal preference. Trace and cut out.

3. *For the outside:* Study the manner of construction, the particular appearance of the materials on the surface, how shadows emphasize design, and so forth. You may want to include some Egyptian people at the base of your pyramid to indicate scale.

4. *For the inside:* First consider the wall painting—the decorative symbols, glyphs, and imagery. Then, think about the other objects you might include—statuaries, chests, ostrich feathers, fans, ancient musical instruments, and other artifacts. Reference material may be used. Follow the direction of your unconstructed pyramid. Remember that the center is the floor (a good place for ornamental mummy cases). Draw with markers.

5. When the inside and outside are complete, the flaps that join the pyramid walls may be scored. You may want to cut an entrance or windows into the pyramid. One wall may also be removed to allow an inside view.

6. Glue tabs together along seams. Masking tape may be used to hold sides together until glue dries.

7. Tiny powerful pyramids! Display in groups, using reference material to produce original arrangements of structures along the Great Nile!

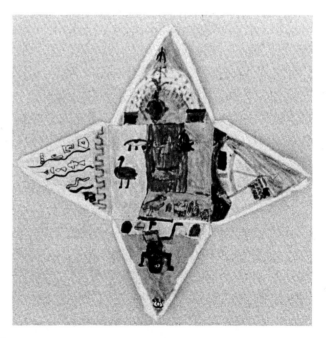

FIGURE 26. A pyramid revealed before assemblage.

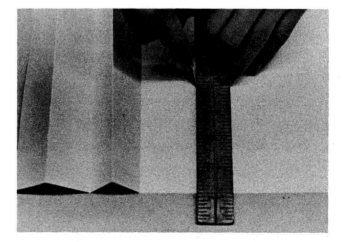

FIGURE 27. Paper scoring is quite easy to do and provides a sharper fold. Simply draw along ruler edge with a sharp object, such as scissors, where the fold is desired. Then fold. X-acto® knives should be used by teachers only!

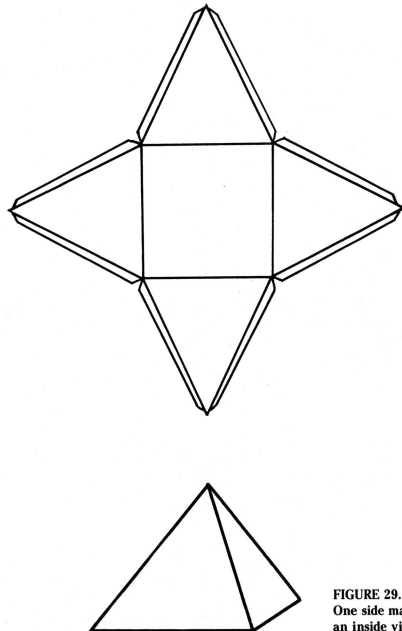

FIGURE 28. Cut the oaktag in the shape shown here. The recommended scale is 5 inches. Paper may be scored and folded when the interior and exterior are decorated. The edges should be folded back and glued for assembly.

FIGURE 29. The complete pyramid. One side may be cut away to reveal an inside view.

SUGGESTIONS FOR FURTHER DEVELOPMENT

It was King Zoser who appointed the first architect to the building of his pyramid. The man was Imhotep, and could very likely be considered a leader of his craft. There are many other fascinating facts that surround the construction of pyramids which could be developed into a study unit. The pyramids we constructed during this activity might easily be used as a basis for a diorama or exhibition that would illustrate the details of "building" art history!

GREEK AND ROMAN

700 B.C.	500-400 B.C.	300 B.C.	200 B.C.	100 B.C.	30 A.D.	400 A.D.
Archaic Period . . . . . Classical . . . . . Hellenistic . . . . . Greco/Roman . . . . . Imperial Rome						

Greek art has become completely enmeshed with our environment and culture. The architecture of public buildings—universities, libraries, museums—are the tangible evidence. Pediments and columns are everywhere it seems! Why?

Greek art and architecture—like Greek philosophy, drama and literature—are at the foundation of our civilization. The word *classical*, synonymous with this ancient period, encapsulates its meaning. The gods and goddesses established a tradition for physical beauty, while the orderly, formal qualities of the Greek temples—the buildings where much of the sculpture resided—set criteria that remain with us today.

Even the drawings on Greek pottery have the classical quality, as evidenced in their exquisite line work. Such aesthetics don't disappear, but become a motif that will renew itself, as in the drawings of Picasso many centuries later. But that is what classical art is about—it is resilient, and it endures.

So where does Rome fit into the art of the classical world?

Often the art of Rome is dismissed as an ambitious copycat of Greek art, leaving it as something of a footnote in the history of art. While the impact of Greece on Rome is undeniable, Roman art and architecture clearly hold up on their own.

It was in Rome, specifically Pompeii, where the art of painting as we know it began to take shape. Painting grew out of mosaics, another art form at which the Romans excelled. These contributions could hardly be considered minor. Nor could Rome's development of the legal system, as detailed in the portrait busts of senators, politicians, orators, and other imperial figures of their time. These sculptures are as uniquely Roman as the Coliseum itself.

Greek and Roman art and culture are singular indeed. Together they form the bedrock of our modern world.

ACTIVITY 11
From Apollo to Zeus: Gods and Goddesses of Mythology

ARCHITECTURE: 3-D Pediments

We must remember that Greek temples were built as shrines for the all-important gods and goddesses of the ancient world. Their influence was awesome; their myths and legends immortal.

FIGURE 30. A Greek pediment, from left to right: god of armor, goddess of hearts, god of fire, goddess of air, goddess of flowers, goddess of sky, and god of bumble bees.

MATERIALS

- White paper
- Colored markers or crayons
- Scissors
- White glue

- Foam board or cardboard
- Tape suitable for heavier mounting (such as double-sided foam tape)
- Masking tape

TEACHER PREPARATION

Obtain foam board from the local art supply store if possible—it's great for construction projects. To make the pediment in which your gods and goddesses will dwell, you may want to precut parts beforehand. A triangular shape with three strips to be attached will do it. An instant architectural detail!

To further familiarize students with Greek mythological deities, you might make reference materials available for their use, such as books and illustrations. (See "Suggestions" for recommended texts, as well as a list of the more important mythological subjects.) The names of the gods and goddesses and their powers can be listed on the chalkboard or on a chart before beginning the lesson.

DIRECTIONS

1. Discuss the role of deities in Greek society. What would such gods and goddesses be like if they were with us today? What would they rule? Invent some gods and goddesses!
2. Talk about the basics of Greek temples (see Activity 12), particularly pediments, and the influence of the gods on their construction.
3. Distribute paper and drawing materials. Students might want to try practice sketches before deciding on the god they will depict.
4. Color and decorate the figures. Consider the compatibility of size to pediment dimensions. Cut out.

5. Attach a group of gods, frieze-style, on the triangle with rolled masking tape. Glue foam board strips to assemble pediment.

6. Secure pediment on wall with heavy-duty tape. Place over a door jamb for greatest architectural effect. Ask students to explain their invented gods and their strengths.

7. Pediment may remain as a fixture indefinitely. The gods and goddesses may be rotated—fame can be fleeting!

SUGGESTIONS FOR FURTHER DEVELOPMENT

Here's a starter set of "who's who" in Greek mythology:

Zeus (ruler of the gods)
Hera (queen of the gods)
Athena (goddess of wisdom)
Aphrodite (queen of love; from the sea)

The stories that come down from Mount Olympus are sure to stimulate student imaginations. Pandora's infamous box of evils; Hercules and the nine-headed serpent; and Prometheus, thief of fire, are but a few forever fascinating Greek myths. For further reading, try *Book of Greek Myths* by Ingri D'Aulaire and Edgar Parin (New York: Doubleday and Co., 1962).

ACTIVITY 12
It's As Greek to Me As the Parthenon!

ARCHITECTURE BLUEPRINTS: 3-D Constructions

The Parthenon is more than a well-designed building. It is, in fact, a temple dedicated to Athena, the daughter of Zeus and the goddess of learning. During the Classical Age of Greece, at which time the temples were erected, standards for human achievement were determined. Greek architecture and its attendant sculpture are tangible manifestations of these time-honored ideals!

SLIDE #4: THE PARTHENON

FIGURE 31. This "blueprint" for a temple places Athena in the very center of it all.

MATERIALS

- Blue construction paper
- White oil pastels
- Rulers
- Shoeboxes (see Teacher Preparation)
- Posterboard (see Teacher Preparation)
- Nonflexible plastic drinking straws
- Applicator sticks (see Teacher Preparation)

- Gesso
- Paintbrushes
- Gold acrylic paint
- Black acrylic paint
- Markers or crayons
- Scissors
- Glue

TEACHER PREPARATION

This lesson will begin with the replication of the floor plan, also known as a blueprint, of the Parthenon (Part One of the activity). You may want to have an art history text on hand that illustrates the blueprint, as well as various elevations and views of the Parthenon and other surrounding temples of the Acropolis. Books on blueprints in general, which come under the broad heading of "architecture," may be of additional interest. Should you be able to acquire a *real* blueprint, bring it in by all means!

Part Two of the activity will ask students to "reconstruct" the Parthenon with the aid of the blueprints. Shoeboxes, with their lids, will be used for the structure. Child-sized shoeboxes work best. One box may be shared by two students who will work as partners. Posterboard can be cut ahead of time into sections to supply parts not provided by shoeboxes. Applicator sticks, suggested for implanting the philosopher in the temple, are available in most drug stores.

Because the temples will display their original purpose, include reference material on Greek gods and goddesses, as well as children's books outlining the important Greek philosophies and their ideologies and roles in Greek civilization.

Although it is not wholly necessary, it is still a good idea to prepare a demonstration model of the Parthenon, as detailed in the lesson, in advance of class construction activity. (NOTE: This lesson will require several class sessions to complete.)

DIRECTIONS

Part One: The Blueprint

1. What is a blueprint? Bring out any examples, maps, or reference materials you have to demonstrate. Compare blueprints to photographs depicting the Parthenon. Try to "translate" from paper to stone by identifying corresponding elements.

2. Distribute blue paper, oil pastels, and rulers. Students may count columns as reference points to help them begin, but should not feel intimidated by exactitude! The object is to broadly interpret what we see in our own terms—as long as there's a reasonable resemblance!

3. You may assist with fabrication of blueprints by offering guidance and names of architectural elements. The circles that represent columns and pediments, as well as spaces that mean the naves, should be understood. The small, innermost rectangle is the statue of Athena. Flesh it out on paper!

4. At the conclusion of the blueprint drawing session, students should have a sense of what a floor plan means to the architect and builder—as well as for their own model constructions.

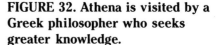

FIGURE 32. Athena is visited by a Greek philosopher who seeks greater knowledge.

Part Two: The Parthenon

5. We will be constructing a simplified model of the original structure (for example, double sets of columns, which appear on the original, would be difficult to install). Present your demonstration model and retain all blueprints and reference materials.

6. Distribute all other construction materials. Follow the instructions shown in Figures 33 through 37. Create the Parthenon roof and base, installing apertures for columns as indicated. Paint with gesso.

7. It should be pointed out that the Parthenon is built in the Doric order (see Figure 38). Our plastic straw columns do mock column fluting—capitals may be included if desired. Here's how to make the central column body:

    a. Place six drinking straws in the palm of your hand. Have a partner apply glue generously to the seventh, then position it in the middle as the "core."

    b. Close hand, gently pressing all straws together. A clustered column will be formed.

    c. Once the seven straws are glued in place and stable, paint with gesso.

    d. You'll need twelve columns for each Parthenon.

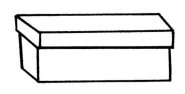

FIGURE 33. To make the Parthenon roof, start with the shoebox and lid. (See Teacher Preparation.)

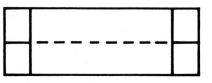

FIGURE 34. Use a proportional piece of posterboard. Cut approximately ⅓ inch on each side. Fold along the dotted line.

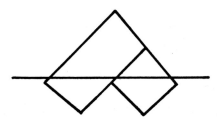

FIGURE 35. Here is the front view of the posterboard. Cut along the solid line. Fix in place.

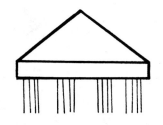

FIGURE 36. Place the roof on top of the drinking straw columns.

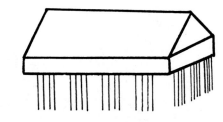

FIGURE 37. Finished!

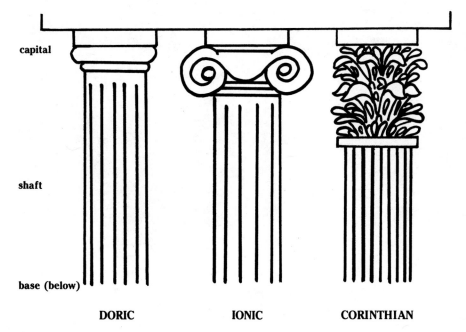

FIGURE 38. Three column orders.

This method teaches the basics *core construction* in architecture.

8. Insert columns through the base in allocated spots, adjusting as necessary. Be careful not to cut too much space, try for a snug fit. Glue the columns to the spots to further secure them in place and then let dry.

9. Cut out a figure from posterboard to represent Athena. Consider her gigantic size. Attach the figure to applicator sticks. Using reference material provided, decide on a Greek philosopher (Plato? Socrates?). Then draw and cut out to dramatize Athena's great scale. Glue the philosopher onto an applicator stick and let dry.

10. Pierce slots into the base of the Parthenon with scissors to insert Athena and the philosopher. Place the roof on top of the columns. Paint decorative Greek motifs on the pediment, base, and other appropriate areas. (See Activity 13 for suggested designs.) Add any other architectural details you wish. Let dry.

11. Students should have the opportunity to discuss their selected philosophers and the particular contributions they made to society.

12. Perhaps the Acropolis plan may be used for your display arrangement. Enlist students' ideas for exhibition possibilities. Don't forget, the Parthenon was at the very apex of Greek civilization!

ACTIVITY 13
Priceless Greek Urns

"VASES": Drawing

What we know of Greek painting today is primarily due to the survival of decorated pottery. The exquisite line work depicts figures in classical profiles. Black figure vases show silhouettes against reddish backgrounds. The color scheme was later reversed to reddish figures against black backgrounds. Many artists of this period created dynamic combinations of graphic schemes, patterns, and action figures.

SLIDE #5:   OLIVE GATHERING

MATERIALS

- Drawing paper at least 12″ × 15″
- Pencils
- Crayons or markers
- Scissors
- India ink or black poster paint
- Brown butcher paper (optional)

FIGURE 39. "Black figure ware" amphora shows off athletic action figures and dramatic design motifs. Contour of vase is respected.

TEACHER PREPARATION

The graceful, heart-shaped amphora (see Figures 39-40, as well as the March calendar on page 16) is a basic vase shape that does nicely for this lesson, although other classic shapes may be used. Students can cut their own paper vases, but receiving a precut shape is challenging and motivating!

To best achieve symmetry, fold paper first, draw *half* of the vase (use pictorial illustrations as a guide), cut, and open. This paper may also serve as a template.

FIGURE 40. "Red figure ware" continues wrap-around motion and decor on the reverse side. Note the soccer ball pattern! Circa 1987. Artisan: a sixth-grader.

FIGURE 41. Greek motifs.

DIRECTIONS

1. Consider the themes for vases with students. Vases will be treated as if they were "in-the-round," with wraparound designs that go from *front* to *back*. Plans might include leaping dancers, sports (for example, roller skating), sailing ships, parades—any topic which requires continuous action will work well.

2. Because student will reverse figure-to-background on opposite sides of vase, some thought should be given as to which part of their drawing will be in silhouette and vice-versa. Line work may suggest the illusion of a curved surface.

3. Once drawing has been blocked onto both front and back in pencil, execution of reddish and silhouetted figures may begin. Don't forget border motifs. (See Figure 41.)

4. When the entire vase is completed, the reversal of color schemes should be visually dramatic. Ask students to respond to differences between drawing "naturally" (into the reddish-earth tone), as opposed to the black silhouettes. Which one lends itself to greater detail and dimensionality?

5. What goes around comes around! Perhaps a likely display for these "vases" is brown paper panel "showcases"—use thick marker lines to indicate "shelves" on which these archaeological treasures sit. Label your museum "cases" to identify student artists and historical period. Students may select the side of vase they wish to exhibit first; they can reverse sides later if desired.

SUGGESTIONS FOR FURTHER DEVELOPMENT

"Priceless Greek Urns" may be presented as a crayon scratch-out activity. Cover one side in thick red (or tan) crayon, then paint with black ink or poster color. To keep the paper intact, design only one side with this lesson.

When ink is dried, use a stylus, bobby pin, or large opened paper clip to incise the drawing. Although it may be more challenging to control line work in this way, the scratch-out technique is probably closer to the actual method used by ancient Greek artisans on their pottery.

ACTIVITY 14
Caryatids: Women Who Hold Up Under Pressure!

ARCHITECTURAL COLUMNS: Stuffed Paper Sculpture

They are just as tough as they are lovely—truth to tell, they're really columns! Caryatids are considered part of the Ionic order and are charged with the same task as their less sinuous counterparts—to withstand the weight of the temple. So don't be fooled by their charm and grace; these ladies can surely hold their own!

FIGURE 42. A pillar of the community!

MATERIALS

- Brown butcher wrap (see Teacher Preparation)
- Scissors
- Pencils
- Newspaper
- Gesso
- Poster paint, black and white
- Brushes—all sizes
- Trays and containers for mixing
- Small sponges (see Teacher Preparation)
- Dowels (see Teacher Preparation)
- Staples

TEACHER PREPARATION

Recommended height for the stuffed paper sculpture caryatids you'll be constructing is three to four feet. You might precut butcher wrap in accommodating lengths. Remember, this is a project with two sides, front and back!

Dowels may also be sectioned in advance of class with a saw. Leave about a foot for possible "planting" of caryatids. Dowels will essentially serve as cores, just as they are used in architecture.

Small sponges will be helpful in replicating the stony quality of the material surface of caryatids. They will be used to apply some of the paint.

Reference books on Greek column orders (see Activity 12 for examples of orders), as well as illustrations of early weight-bearing figures in particular are recommended. "The Porch of the Maidens (The Erechtheum)" on the Acropolis in Athens is the model we have used for our project.

Books themselves will also be used for their own weight, as well as for their content, in this activity!

This lesson will take several sessions to complete.

DIRECTIONS

1. Have all reference materials ready. Consider the "Maidens" and the burdens they have on their heads! Yet they were designed to look effortless in their chores. If you have any Atlas (also called "Atlantes") examples, compare the caryatids to the strain that some of these figures register.

2. What does it mean to carry such weight? Students will take turns balancing the larger reference books on their heads. Try to shift your posture slightly, as in the pose of the caryatids.

3. Distribute butcher wrap and pencils. Students should work in pairs. Based on observations of caryatids (their posture, the fall of their costumes, the folds, etc.), create a simple contour. Outline it and cut it out. Don't forget the "capitals."

4. Take newspaper and tear it for stuffing. Staple the two sides of the figure together in sections, stuffing newspaper into it as you go along. (See Figure 44.) You may want to assist students. Leave a small opening at the bottom to insert the dowel. Continue stuffing and stapling until the side seams are shut. Then insert the dowel and close with staples.

FIGURE 43. It's the original Greek chorus line!

FIGURE 44. Stuff caryatid section by section with crushed newspaper, then staple it closed. Continue until completed.

5. Gesso the figures with a flat, wide brush on both sides. Let dry.

6. Mix shades of grey from black and white paint. Using sponges and various brushes, create a "sculptural" surface, such as granite, giving it a stony appearance. Use shadows also.

7. "Carve" out features and details with your brushes! Refer to reproductions for suggestions. Notice styling and modeling details. Do both sides, working in the round. Let dry.

8. The maidens may be installed any place that needs to be rescued from boredom. (Dowels may need adjustment to adapt to available surfaces.) An outdoor area that is protected from the elements, perhaps under a shelter, is ideal. Here, caryatids may be "planted" in a Greek chorus line where their beauty will bloom!

ACTIVITY 15
Greeks Bearing Gifts

ORNAMENTAL ART: Jewelry, Necklace

You can paint them, sculpt them, use them decoratively. You might make them the subject of a still life, or pluck them and wear them ornamentally! They are the organic forms of nature—plants, pods, seeds—and their influence on art has been considerable. A kinship between plant life and art strongly existed in the ancient world, where the presence of leaves, for instance, was quite noticeable. What do you think of when you see an olive branch? Why, Greeks and Romans, of course!

FIGURE 45. A necklace made from all natural ingredients.

MATERIALS

- Baby pine cones, acorns, and other organic items (see Teacher Preparation)
- Heavy sewing thread, such as coat thread
- Sewing needles (make sure the eye size is large enough for thread passage)
- Scissors
- Gold acrylic paint
- Brushes
- Oaktag (optional; see Teacher Preparation)
- Jewelry clasps, called "barrels" (optional; see Teacher Preparation)
- Acrylic gloss varnish

TEACHER PREPARATION

The Greeks and Romans used organic themes frequently in their design motifs as the history of jewelry bears out. Books that illustrate the chronological development of the ornamental arts will provide interesting information and stimulate ideas for this jewelry activity.

The materials students gather for their natural necklaces will depend on the region in which they live and on the season. Fall, of course, will generally offer the greatest variety of cones, acorns, and the like. But if your immediate resources include shells, for instance, check the possibilities in the jewelry history books for adapting specific materials to Greek/Roman necklaces. Failing all else, oaktag may be cut into olive leaves, painted gold, combined with other materials, and strung as directed.

A nature walk, if it is practical, is the best way for students to collect materials. Otherwise, students and teacher may gather interesting organic objects on their own and bring them to class. Hollow acorn tops are great, and were used for this lesson.

Jewelry clasps, or necklace "barrels," may be purchased at dime stores or hobby and notion shops. Thread may be cut in advance into suitable necklace lengths, leaving room for joining ends to clasp. If clasps are not available, necklaces should be made long enough to slip over heads, therefore, they may be knotted instead of clasped closed.

DIRECTIONS

1. Study jewelry reference materials. Can you identify the direct and indirect sources of nature's inspiration on the Greek and Roman jewelry? Name some specifics, such as birds, crescents, animal heads. What was a common material? Gold!

2. Distribute all materials. Thread the needles. Consider the materials before you shift them around. When you have an arrangement that pleases you, start sewing! Press needle gently through your organic materials and string them. (NOTE: Some materials may require piercing, so use your discretion with appropriate tools. You may want to use an awl or drill on harder materials.)

3. Join ends with clasp or tie together. Thin the gold paint down a bit with water, apply with brush. Let dry.

4. Apply varnish (teacher only should do this). It will preserve your work.

5. You can wear your art or give it as a gift. Put jewelry in the showcase for all to see. It's straight from the "Golden" Age!

ACTIVITY 16
Frieze! Classic Poses

FIGURE GROUPS, MOVEMENT EXERCISE: Full-size Painting

The classic sculpture of ancient Greece has given us a standard for the ideal human form. This concept of physical perfection remains with us even to this day. The gods and goddesses in their superior beauty were strong and athletic; yet graceful and natural, as well.

SLIDE #6:   VICTORY

FIGURE 46. "Students who paint themselves into a frieze are definitely cool!" —Ancient Greek proverb

MATERIALS

- Brown butcher paper or other wide paper from a roll
- Scissors
- Markers
- Poster paints
- Brushes—regular to one-half-inch flat
- White glue
- White or pastel bedsheets (optional)

TEACHER PREPARATION

Cut vertical lengths of brown paper to accommodate students' heights. Tape up to wall, placing in two's, side-by-side.

Having bedsheets or yards of plain fabric on hand will help to dramatize this activity. Reference materials, which depict various classic poses, should be made available for discussion.

DIRECTIONS

1. Examine the characteristics of the classic pose. Where is the weight distributed? Which is the weight-bearing or "engaged" leg? Ask students to assume several poses to emphasize this concept. Point out the invisible "S curve" known as "contrapposto."

2. Ask students to drape sheets over themselves and try out some more poses. Notice how the folds accentuate the direction of their body movements.

3. Game time! Select or assign partners. Teacher declares "Begin" and students move in continuous Greek poses. Teacher states "Freeze!"—in this case, it's "frieze" actually. Instruct students to stop action in their poses.

4. One of the partners will pose against the butcher paper; the other student traces first partner with marker. Second student reassumes frozen pose for tracing by first partner. Teacher may assist.

5. Once contour outlines are established, paint your self-portraits in the classical style! The pull of the folds needs attention—this tells us of the pose beneath the cloth.

6. Classic self-portraits may be displayed in groups, forming an impressive wall frieze. Cutting them out along their contours lends greater realism as statues.

SUGGESTIONS FOR FURTHER DEVELOPMENT

For an off-beat and lively variation of this activity, faces may be cut out from completed paintings, leaving a space behind which students can stick their heads! The effect is that of those corny but ever-popular devices that boardwalk and amusement park photographers use for a funny, pseudo-believable image. An instant camera will top off the day for your young Greek imposters!

FIGURE 47. Don't try this at home! It can be done only where ancient ruins are found; otherwise, recreate statue torsos from cardboard. The author stopped traffic along the Appian Way on a Roman holiday with this heady idea!

ACTIVITY 17
Breathtaking View from Mount Olympus

ARCHITECTURE: Greek "Real Estate"

Greece may exist in our imaginations as well as on the map at the very same time—for it is both real and mythical. Once believed to be a home for gods, Mount Olympus is indeed an actual mountain in Northern Greece. The Oracle at Delphi was a real personage, considered to be a kind of medium, whose edifice still stands today. Temples have paid tribute to their gods and to the formation of Western architectural principles. The formal intelligence of Greek society is clearly acknowledged, along with its provocative myths and legends. We are fortunate to have such a wise and magical place at the source of our own civilization.

FIGURE 48. *The Greek Times* offers "a luxury property overlooking the Adriatic. Sculpture by Praxiteles included in price. One million drachma."

MATERIALS

- Black fine-tipped markers
- Pencils
- Rulers
- T-squares (optional)
- White paper (11″ × 18″ approximately)
- Scrap paper for practice sketching
- Scissors
- Glue
- Real estate pages, such as *New York Times Magazine,* daily newspapers, etc. (see Teacher Preparation)
- Nontoxic correction fluid (optional)
- Correction and cover-up tape (optional)
- Computer access (optional; see Teacher Preparation)
- Typewriter access (optional; see Teacher Preparation)
- Nonreproducible blue line graph paper (optional)

TEACHER PREPARATION

This activity is a real imagination tickler. It will introduce elements of Greek architecture while teaching the basics of newspaper layout, specifically the classified sections! Computers may be used (as indicated in directions) as may typewriters but they are not essential.

You will need some "tear sheets" from the real estate section of the newspaper, and from other "For Sale" classifieds too. The *New York Times Magazine* is great because it includes pictures of the homes. You might also pick up flyers and brochures distributed by realtors. These are sometimes mailed or are available at real estate agencies. They show photos accompanying descriptions and prices. Include some *regular* front pages as well to demonstrate headline types.

Graph paper (light blue) is helpful for the layout, but not critical. Tapes and correction fluids do help. The newspapers we'll be designing—our "classified classics"— may be reproduced at a copy shop. The lesson is geared accordingly, but is not exclusive, to that end.

Reference materials may include:

- Greek architecture
- Greek motif designs (shown in Figure 41)
- Maps of ancient Greece
- Books (such as encyclopedias, atlases) outlining highlights of life in ancient Greece: the money system, the trade, communication, and so forth
- Illustrations of Greek art (for example, sculpture) and artifacts (vases, coins, jewelry, etc.)
- Examples of Greek alphabet (check the dictionary)

This lesson will require several sessions to complete and is a great deal of fun.

FIGURE 49. *The Sparta Express* claims this island villa is a "steal." The owner will even throw in a chariot as an extra. Must be seen!

DIRECTIONS

1. Bring all reference materials forward, both ancient and modern. Ask how many students have ever moved and remember selling or buying a house. Can the experience with any real estate brokers be recalled? What was their job? Discuss.

2. What if we lived back in old Greece and were trying to sell a house or building? Knowing what we do today, how would we—acting as the real estate agent—advertise our property? Where would you advertise it? How would you describe it? Check real estate reference for proper wording.

3. Distribute all materials. Keep maps in prominent view. Students will work as partners in marketing the sale of their villa. First, agree upon a desired location. By the sea? On a hill? Discuss architectural order (see Figure 38 for columns), size, special features, price, and "extras." Sketch out and make notes of your ideas. Use "real estate language" and abbreviate!

4. Determine which *views* of your property will look most attractive to the prospective buyer (sometimes called "elevations"). Perhaps a sculpture garden will "show" best? Rough out your sketches further, leaving room for "copy" (printed information).

5. Turn your attention to ad size before you transfer drawings on to graph paper (plain paper may be substituted). Measure the spaces allocated to ads in the real estate pages. Select a specific dimension, for example, five by six inches, and make them close to actual measurements. Cut the square or rectangle out to work on it.

6. Use black pen on the "good" illustration of your property. Include copy—hand-printed (or typed, and then cut out and dropped in). Make your property sound terrific! Again, check real estate pages for inspiration.

7. One sheet of 11″ × 18″ paper will suit two students. Plan the page layout. Move your completed ads around page (*before* gluing) and decide what other classifieds you might include. A summer home? A rare coin collection? A used chariot? Review Greek art and artifacts books for ideas.

8. When all classified ads have been completed, give your page a heading (computers may be used here and many have Greek typefaces). Titles should be bold and creative! Use Greek-style lettering.

9. Paste up all art with glue. Use "galley"-style arrangement (page columns) found in real newspapers as your model. Correction tape can hold ads in place and correction fluid will assist with errors. Decorative borders should be used. Clean up smudges with erasers (or correction materials).

10. Pages may be taken to a print shop with a large copy machine, where you may make enough copies for an art room newspaper. They may also be reduced in size for further copying. Are these not the classiest classifieds ever? It surely will be a collectors' edition. Distribute and display.

ACTIVITY 18
Mosaics: Small Beginnings

MOSAICS: "Pompeii"

Romans have earned the reputation as superb crafts-people. Respect for this ancient Roman tradition is indeed etched in stone, and reflected in marble, too. Small cubes of marble and other stone, called *tesserae,* were part of the earliest mosaics, often used for decorative architectural effects. Here is where many feel that painting as we now know it had its start.

FIGURE 50. Single mosaic works, such as this convincing still life, may be later joined with other mosaics for a group display. Lengths of butcher wrap (or posterboard panoramas) will turn your hallway into the walls of Pompeii!

MATERIALS

- Brown butcher paper
- 9″ × 12″ manila paper
- Colored construction paper
- White glue or library paste
- Scissors
- Pencils
- Ceramic tiles (optional)
- 9″ × 12″ cardboard or posterboard (optional)

TEACHER PREPARATION

Precut several lengths of brown butcher paper, enough to accommodate the mounting of manila papers later. Providing students with construction paper that has been cut into strips will also speed up the activity.

Should you wish to carry out the lesson with real ceramic tiles, these may be purchased fairly inexpensively at floor supply stores. Hobby and craft shops also carry small ceramic squares.

DIRECTIONS

1. Demonstrate the lesson by forming a simple, recognizable shape, such as a fish, from paper or ceramic mosaics. It is not necessary to use glue for the demonstration—just organize the paper pieces or tile squares within the desired configuration against a contrasting background.

2. Class should practice this technique before attaching tiles to the surface. Topics may be explored through drawing first. The popular subjects for Roman art include Emperors, mythology, or themes from nature, such as a flower, the sun and so forth. Keep it simple.

3. Upon selection of a subject matter, students doing paper mosaics will cut the desired colors of paper strips into little squares.

4. If ceramic tiles are being used, squares may be affixed to posterboard with white glue (the method of application is the same for either paper or ceramic mosaics). NOTE: There is no "right" way to organize mosaics. Students should feel free to find the approach that works best for them. The main thing is to be sure to *separate* areas of color when arranging the squares. Otherwise, you might be heading for something that looks more like an explosion in a confetti factory than an eye-pleasing mosaic!

5. At the completion of the project, students should be asked to help decide which subjects are most compatible with each other for a group arrangement. Once a workable conclusion is reached, paper mosaics can be attached to butcher paper.

6. Ceramic tile works mounted on posterboard can be displayed as standing fan folds by joining boards together from behind with heavy masking tape. You will have a panorama with all the glory that was Rome!

ACTIVITY 19
The Noblest Romans: Stand-Up Guys!

PAPER SCULPTURE: Stand-Up "Busts"

Emperors, senators, and aristocrats were the favored subjects of Roman portrait busts. The intelligent and the brave—men and women of action—were the heroes of ancient Rome!

MATERIALS

- Manila paper
- Lightweight gray posterboards or bristol boards
- Scissors
- Markers (optional)
- Glue
- Colored pencils, including white
- Masking tape (optional)

FIGURE 51. It isn't easy to turn cardboard into marble, but Dheen managed to do just that! Notice his pedestal "carving" which states "Dheen, Emperor, 1987."

TEACHER PREPARATION

Books on history of costume or specifically on the costumes of the ancient world will prove to be of great value for their details.

Try to bring in some examples of *real* marble, such as an ashtray or a tile, to demonstrate the quality of the materials commonly used for Roman portrait busts.

FIGURE 52. A section of cardboard, borrowed from a box, makes a sturdy stand. Cut the cardboard into a triangular shape, fold, and attach with white glue as shown here.

DIRECTIONS

1. After studying examples of Roman portrait busts, ask students to practice on manila paper. Ideas for portraits can pay tribute to the noble, ancient Romans or real people. The school principal, teachers, and friends are all worth trying!

2. In cutting and designing paper portrait busts of cardboard, be sure to give ample space and attention to the frontal area. Here you may create a vest that might show, as in an allegory, the important feats of the portrait subject. Outside contours may include elaborate helmets as well.

3. Block in the design with markers or colored pencils, attending to the details, such as expression, hair style, and so forth. Try your best to imitate marble or stone by observing the surface, then drawing the veined pattern to realistically imitate marble.

4. The base may be treated in a similar manner, perhaps reversing the color scheme, for example, a pink or black marble base against white or tan portrait figure. You may fool the eye by drawing "carved-looking" Roman names and numerals.

5. When the bust drawing is finished, you are ready to make portraits stand up and be noticed.

ACTIVITY 20
Heads Up! Roman Coins

COIN RUBBING: Jewelry, Pins

Money slips right through our fingers without our giving it too much attention. Yet the images on coins may be rare and special, particularly the ancient coins that carry idealized portraits of once-mighty rulers. Coin collectors, archaeologists, and historians place great value on these coins. As someone observed wisely, time is money—but in this case, money is art!

FIGURE 53. Money talks! Ancient coins double as jewelry.

MATERIALS

- Metallic color foil paper
- Scissors
- Lightweight cardboard (see Teacher Preparation)
- Stylus pens (see Teacher Preparation)
- Liberty silver dollars (see Teacher Preparation)
- Blunt object, such as clay tool or brush handle (see Teacher Preparation)
- Pin backs or safety pins (see Teacher Preparation)
- Glue
- Tape
- Pencil

TEACHER PREPARATION

You will need Liberty silver dollars or similar coins on which rubbing can be done. Cardboard and paper craft foil should be precut into small sections to accommodate this size. Stylus pens will work best for "engraving," but may be substituted with ballpoint pens. Blunt wooden handles, such as paint brush handles are suggested for rubbing coin images into foil.

Pin backs may be inexpensively purchased in jewelry, craft, and notion stores. Good-sized safety pins may be used where jewelry pin backs are not available.

Coins are, in themselves, an area of great intrigue, associated with buried treasures and fabled ruins. Books provided on the subject will fire students' imaginations, and may be garnered under the headings of archaeology; coin collecting, otherwise called numismatics; and even anthropology on occasion. Art reference material on Imperial Rome will provide some noble profiles. Such proud faces may also be found in Roman mosaics. Illustrations of ancient Roman coins are strongly suggested for lesson presentation.

If any students or teachers are coin collectors, urge them to bring information or examples to class. And, of course, a teacher who can coordinate a trip to a mint or coin shop with this lesson is to be lauded!

DIRECTIONS

1. Study all reference materials on hand. Consider size of coins, their shapes, and images. Compare them to our modern currency. Coins are often made to glorify or idealize leaders of a given period. Do the examples you see support this? Notice the profiles of Roman coins and their decorative details as well as numerical signs.

2. Distribute materials. Liberty silver dollars (or reasonable facsimiles) will be needed for rubbing, so if sharing must take place arrange the room accordingly.

3. Place square of foil paper over profile side of the silver dollar. Rub with fingernail and blunt handle until faint image comes through.

4. Transfer silver dollar to piece of cardboard. Trace circle and cut out. Place foil over, gently taping edges to back of disk. Roll along table to give roundness to the coin's edge.

5. Using stylus and reference materials, along with the outline borrowed from the silver dollar profile—"counterfeit" a coin! Your chosen subject may be the profile head of a real Emperor or an invented one, your own, for example, with an olive branch garland or maybe a football helmet! "Etch" details, such as patterns, Roman numerals, borders, and so on.

6. Completed coins should receive pin backs. Apply glue generously and position in place. Let dry. Tape may be used for reinforcement.

7. Before students wear their badges of honor, ancient Roman coins in a showcase would make a splendid display.

THE MIDDLE AGES

.....500......... 1100......... 1150......... 1200......... 1300......... 1400.....
Early Christian & Byzantine	**Early Gothic**	**High Gothic**	**Late Gothic**

It's hard to imagine that unicorns, fair maidens, knights, and dragons—as charming as they are to us—could come from a period in time often referred to as the Dark Ages! It was a time of considerable superstition, but the implications of this term gives us reason to pause.

After all, it was not as though the people of the Middle Ages were entirely without humor or playfulness! One has only to leaf through an illuminated book on love, observe the millefleurs of a Medieval tapestry, or stand in a shaft of colored light as it passes through a pane of stained glass to believe in the magic of this particular era in history. Also, it was a time of growth—towns and cities were rising and great castles too!

Paradoxical, in a way, were the Middle Ages. Painting itself seemed to take a curious turn. It appeared that the classical standards were set aside in favor of a stiffer, more severely stylized form. Much of the art was of a religious nature, and was usually built right into the architecture of the great cathedrals. Most painting had a primitive quality, one which represented space in a way that was symmetrical, rather than natural. Of course, there were some painters who took exceptions to this rule. One of them was Giotto.

Giotto was extremely important, not only because he was a fine painter, but for his early understanding of picture space, composition, and perspective! In this sense, Giotto could be regarded as the precursor of the great watershed period that would soon begin—the Renaissance.

ACTIVITY 21
A Castle Fit for a King

3-D CONSTRUCTION: "Castles"

Castles played an important role during the Middle Ages. They were sources of security to the towns and stately homes for kings and queens, lords and ladies. Their mighty appearances alone were responsible for much of the protection they provided. The architecture of castles represented power and strength.

FIGURE 54. A stately castle by "Lady" Allison, age 8.

MATERIALS

- 12″ × 18″ white paper
- Waterbased colored markers (fine to medium points)
- Round salt boxes (or oatmeal containers)
- Shoe boxes
- Tape
- Scissors
- Colored construction paper
- Applicator sticks (or beverage stirrers)
- A deck of playing cards (optional—see Teacher Preparation)

TEACHER PREPARATION

Precut a four-inch strip from the end of your 12″ × 18″ white paper, leaving a 12″ × 14″ format for castle tower design. The four-inch strip will be used for texture swatches. Keep extra white paper on hand for other details, such as banners.

Collect empty round and square boxes—salt boxes are best for castle towers, shoe boxes are great for walls. Each student should have *two* round containers and one square box.

Reference material featuring castles and medieval life, as well as 3–D models, will be excellent for students to study. A deck of ordinary playing cards will help with illustrations of kings and queens.

This lesson will require more than one session to complete.

DIRECTIONS

1. Using a black marker, design the top of the castle tower on the 12″ × 14″ paper, drawing right to the top edge. Measure paper against height of the two stacked salt boxes so that pattern will clear the edge of top salt box when cut without revealing the box inside.

2. Discuss styles of castle windows. Draw their contours, allowing enough space for "castle dwellers" to be seen inside. Other elements, such as stained glass panels, niches, and gates may be included in the overall planning.

3. Fold the four-inch white paper into four quarters (fold in half, then in half again); open. Design four different textural patterns with the black marker that would suit a castle wall—stone, brick, slate, etc. Cut in four cards, use as "texture swatches." Decide which pattern best fits your castle by sharing various swatches and holding each one against your castle design.

4. With the black marker, create the chosen surface pattern and draw the castle dwellers into windows. Kings, queens, servants, and so forth, should appear along with descriptive details.

5. Apply color, with attention to appropriate choices. You may want to retain the textural line drawing as is, or add grays and browns to it. Costumes, stained glass (and later, banners) should be bright and colorful.

6. Tape the two stacked salt boxes together at the middle. The top outside shape of the completed castle tower drawing may be cut. Wrap around the cylinder and tape back.

7. To design adjoining castle wall, measure paper to wrap around the front and two sides of shoebox. Carry the selected texture and architectural style from tower to castle wall. Consider placing figures *in front* of the wall, such as knights or guards on horses. Tape paper to shoebox when finished. Assemble castle parts by moving them together.

8. Top off the tower by placing the dome on it. (See Figures 55A and 55B.) Cut little banner shapes out of white paper, and create simple colorful patterns. Tape the banners to sticks, insert into the dome, and tape in place.

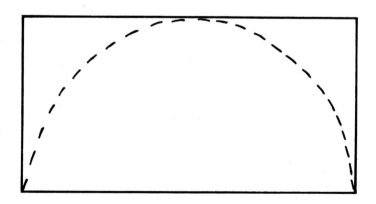

FIGURE 55A. Cut a piece of construction paper into a rectangular shape. Fold down the center vertically. Then cut (as shown by the dotted line), easing the scissors along the curve and open.

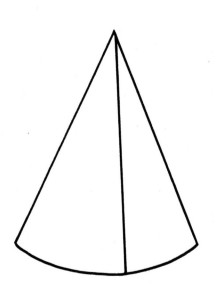

FIGURE 55B. Now fold the curved paper to form a cone. Tape or glue the ends together. Place the base on top of the salt box inside the tower ledge.

ACTIVITY 22
Rose Roundels

WINDOW HANGINGS: "Stained Glass"

Stained glass originated within the walls of the great cathedrals. Pieces of tinted glass were assembled in a lead framework to form a picture or design. Then— presto! Like magic, ordinary daylight was instantly transformed as it passed through the stained glass, into an array of dazzling colored light!

SLIDE #7: ROSE WINDOW

MATERIALS

- White glue
- Black construction paper squares
- Colored tissue paper (Colored cellophane is excellent, if available.)
- Scissors
- Tape (masking or transparent)
- String
- Hole-puncher
- Rulers

FIGURE 56. A stained glass roundel by James, age 11.

TEACHER PREPARATION

Precut a good number of squares from black construction paper allowing enough for practice, and for extras. You may also want to save some completed roundels for Activity 23. This will give students the opportunity to "install" their paper stained glass works as windows.

You may want to cut the colored tissue ahead of time as well, for conveniences.

DIRECTIONS

1. Distribute paper squares, tissue, and scissors. Explain that a circle will be cut from the square. (See Figures 57 and 58.) Demonstrate how this will be done. If necessary, draw Figures 57 through 60 on the chalkboard. (NOTE: You may want to seize this opportunity to teach symmetry, as in Figures 59 and 60, in which case you'll need designs with equal, corresponding parts. Symmetrical motifs are often found in Gothic traceries.)

2. Discuss stained glass and its properties. Compare this to colored tissue which can, on a more limited basis, also emit light. Consider similarities between the way a stained glass artist fits pieces of glass into a lead frame, and the method you will use with paper and glue.

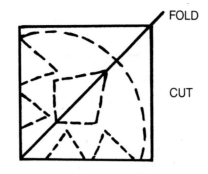

FIGURE 57. The first step in making a roundel.

OPEN

FIGURE 58. The open paper.

3. Now, the design problem! You have a roundel, a circle, out of which an appropriate subject must be cut. What are some good ideas? A rosette? A snowflake? A flower? A radiating sun? Other elements of nature, such as the crescent moon and stars, might do as well.

4. Practice individual subject choices with your scissors, using the paper circle. Cut into folds.

5. Colored tissue will need to be trimmed to fit particular spaces within each roundel. Establish a "wrong" side where pieces are to be glued or taped into place. Try to be as neat as possible with the glue; it doesn't take much to afix these tissue pieces.

6. Punch hole at the top. Insert string. (Remember, keep some roundels aside for Activity 23, but these won't need a hole for hanging.)

7. Roundels should be hung in a sunny window, facing the inside of the room. They should certainly help to brighten your day! NOTE: Colored tissue will eventually fade from direct sunlight. It is unavoidable, but there's certainly enough time for the project to be enjoyed and admired.

FIGURE 59. A symmetrical design. Quatrefoils, a popular floral clover-like medieval motif, might be considered.

FIGURE 60. An asymmetrical design where "anything goes"!

ACTIVITY 23
Windows and Doors

MIXED MEDIA: Elements of Architecture

You can't judge a book by its cover, but you can tell a great deal about a structure by its windows and doors. When you enter a building, the first physical element you'll encounter is the door. If you take a good look at it before turning the knob, you should have a strong clue about the style of architecture you can expect to find inside.

FIGURE 61. A door is also the sum of its parts. Can you see how many elements comprise this imaginative example?

MATERIALS

- Brown butcher wrap
- Pencils and erasers
- Yardstick
- Poster paint or acrylic paint
- Wide and flat paintbrushes
- Colored tissue
- Masking tape
- Black plastic-coated or wide cloth tape
- Glue

TEACHER PREPARATION

The doors we'll make are most effective when sized to fit the classroom door(s). Because the lesson will then require our covering a large area, we will construct our door facade in parts (in the furniture trade, this is known as "knocked down," meaning pieces that are later assembled to form a whole item). Measure dimension of your classroom door (and a closet door also, if available). You'll be making three door facades. Cut your brown paper to the lengths indicated. Move student desks together to create workable flat surfaces. Have all materials ready and available for your class, and extra butcher wrap for any "reconstruction" that might occur. (NOTE: This lesson may take several weeks to complete; however, it has not been broken down into "parts." You will need to judge how much time is necessary for this project according to individual class schedules.)

DIRECTIONS

1. Divide class into three planning committees. Give each group a length of brown paper.
2. Discuss the various architectural elements and details that comprise a door. What parts may doors in the Gothic style contain? (Front panels, windows, handles, hardware, hinges, and so on.)

3. With some input from the teacher, groups will decide how to divide parts and labor. One or more students will need to be the "cutters" to begin the group's work.

4. Sections of brown paper will be cut and distributed. These parts may be designed by a couple of students, while other larger areas may require more hands. Teacher will determine the most practical way of doing this step in accordance with class size and available room space.

5. Fabricate your door. Don't forget to leave space for the traceries (roundels) you created in Activity 22. You might want to use them to outline appropriate circular spaces in your door front.

6. Paint and glue. Add details.

7. Install windows and assemble parts. Use black tape to reinforce the sections as well as to accent motifs.

8. Hang your paper doors over the actual ones in your room if possible. Try to coordinate this with other activities you've completed from the Middle Ages and are displaying on your walls. Thus, the illusion of entering a corner of a medieval castle will be created.

ACTIVITY 24
Ugly Guys!

GARGOYLES: Clay Sculpture

Some very suspicious characters sprouted from the walls of otherwise respectable buildings during the Middle Ages. These beastly creatures were called gargoyles. Their original purpose was to replace deteriorated rain gutters, but gargoyles were later valued for their own unique appeal. However, they were not the only "uglies" that hung around the architecture. Other stone monsters, known as grotesques, hid in niches, perched on columns, and generally lurked about—so beware!

FIGURE 62. Horrors!

SLIDE #8:   GARGOYLES

MATERIALS

- Modeling clay (see Teacher Preparation)
- Clay tools
- Manicure sticks
- Garlic press (optional, but recommended)
- Textural objects, such as empty sewing spools, tacks, meat tenderizing mallet, cheese graters, nail files (see Teacher Preparation)
- Wire, such as piano wire, for wedging and slicing clay

TEACHER PREPARATION

Refer to "The Clay Studio" in Section One for complete instructions in classroom clay preparation and techniques. You will need to set up your room for a wet clay activity by covering desks, utilizing wooden work tables, and so forth. Garlic presses will produce a kind of clay angel hair, which can be used for animal fur texture, or flames—whatever the imagination yields! You can never use the same press for garlic again, but you'll gain a wonderful addition to your clay tool collection! Other household objects (suggested under Materials) are excellent for creating distinctive patterns when applied to clay surfaces.

You may want reference materials on animals, as well as fantastic beasts, to help introduce this lesson.

FIGURE 63. Attention is paid to backs as well as fronts. Musculature is also noted.

FIGURE 64. Notice the surface texture as well as the perched posture of this little beast.

FIGURE 65. A quizzical look from a questionable character!

FIGURE 66. What—or who—is providing a snack for this clay creature?

DIRECTIONS

1. Creepy, scary, weird, spooky, even silly, but not pretty were these ornamental beasts! You will sculpt some fantastic monsters that fit the same description.

2. Give each student a fair portion of clay—at least the size of a grapefruit. Clay tools and textural objects should be made available to the class. Demonstrate use of the garlic press.

3. Experiment by sculpting several combinations of beasts from your clay. Students may want to first make one *whole* animal (e.g., a lion, eagle, lizard), then exchange parts of their sculpture with each other, creating their own special mythological beasts. (NOTE: Griffins, for example, had the body and hind legs of a lion, and the head and wings of an eagle.) Other ideas might include multiple faces, exaggerated features, even little "nobodies," who are heads with only arms and legs. Let students' imaginations run wild!

4. As students get closer to their realized piece, they may want to incorporate a base. A triangular or square bottom may be shaved and sculpted to resemble an architectural element, such as a cornerstone. This should be integrated into the overall concept. Nonetheless, figures must be planned to stand—legs and necks should be supportive. (NOTE: Suggestions for this are given at the end of this activity.)

5. Manipulate clay surface with textural tools to represent scales, fur, feathers, etc. Add other details, like tails, wings, horns, and spikes. NOTE: Sculptural protrusions are the first to break, so handle sculptures with care!

6. Scoop out center of clay with proper tool, fill with crushed newspaper, or pierce with pencils. Let dry. (NOTE: Air-hardened clay is extremely fragile, so be careful.) Kiln fire, if possible.

7. Ugly guys are fun to display in unexpected nooks and crannies!

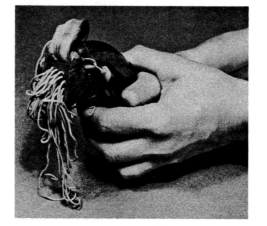

FIGURE 67. The garlic press is a favorite trick to achieve texture in clay or plasticine (shown here), but there are others! Clay may be pressed through screens and sieves, too. Clay extruders, not unlike pastry tips, are available through fully stocked art supply catalogs. Check them out!

Clay Gargoyle Techniques

Instead of scooping out the center for drying, well-wedged clay may be pierced with pencils as shown in Figure 68. The thicker the body, the more pencil holes will be required.

Note that the "nobody" head in Figure 68 may lack arms and legs, but it is still made to stand. In forming any clay gargoyle, it is essential to create a bottom. The base, or legs, might take the form of a fat tooth "molar," on which a ball-like center body and head may be added. Students can roll out sausage-shaped tubes of wet clay, then cut away needed sculptural parts, such as appendages, with a clay knife.

Scoring clay for joining body parts is not essential if clay is generously "dragged" (pulled) over the wet surface during construction. Working "round-to-round," for example, pressing one rounded end against another rounded surface then dragging the clay, will join parts together effectively. Watch out for air pockets!

Finally, remember that plastic sheets, if securely wrapped around unfinished wet pieces, will keep work fresh until completion.

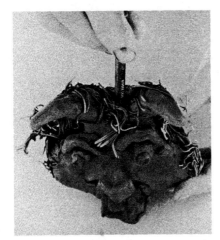

FIGURE 68. Piercing a clay figure with a pencil.

ACTIVITY 25
Please Watch Your Coat of Arms!

HERALDRY: Cut Paper

Individual knights could not be recognized behind their helmets. How to solve this problem? Pick bold colors and strong designs, called heraldry, with which individual knights could be identified. The shields, helmets, and horses' coverings that bore these emblems were known as coats of arms. This use of personal symbols spread from knights and kings to trade guilds, and were passed on to families, too, where the coat of arms was considered a proud sign of aristocracy.

MATERIALS

- Construction paper in bold colors
- Scissors
- Practice paper
- Pencils
- Rulers and yardsticks
- Glue
- Thick black markers

FIGURE 69. East meets West in this symbol of Nicole's favorite hobby—karate.

TEACHER PREPARATION

You may want to cut sample shapes of the shields ahead of time, or draw the suggested shields on the chalkboard.

DIRECTIONS

1. Ask students to name some versions of the coats-of-arms that they may have seen. How about school colors and insignias, team mascots, government seals, crests on military garb, or even business trademarks?

2. Distribute pencils, rulers, bristol boards, and all other supplies needed for this activity.

3. The backgrounds of shields should be simple. Checkerboard squares, diamond patterns, wide bands, etc., are recommended. However, you may wish to create a *quartering,* which would mean dividing your shield into four quarters and planning your designs accordingly.

4. Each student should select *two* bold, contrasting colors. If the colors have a meaning for the students, for example, camp colors or personal favorites, all the better!

5. Discuss selection of symbolic emblems. Ask what animal, bird, or reptile do you most admire? What's your hobby? Special interest? Favorite subject? Have students take out practice paper and pencils as they think about this. *Questionaire to set ideas*

6. Sketch some simple objects and shapes that reflect choices. For example, if a student likes dancing, he or she could try illustrating ballet (or jazz) shoes. If one likes hockey, draw a face mask and puck. (See Figures 70 through 72 for suggestions.)

7. Switch over to scissors and construction paper. Pick *one* strong color. Cut out your *one* favorite image. Think big and bold! Cut out patterns and symbols, too.

8. Glue your symbolic emblem and design elements to the shield. Use the marker to strategically add student's name in Gothic-style letters (see Activity 28) if you wish. Medieval motifs, such as the fleur-de-lis, may be used for accents, but don't overdo it!

9. There you have it—all you need for your own classroom Hall of Fame. Be sure to give students a chance to talk about their choices and to respond to each other's work.

FIGURE 70. Sample shield.

FIGURE 71. Sample shield.

FIGURE 72. Sample shield.

ACTIVITY 26
Unicorns Unlimited

STITCHERY: Wall Hanging "Tapestry"

What looks like a fine white pony, has a long sharp horn jutting from its forehead, and is a symbol of purity? The unicorn, of course! This beloved beast grazes in the land of make-believe. You will find our mythological friend woven into the tapestry of medieval legend.

SLIDE #9:   THE LADY AND THE UNICORN

FIGURE 73. Students will be enchanted with the images of unicorns from fifteenth-century tapestries as this joyful interpretation demonstrates. On burlap.

MATERIALS

- Practice paper
- Pencils
- Embroidery-type sewing needles
- Embroidery threads (red, deep blue, green, and tan are common to medieval tapestry)
- Fine-tip and regular markers
- 90-lb. weight drawing paper
- Scissors
- Dowels
- Staple gun
- Masking tape
- Yarn (optional)

TEACHER PREPARATION

Essentially, you'll be creating stitchery pictures on paper. However, there's no reason why you can't translate this activity into a real embroidery project. To accomplish fabric stitchery, add burlap (or similar cloth) and embroidery hoops on stretchers (optional, but recommended) to your materials list. If you choose this alternative, replace drawing paper with fabric when following the directions. (NOTE: You will probably find that fabric yields more readily to the needle than paper generally does.)

For either paper or fabric stitchery, students and teachers should bring to class examples of embroidery and similar textiles for scrutiny. You may also want to secure reference books that illustrate varieties of stitches. Such information is readily available in "how-to" sewing and craft books.

Make sure your needles are not exceptionally blunt or thick. Needles that are too thick make sewing on either paper or fabric tougher to manage (although you'll want to avoid very sharp ones for safety reasons as well).

Cut the dowels to twelve inches ahead of class time. You may need to enlist your industrial arts teacher here.

You might want to provide other examples of unicorn tapestries for further motivation. NOTE: medieval tapestries were *woven*, not embroidered. However, the stitchery project, as outlined, is probably a more direct technique for students to produce suggested images.

FIGURE 74. Whether the unicorn is engaged in a hunt or admiring its reflection in a Lady's hand mirror or simply grazing, this creature is always unique! Paper "tapestry."

DIRECTIONS

1. Discuss the representation of unicorns in tapestry. Examine examples of textiles and the possibilities for your subject. You may want to point out the differences and similarities between tapestry and embroidery.

2. In what ways can unicorns be shown? Prancing, dancing, leaping, or even looking at their reflections in a mirror or a pond? Also, think about the many surrounding flowers and woodland creatures that you can include in your design. Name some that you think are appropriate, such as rabbits, squirrels, and birds.

3. Begin your drawings on practice paper. Remember, this is a *flat* design. It should not be too complicated. Deep picture space is *not* suited to this activity.

4. Once you are satisfied with the practice sketches, begin your drawing with markers on the paper (or fabric) to be used for stitchery. Marker lines may indicate chosen stitchery patterns. The flowers and foliage of medieval tapestry, known as millefleurs, are the perfect shapes for stitches. You may even want to experiment with stitching some patterns on a separate section of paper before proceeding to the next step.

5. Sew directly into drawing paper, combining stitches with drawings. Don't be afraid to combine both techniques of drawing and stitching, for they should assist each other. Threads may be stitched to outline contours and to fill in various shapes. Use any manner that works.

6. Try to avoid overworking areas as well as poking and pulling the paper. This will break it down and tear it. Stop when a convincing overall effect has been achieved. Your drawing should read like a tapestry.

7. Staple the top of tapestry edge around a horizontal dowel, covering the wood. Secure yarn (or embroidery thread) to either end. You may need to apply masking tape to the back of the paper to keep it hanging straight and flat.

8. Display your wall hangings proudly!

ACTIVITY 27
A Good Knight

MIXED MEDIA: Cut Foil Paper Pictures

Armor is an art form in its own right. While some armor is plain and basic, other suits are highly decorative. Knights counted on their armor to protect them and to move easily with them, but they also cared about their appearance, too. Dress armor was designed for such events as games and tournaments where both the knight and his horse could shine!

FIGURE 75. This brave knight in the plumed helmet sure has his work cut out! Note the length of the dragon behind the castle and the fair maiden in distress!

MATERIALS

- Foil paper
- Scissors
- Glue
- 12″ × 18″ paper
- Pencils (stylus pens are even better)

- Markers
- Crayons
- Newspapers (see Teacher Preparation)
- Fabric scraps (optional)

TEACHER PREPARATION

You may need to do a small paper drive in your class to gather enough newspapers for one wad of newspaper per student. Newspapers will be required as padding for your armor "engraving."

DIRECTIONS

1. Discuss the role of knights in medieval society. What was their function? To guard castles, to defend towns against enemies, and to rescue fair maidens from ferocious dragons! Knights also participated in contests and attended royal events.

2. Now what about the armor itself? What was it made of, besides steel? There was mail, and sometimes velvet, and often a variety of materials combined. Was it a stiff suit, or was it put together in parts that could bend at the right places?

3. Distribute materials, withholding newspapers only.

4. Considering the above suggestions, let us begin by constructing our knight's shining armor from foil paper. Cut out the various parts, with attention to such details as helmets, breastplates, shields, even gauntlets (those pieces that fit over the hands). You might think about a symbol for a coat of arms, say a lion, and carry the theme into the knights' helmet and the horse's garb.

5. Students can make one or more knights, but should plan to include at least a horse or a damsel in distress. Students should have a basic idea of where and how they want to show the knights—either marching in a crusade or bowing to the king.

6. Assemble picture parts. If you have them, add fabric scraps for finery. Draw with crayons and markers as needed in the composition.

7. Bring out the wads of newspaper and place them under your drawing papers. With your pencils or stylus pens, inscribe designs into the armor. Try patterns and elements that suit the Middle Ages. Apply enough pressure with your pencil so that your patterns show.

8. How does it look? If you are finished, flaunt it!

FIGURE 76. Detail of foil "armor" that has been inscribed and decorated.

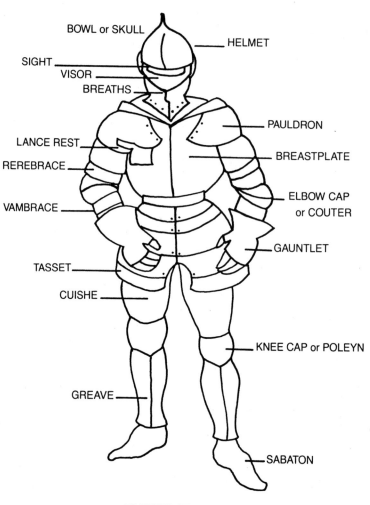

FIGURE 77. Armor.

ACTIVITY 28
Medieval Alphabet Soup

ILLUMINATION: Bookmarks, Book Labels

Welcome to the zoomorphic world of the Medieval alphabet! It's a place where real and imaginary creatures of land and sea combine with decorative designs and letters of the alphabet. The results are truly illuminating!

MATERIALS

- 9″ × 12″ oaktag or bristol board
- Self-stick mailing labels (see Teacher Preparation)
- Scissors
- Rulers
- Markers
- Lined writing paper
- Pencils
- Clear self-stick vinyl (see Teacher Preparation)
- Gold and silver watercolors or acrylic paints (optional)

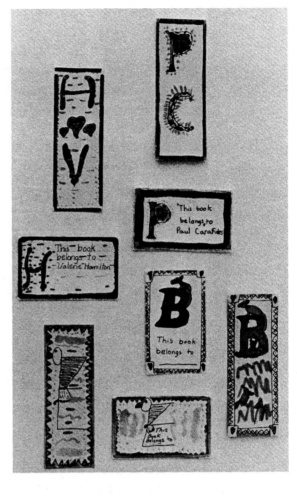

FIGURE 78. Students were encouraged to select endangered animals for their bookmarks and labels, such as the bobcat wrapped around the letter B. Illuminating and enlightening!

TEACHER PREPARATION

To familiarize students with Gothic letters and other typefaces, you can make use of library reference materials. However, your art supply store may have typeface selection catalogs that are often free for the asking. Printers, too, will sometimes give you typestyle charts. These materials will contain examples of the Gothic alphabet, which can be used later for art room reference, too.

Precut the oaktag (on a paper-cutter) into 2½″ × 7″ strips, one per student. Self-stick (peel-off) labels, approximately 3″ × 5″, that are available in the stationery store will be ideal for our bookplates. If this isn't feasible for you, unlined 3″ × 5″ cards will do, but add glue when applying them to the inside of a book, of course!

Clear self-stick vinyl will not only preserve your bookmarks, it will enhance their appearance and please your students! You may want to laminate both sides (sandwich style), although it isn't critical that you do. This sealing step can be done by students or by you with some student assistance.

DIRECTIONS

1. Introduce examples of Gothic alphabet style. Talk about some of the beasts, e.g. birds and reptiles, that figured in the decoration of the times. Examine reference materials for other medieval design motifs.

2. Distribute rulers, pencils, writing paper, and scissors. Practice letter forms freely. Students may cut practice paper to the dimensions that will be used in their final products. (Refer to Teacher Preparation for sizes.)

3. Sketch some ideas for decorative borders on your practice papers. Try letters that represent your initials or those of someone to whom you might want to give these items as a gift, such as a teacher or a parent. Think of a subject you could use that starts with the same letter and incorporate it, as in K for Kenny—also for King. These kinds of images can be mixed in, too.

4. When satisfied with the practice work, move on to the final copies. Distribute markers, oaktag, labels, and the rest of the materials, saving the plastic for last.

5. Bookmarks should have a recognizable motif, a border, and one or two selected initials with medieval design elements intertwined. Book labels should have their borders drawn first. The center area will state "This book belongs to _____." Students will use their best hands at writing out that statement and will be as decorative as possible in embellishing it. Bookmarks and labels should have corresponding motifs.

6. Use gold and silver paint, if you have it, for larger spaces and for accents. Fill your bookmarks and bookplates with design and color. Lend your special touch.

7. Laminate (see Teacher Preparation).

8. Completed illuminated items may be presented as sets for a lovely gift or kept for students' own use. Either way, you've made your mark!

FIGURE 79. Medieval illuminated alphabet sample.

FIGURE 80. Medieval illuminated alphabet sample.

ACTIVITY 29
Book of Days: The Illuminated Seasons

ILLUSTRATION, MIXED MEDIA: Calendars

The illuminated manuscript was a very artistic fore-runner to the printed books we read today. Manuscripts were illustrated by monks and traveling artists who told many different tales with their elegant letters and fine small paintings. Stories from the Bible and from life in the royal courts were popular during the Middle Ages. Fantastic beasts put in their appearances, too. But among the most charming of scenes were those of life in the country, which could be found in the illuminated calendars of the changing seasons.

SLIDE #10: NOVEMBER

MATERIALS

- Pencils
- Scissors
- 12″ × 18″ white paper
- Markers
- Watercolors
- Gold watercolor (optional)
- Hole puncher
- Ribbon (see Teacher Preparation)
- Stapler or paste
- Calendars (see Teacher Preparation)

FIGURE 81. The four seasons as Melissa, age 9, imagined them to be *in the days of olde, when knights were bold.*

TEACHER PREPARATION

You will need calendar pages for your students. This can be accomplished by making photocopies from a preexisting calendar—a single page that shows all twelve months can't be beat for cost and time effectiveness. Other suggestions include copies of calendars made from a master stencil you can produce by directly replicating a calendar, or simply ask students to bring in calendars they'd be willing to donate (perhaps free ones with company advertising). Finally, little calendars can be purchased by the dozen from stationery stores and some notion specialty shops. Thin ribbon that will be used for hanging may be substituted with string, but it really does add the crowning touch. You may also wish to have some reference material available that shows life on the farm during the different seasons, particularly. Books on astronomy, the zodiac, and illustrations of phases of the moon will help with the arch design, too.

NOTE: You may find that younger students will appreciate precut arch-shaped paper. Be prepared to offer assistance in folding if you do not prefold pages.

This lesson may take several sessions to complete, and is presented here in two parts.

DIRECTIONS

Part One

1. Distribute the paper, pencils, and scissors. Ask students to fold their papers into rectangles as shown (see Figures 82 and 83), leaving space at the bottom for calendar attachment.

2. Consider the empty blocks. We will soon fill them with our ideas for the four seasons. What's the first thing that distinguishes one season from another? The changes in the weather, of course. How can we best show those changes—spring showers? Autumn leaves? Snow on the rooftops? A suntanned swimmer at the beach? That would certainly be close to our daily lives.

3. What do you think the seasons mean to farmers in their fields? Do their tasks change with the weather? In the calendars of the Middle Ages, we can see planting, plowing, and harvesting. The illustrations often told the weather and time of day by the color of the sky.

4. Pencil in your ideas. You may represent four seasons in the present time or as the seasonal changes may have appeared in country and town long ago.

5. If time allows in Part One, sketch an appropriate motif into the arch space, such as the Zodiac, which was a part of the original "Les Tres Riches Heures du Duc de Berry" illumination. Carry a corresponding motif below to bottom band.

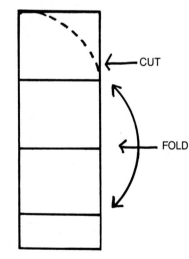

FIGURE 82. Fold paper vertically, then over again horizontally into four rectangular spaces. The bottom fold provides band for calendar attachment. Block sizes may be measured or estimated through folding sample pages.

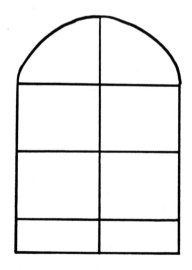

OPEN

FIGURE 83. Open the fold. Turning the paper over or bending it against the folds will flatten the work surface.

Part Two

6. Finish any work that has not been completed in Part One. Distribute needed materials, along with watercolors, markers, etc.

7. Illustrate your seasonal calendar. Pencil lines should be obscured by markers and paint. Remember details! Trees, animals, gardens, and people's clothing tell us much about the seasons!

8. Add special effects, like gold paint. Stars painted gold against a deep blue sky are not only dramatic—they are truly reminiscent of medieval manuscript art.

9. When all seasonal composites—as well as top and bottom motifs—are complete, punch up your calendar art! A hole in the center of the arch will do. Attach ribbon and tie in a loop.

10. Distribute calendar pages. Affix with stapler or paste. Hang!

ACTIVITY 30
3-For-1 Triptychs!

PAINTING: Narrative Panels

Many painters of the Middle Ages used their art to tell a story. Lives of saints and other religious subjects were often portrayed, as well as tales of crusades and of bold knighthood. These paintings were done mostly on wooden panels of arched and curvy shapes that were attached to each other, and sometimes they served as altarpieces. This was often the case with the triptych, a three-part panel that was quite popular with artists of the time.

FIGURE 84. The front of the triptych. Panel number one finds a sad and lonely princess who pines for a handsome prince. The turtle on the windowsill behind her also weeps. We'll soon see why....What terrible magic has trapped a handsome prince inside a turtle shell? The Wizard, who is trained for such things, cracks both shell and spell with a wave of the wand. One lonely princess is bored no more. By panel number three, we have our royal wedding!

MATERIALS

- Brown butcher wrap
- Scissors
- Pencils
- Markers

- Poster paints
- Gold acrylic paint (or gold foil)
- Gold doilies (optional)
- Glue (if doilies are used)

TEACHER PREPARATION

Divide the number of students in your class by three. Cut lengths of one yard from your paper roll in the number you require. Set your room up for painting and related activities, with all materials accessible. You may want to have a demonstration piece—along with pictorial references—to introduce this lesson. You might also cut the panel shapes ahead of time, depending on size of class and age level of students.

DIRECTIONS

Part One: Three-Part Panels

1. Explain the purpose of triptychs and other panels (polyptychs)—they were architectural elements of cathedrals that told stories through painting. Perhaps some students know of painted panels in churches they've attended. Discuss.

2. Distribute pencils and paper panels with three students to a panel. Put together students whom you feel will work well together. Identify panel "parts" where story action will take place, much like a book. In the *open* 3-fold panel: panel 1 is the beginning; panel 2, the middle; panel 3, the end.

   Student teams of three will need to collaborate on stories with each assigned to panel 1, 2, or 3, respectively. There are many characters and adventures from this period in time that would build a good story: kings, queens, jesters, loyal pages, wizards, magicians, and fiery dragons, to name a few.

   NOTE: If students have difficulty getting their three-part story started, the teacher may evoke a story-telling exercise. Give Student 1 a verbal opener, like "Once upon a time in the Land of _____, there was an evil _____, who—etc." Student 2 can pick up the story thread, and Student 3 draws the story to a conclusion. Teacher may interject similar plot "problem-solvers" in instances where students seem stumped.

3. Each student will sketch in his or her illustration ideas. Students should be encouraged to help with each others' panel illustration within their teams. Pictures—not words— will tell your story!

4. Begin painting. Give thought to the contours of the frames in which the panels are placed. Create curved borders! Flesh it all out.

5. Let dry.

Part Two: The "Cover" Art

6. Return work to student teams. The panels (now dry) should be turned over for completion on other side. This side will serve as a pictorial *cover.*

7. Distribute the same materials as outlined in Part One. Plan the cover to include characters and scenes from inside the "book." These may be designed in a panoramic or wraparound fashion, but should form a *specific fronticepiece* facade design when the panels are closed. Fold the paper triptych as much as needed to assist in the planning stage.

8. Students may study examples of corresponding (parts of) triptychs in reference materials provided for design ideas. Teams once again determine overall cover art for their particular story. Images may or may not be sequential, but should be clear, and best represent story content.

9. Teams may find this side easier to work on together, rather than in a student-to-a-panel ratio. Again, consider the panels' framework contours.

10. Colors should be bold and bright. Gold is great for details and frame design. Finish all painting. Let dry.

11. Students should have an opportunity to reveal their fantastic fables! Exhibit like real triptychs and let the tales unfold.

FIGURE 85. The back of the triptych. See how well things can work out sometimes? Prince and princess are now king and queen.

FIGURE 86. The closed triptych displays cover art. The man on the left needs no introduction...but the little ones on the right? Why, they're the children of our royal couple! Needless to say, everyone lives happily ever after.

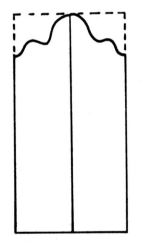

FIGURE 87. Step one for cutting a triptych. Establish the center of the cut length of butcher wrap. Fold in two flaps and cut the top in a curved contour.

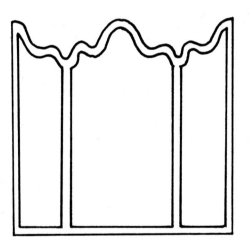

FIGURE 88. Step two in making the triptych. Open and decorate.

SUGGESTIONS FOR FURTHER DEVELOPMENT

The allegorical and symbolic aspects of medieval panel painting may be particularly fascinating for children. For instance, a rabbit in a picture may signify fertility; a dog may suggest loyalty. Students might want to research medieval symbolism further and use this information in their own work. Allegory, or personal symbolism, may also be integrated.

Who knows? Enthusiasm for panel painting could even lead from triptychs to polyptychs!

THE RENAISSANCE

.....1400............. 1500............. 1510............. 1520............. 1530.....

| Early Renaissance | High Renaissance | Late Renaissance |

Renaissance, as we all probably know by now, means "rebirth"—a renewal of interest in the antiquities. Once again, art looked back into the natural world. Although Papal Rome still exerted great influence, secular and mythological subjects were taken up with enthusiasm. The spirit of art was one that celebrated earthly pleasures and displayed healthy curiosity! Art and science joined forces. It was a time of intelligence, growth, and progress.

When the Renaissance began, there was an overlap between its introduction and the ongoing Medieval style in Northern Europe, also called Late Gothic Art. There were, at the time, many excellent Flemish painters, like Pieter Brueghel the Elder, Jan van Eyck, and the ironical Hieronymus Bosch! Germany had its own school, too, and gave us painting greats, such as Hans Holbein the Younger, Dürer, and Lucas Cranach. But, to this day, it is Italy that we think of when we speak of the Renaissance.

The starting line, if indeed there was a definitive one, could have been drawn in the city of Florence. More than an urbane center, Florence was the cradle of a specific art tradition—the Florentine school. There were recognizable characteristics of the Florentine style: portraits were often shown in sharp, clean-cut profile, with a good understanding of the perspective behind the figure. Patterns and textures were somewhat flat, but decorative and lively. And there was a real sense of fine drawing behind the painting of the Florentines. Yet the Renaissance was to advance even more, much later, in another Italian city—none other than the famous city of waterways and canals—Venice.

The Renaissance may be said to have reached its zenith in this place where a style called the Venetian tradition emerged. It was an unparalleled school of painting, especially reflected in its structural color, which had about it a rich glow, as well as the use of harmonious compositional space. An earthy, naturalistic tradition, Venetian painting was expressed in warm human terms.

The Venetians had artistic giants amont them: Bellini, Giorgioni, Tintoretto, Titian, and Veronese. The list of famous Florentine painters is long and also illustrious, for it includes Michelangelo and Leonardo da Vinci—along with Botticelli, Uccello, Piero della Francesca, and Raphael—to name a few. With the strength of all these artists behind it, it is easy to understand why the Renaissance was destined to change the face of art history forever.

ACTIVITY 31
The Art of Invention

DRAWING; 3-D ASSEMBLAGE: "Inventions"

It was during the Renaissance that art met science head on. Perhaps no man embodied this union better than Leonardo da Vinci, a scientist and inventor, and a great artist, too. Through his many successes, Leonardo proved that art and science can grow from the same seed of creativity. The result of combining these forces? We call it progress!

MATERIALS

- 9″ × 12″ paper
- Pencils
- Shoeboxes (see Teacher Preparation)
- Poster or acrylic paints
- Glue
- Colored paper
- Scissors
- Tape
- Gesso (see Teacher Preparation)

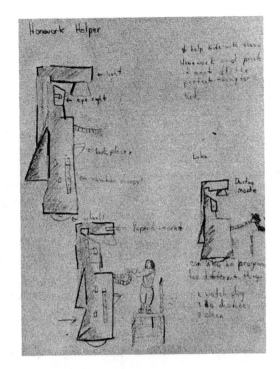

FIGURE 89. Ah, the "Homework Helper," the perfect thing for the overworked student!

TEACHER PREPARATION

Students will need shoeboxes to do a mock-up of their inventions. They also may want to include other spare parts, such as wheels (from old toys), hardware odds and ends (nuts, bolts, screws), stationery supplies (paper fasteners, rubber bands, etc.), as well as other scrap materials. Teacher and students may collect various items in advance of lesson.

NOTE: Gesso painted on shoeboxes in advance of paint application will allow the paint to cover the surface brightly and more evenly.

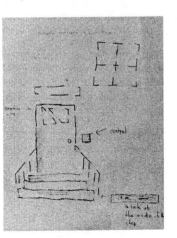

FIGURE 90. Tired of rushing to answer the door? Here's a remote control device with a built-in scanner that will solve all your problems!

DIRECTIONS

Part One

1. What is an invention? It's a device that eliminates work or improves an existing condition. Do you have something you want to correct or improve? Here are some idea starters:

   • Dog walker
   • Cat feeder
   • Automatic homework doer
   • Portable lie detector
   • Calorie remover (grown-ups would like this one!)
   • Instant fabric restoring machine (fixes tears and rips, makes clothes brand new)

2. A list may be developed on the chalkboard. Another way to stimulate responses is to ask for pet peeves, then invent an "anti-" device or "buster" to fix the problem. Inventions can also take the form of transportation vehicles.

3. Distribute paper and pencils. Just like Leonardo, we will make notes and various sketches of several ideas. Thumbnail (small) sketches and see-through diagrams are excellent here.

4. After sketching several ideas, select the one that will translate most successfully into the 3–D (shoebox) model. Include brief instructions on how to use your invention.

Part Two

5. Bring out the paint, glue, scissors, tape, colored paper, shoeboxes, and other materials.

6. Construct your model to represent your chosen idea as best you can. It's great if your model will have working parts, but it's not essential. We can use our imaginations.

7. Add any special features (flaps, antennae, arrows, push buttons, etc.). Finish painting and affixing parts as needed.

8. Eureka! You are a patent genius! Display the inventions in a visible place with the plans and schemes to back them up.

FIGURE 91. Carlo, an intrepid eighth grade inventor, answers the call for building a better mousetrap. In his own words... "This wonderful piece of machinery easily lures a mouse and catches it with no problem. Walls close in and, well, you know the rest. The box is disposable." Affordable... portable... and best of all, no mice!

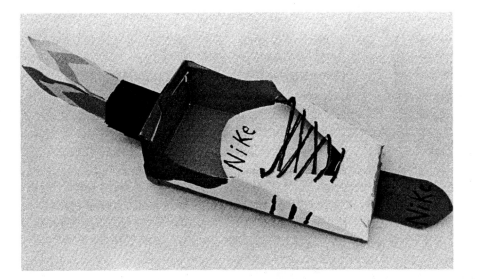

FIGURE 92. THE ATOMIC RUNNING SHOE. "High powered sneaker designed to give runners the competitive edge."

ACTIVITY 32
I Remember Mona

MIXED MEDIA: Portrait and Frame Design

Mona Lisa has almost become a figurehead for Renaissance art. Yet she was not a duchess or a queen. She was the wife of a banker whose portrait became the most famous ever painted! In immortalizing his model Mona Lisa, the artist Leonardo da Vinci also preserved a part of the world that surrounded her. So look just beyond that secret smile for a glimpse into sixteenth-century Italy.

SLIDE #11:   MONA LISA

MATERIALS

- Illustration board (or posterboard)
- Oaktag
- Markers
- Crayons
- Watercolor (or poster paint)
- Masking tape
- Scissors
- Ruler
- Pencils

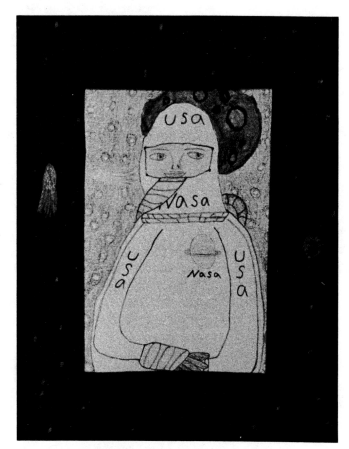

FIGURE 93. Mona of NASA. You can't get any more current than this intergalactic portrayal.

FIGURE 94. Yo! Mona! A student's candid twentieth-century view of La Giaconda.

TEACHER PREPARATION

Illustration boards (or posterboards) should not be too large—9″ × 12″ is more in scale with the original painting of the Mona Lisa. Oaktag will be your picture's mat, so it will have to exceed your illustration boards by three inches (e.g., 12″ × 15″). The teacher may precut the mats. Establish center of oaktag by drawing diagonal lines in pencil from opposite corners, going from lower left to upper right and vice versa, forming a big X. Place illustration board on the center of the oaktag, using your eye as your guide. Trace and remove. Measure ½″ *inside* the outline of the traced rectangle. Fold in half. Cut out the inside rectangle. Your mat will remain when you remove the paper from the center. (NOTE: You may want students to cut their own mats. Have them follow the same instructions as above.)

DIRECTIONS

1. If we were to create a portrait for our era, what could we include in it that would identify the time and the place? Think of some monuments and landmarks of America. Mt. Rushmore? The Statue of Liberty? The Liberty Bell? Maybe you can think of some specific sights in your home town.

2. What could help establish a specific period of time in this portrait? Name some trends and styles of the 1980s. Distribute materials.

3. Do a contour pencil outline of Mona Lisa's outside shape. Regard her placement on the page. Draw the pose, replacing Renaissance fashion with a snazzy contemporary outfit. You may try to make your portrait's face look like Mona Lisa's, or you can substitute another face (your own? a friend's?) if you wish.

4. In creating your modern-day Mona Lisa, consider popular patterns and designs of fabric, clothing styles, eyewear, jewelry, etc. Use the mix of media that best suits your ideas.

5. The background is a very important part of the picture. Show a part of America! It may be the West or a great city—don't be afraid to divide paper to include several pictures and images.

6. When the portrait is finished, take out your oaktag mat. Again, our frame will reflect current styles. Pick motifs from some of the designs or images you used for your Mona Lisa. You can combine abstract patterns with realistic representations.

7. Tape your portraits behind your mats when finished. Display your many interpretations of the Mona Lisa in your classroom *galleria*.

FIGURE 95. Mona of the suburban mall.

FIGURE 96. Mona on vacation. The "Mauna Lisa" maybe?

SUGGESTIONS FOR FURTHER DEVELOPMENT

It's fun to reveal a period of time in the manner described in this activity. Some of your students may enjoy focusing on other decades, such as the 1950s or 1970s. There is much material to choose from in these periods, particularly with our love for nostalgia these days.

ACTIVITY 33
Banner Days!

FABRIC ARTS: Banners

Pageants, processions, and festivals! People marched through the streets of Renaissance cities with many banners ablaze. A celebration, a victory—even the proclamation of a new territory—all of these events were enhanced by flying flags. In fact, the Italian word *pallio* not only means banner, but has come to be the name of a particular sports contest in which the winner is awarded a banner. A handsome banner can be a prize indeed!

MATERIALS

- Felt (see Teacher Preparation)
- Manila paper
- Pencils
- Scissors
- Yardstick
- Glue
- Wooden dowels
- Magnifying glasses
  (see Teacher Preparation)

FIGURE 97. Renaissance motifs culled from paintings and costume design need not be elaborate to be visually effective.

TEACHER PREPARATION

You will need some good lengths of felt, preferably from a bolt. Measure and cut felt into two-foot sections, figuring on half the number of your class size (students will work as partners). You'll also need squares of felt to be used later for the banners' designs.

Because we'll be hunting for Renaissance design motifs in fabric and dress, try to have some reproductions of Renaissance portraits on hand. Also, costume books often illustrate popular patterns throughout history. Magnifying glasses will assist students in their search.

Cut dowels to fit the felt banner sizes.

This lesson will require more than one class session.

DIRECTIONS

1. Bring reference materials forward. Examine reproductions, books, etc., for examples of Renaissance motifs used in fabric.

2. Distribute practice paper. Try drawing several design motifs, adding your own ideas and variations. Also practice cutting these shapes out with scissors.

3. Match students with partners. Provide them with felt, along with other necessary materials. Cut the banner contour as desired. (See Figure 98 for suggestions.)

4. Students will decide on their banner design in pairs, selecting particular motifs. Color contrast, compatibility of shapes, and their relative sizes should be considered.

5. Before gluing design elements to banner, students should try various pattern arrangements. Simple geometric shapes may be added. Glue all elements to surface when a pleasing design has been reached.

6. Banners may be hung on wooden dowels with loops cut from (2″ × 4″) pieces of the felt. Glue both ends of fabric pieces together, attach to banner edge. Create about four felt loops—they should fit the dowel snugly.

7. Ready to run it up the flag pole to see if anyone salutes? A school event, an assembly, or even a parade would be enlivened by the presence of your banners. Another display suggestion: establish your very own Hall of Flags!

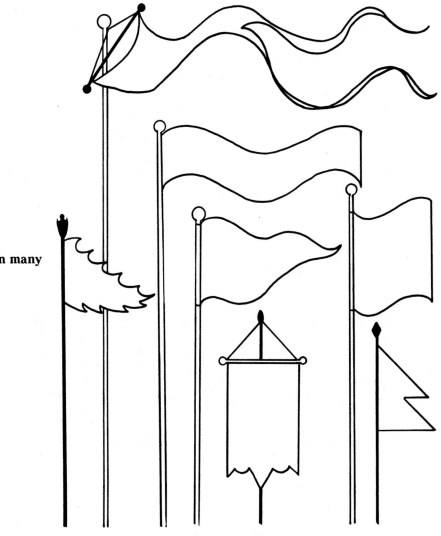

FIGURE 98. Banners come in many shapes and sizes!

ACTIVITY 34
Carnival Masks

PAPIER-MÂCHÉ: Masks

Where can you find wandering minstrels, dukes, jugglers, and fools? Harlequins, jesters, and other madcap characters from the Commedia dell'arte? Only one place, with its narrow, ancient, cobblestone streets, surrounded by canals and gondolas—Venice at carnival time! An old custom which was so beloved that it is still held once a year in the same Italian city today.

FIGURE 99. Venice and the Commedia dell'arte are recalled in these theatrical masks. Students may want to represent specific characters, such as clowns and witches, in their own interpretations.

MATERIALS

- Flour and water for papier-mâché
- Newspapers (see Teacher Preparation)
- Glue
- Acrylic paint
- Paintbrushes
- Acrylic gloss varnish
- Ribbons
- Bells, fabric scraps, etc. (optional)
- Nails (see Teacher Preparation)
- Commercial face masks, such as Halloween masks (see Teacher Preparation)

TEACHER PREPARATION

You'll need the ingredients for papier-mâché. Here are the recipe and instructions:

1 cup flour
1 cup water
black-and-white newspaper
white glue (optional)

Mix flour and water a little at a time in a bowl. Some people prefer adding flour to water, believing that it makes a smoother paste. Add white glue if desired. Avoid "puffs" of flour in air by sifting it directly into water. Tear newspaper into strips. Be sure to cover work surface with newspapers.

When lumps in mixture have disappeared, dip strips in. Slip excess paste off strips by pulling them through two fingers. Apply strips to mask form and build features. Add dry paper strips between very wet ones to absorb extra wetness if necessary. Squeeze and manipulate to control shaping. When complete, let dry. Coat with acrylic gloss varnish.

It is suggested that this lesson be presented near Halloween when inexpensive face masks are readily available. Old used ones will do just as well, but each student will require a face mask form on which our *carnevale* masks will be built. Limp rubber masks are not usable for this activity; hard plastic, molded paper, and rigid fabric forms sized with glue are fine. Books on costume (the history of; theatrical, e.g., the Commedia dell'arte, etc.) will provide good information and character ideas. Also, get out the fabric scraps. Set your room up for workshop activity.

Large nails are handy for perforating holes in masks. Be sure you closely supervise the students.

If you are unable to perform the activity with your class as it is suggested so far, please don't despair! Cut facial mask shapes from bristol board. Cut appropriate vents for eyes and mouth. Decorate with markers, using the Venetian *carnevale* as inspiration for your characters. Staple finished mask directly to tongue depressor. It's not papier-mâché, but still respectable—and you've saved face!

DIRECTIONS

Part One

1. Discuss the cast of characters that might be present at a Venetian *carnevale*. Use reference materials.
2. Decide on a specific idea for the individual mask. Bring out the ingredients for papier-mâché.
3. Build up the face on your mask form as suggested by the basic papier-mâché technique. Exaggerate! Select features to emphasize. That is, after all, the beauty of a mask—it *can* be outrageous.
4. Perforate areas that need it, including holes for hanging masks on the wall.
5. Let dry.

Part Two

6. Paint the mask and glue on details (such as fabric, bells, and so forth). Checkerboard and diamond patterns, wherever they can be inserted, are very authentic for this activity. The use of "clown white" (painting the mask face white) makes an effective harlequin mask.
7. Seal the *dry* paint with acrylic gloss varnish, under teacher supervision. Add ribbons for decoration and hanging.
8. Masks can turn an ordinary wall into a festival of faces!

NOTE: Masks should essentially be used for decoration. Although they may be worn by students, they are fragile. It is best to treat them accordingly.

ACTIVITY 35
The Merchants of Venice: Portraits of the Rich and Famous

MIXED MEDIA, COLLAGE: Portraits

Venice was the center of trade during the Renaissance. Goods from around the globe came to this city of waterways and canals. Venetians enjoyed prosperity along with their art. An important style of painting emerged, often simply referred to as "Venetian," reflecting the richness of the material world. The Venetian style was soon to become a major influence in the history of fine art.

SLIDE #12:   RANUCCIO FARNESE

MATERIALS

- Oil pastels
- Scissors
- Glue
- Bristol boards
- Wallpaper sample books
  (see Teacher Preparation)
- Magazines and catalogs
  (see Teacher Preparation)
- Fabric scraps
  (see Teacher Preparation)

FIGURE 100. A Venetian gentleman complete with an anachronistic watch on his noble wrist.

TEACHER PREPARATION

Visit a paint store, wallpaper store, or home decorating center and ask for any discontinued sample wallpaper books (on behalf of your students, of course!).

Collect fashion magazines—such as *Vogue, Bazaar, Glamour,* for example—particularly Fall and Winter issues. We're looking for a variety of textures, such as leather, fur, velvet, and silk. Venetians also loved their gems, so save those jewelry catalogues and promotional sale flyers you receive in the mail from department stores. Needless to say, the addition of real costume jewelry to this lesson (the kind that would otherwise be discarded) will produce dazzling results! Your students and colleagues could donate to the cause, just be sure there's enough to go around for every pupil in your class. Buttons, especially the studded and sparkling sort, are fabulous too!

Stock your fabric scrap collection with bits and snips of fake fur, silk and, satin (synthetics can also be used), lace trim, chiffon, velvet, even drapery cords and tassles may be included. This lesson may take several class sessions to complete.

FIGURE 101. The lady wears fur (fake, naturally) and appears behind a proper veil. Third grade students learned the implications of textures in their Venetian portraits.

DIRECTIONS

1. Observe the qualities of the costumes shown in Venetian portraits. These were the finest of fabrics, the most splendid of jewels—describe them in your own words through class discussion.

2. After you've noted the soft, plush furs, the sumptuous velvets, the shiny silver, and elegant brocades, you're ready to see more. Let's examine the Venetian style of composition: often a curtain is drawn behind the sitter to reveal a city or landscape. It is a way to suggest space—and an artist's trick.

3. Distribute all materials in a manner that suits your room arrangement. Oil pastels will be used first to establish the head and upper torso of the portrait. Consider the poses favored in Venetian portraiture when you place the figure on the page.

4. Venetian artists turned paint into velvet and gold with the magic of their brushes! We will cheat a little by gluing photographs of textures and fabric scraps on to our own portraits. In this way, we'll also create a fine costume.

5. How about the space behind your figure? Perhaps some of those wallpaper samples could be cut to resemble a drawn-back curtain. Create some space in your picture with background interest. Mix your media!

6. Add all the goodies. Buttons, hats, cuff links, lace bows, pinkie rings—anything you feel will complete your picture.

7. In the end, you should have a pretty impressive portrait. Hang your proud Venetians where they can be properly admired.

ACTIVITY 36
Getting the Proper Perspective

PERSPECTIVE EXERCISE: "Mechanical" Drawing, Painting

The Renaissance artists quested for knowledge. It is not surprising that they established perspective, a scientific system for viewing deep picture space. Although perspective may take many forms, its most dramatic principle is the vanishing point. This is what appears to happen to railroad tracks when they are seen from the back of the train. Like any two parallel lines, they'll eventually converge and disappear from sight. Many Renaissance painters employed this fundamental method in their artwork and were quite successful at fooling the viewer's eye.

SLIDE #13:   MARRIAGE OF THE VIRGIN

FIGURE 102. The principle of perspective, not fully understood until the Renaissance, is expressed by students in familiar imagery.

MATERIALS

- Pencils
- Ruler
- 12″ × 18″ drawing paper
- Posterpaint or colored pencils
- Paintbrushes (if using poster paint)

TEACHER PREPARATION

This lesson is an introduction to one-point perspective. It is a simple lesson, but it can be, at the same time, conceptually abstract. Therefore, perspective may not be grasped by younger students, who may still represent the sky as a blue band across the top of their page. To these students, the planes of the sky and ground are not perceived as meeting with each other on the horizon. Be patient with these young notions; after all, consider how many centuries passed before grown-up artists got *their* notions about perspective right!

DIRECTIONS

1. Use the chalkboard for demonstration. Draw a horizontal chalk line. We'll call this line the *horizon,* or the ground plane.
2. Distribute all drawing paper, pencils, and rulers. Ask students to draw a horizontal line on their papers.
3. On the chalkboard, draw a box around the line to represent a drawing paper. Place a chalk dot on the center of the line. Have students do the same. This is the *vanishing point.*
4. Construct two intersecting lines to form a wide "X" as shown in Figure 104.

FIGURE 103. A road that leads to the vanishing point.

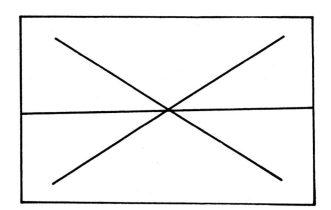

FIGURE 104. The horizon and vanishing point.

FIGURE 105. You might sketch in shapes or grids to keep the horizon on line.

FIGURE 106. Picture space is in place here. The result is perspective.

5. These crisscrossed lines can serve as guidelines for drawing objects that will diminish in size as they recede in space. Lines can help in drawing the scale of houses (see Figures 105 and 106), trees, fences, people, and so forth. You might even want to build a scene around the infamous railroad track!

6. Students can take it from here. Make painting and/or drawing materials available. Here are some reminders about the use of color and light for spatial definition:

   a. Darker shades recede; bright, light colors come forward.

   b. Shadows will push objects back in space.

   c. Softer, blurrier forms appear to be farther away; sharper, more detailed objects look closer.

   d. One object partially obscuring another object will move forward by contrast to the partly hidden item.

7. Use color to not only gain perspective, but to loosen the stiff quality of the diagramatic exercise. Treat it as you would any other painting or drawing. Try some of the effects suggested in step 6.

8. Your finished piece should have left you with a sense of space that you'll use many times over in your future art works. This is your own personal initiation into the rules of perspective!

ACTIVITY 37
Profiles of the Renaissance

PROFILES: "Florentine" Profiles, Perspective

During the Renaissance in Italy, many portraits were painted in profile. Perhaps the noble heads on Roman coins helped to influence the popularity of the profile view.

The face in profile appears more stylized and flatter than a frontal portrait. Renaissance profiles, particularly those by Florentine artists, were painted in a clear, precise manner. What clearly identifies Renaissance profiles is not only their crisp contour, but the way the space is shown behind the face!

**SLIDE #14:   A PRINCESS OF THE D'ESTE
FAMILY (GINERVA D'ESTE)**

FIGURE 107. Flat space complements this fine Florentine head.

MATERIALS

- 9″ × 12″ white paper
- Waterbased black felt-tip pen (thin to medium point)
- Crayons
- Scissors (see Teacher Preparation)
- Construction paper (larger than 9″ × 12″) for mounting (optional)
- Photo copier (see Teacher Preparation)

TEACHER PREPARATION

Teachers with access to a decent copy machine will not need scissors for this activity. Each student will receive *one clean copy* of his or her line drawing after contour is drawn. A supply of sketch paper and pencils may be provided for students who wish to practice contour before final drawing is made.

Reproductions of Renaissance profiles—as well as full portraits—that illustrate various perspectives and backgrounds are recommended as reference materials.

DIRECTIONS

1. Ask a student volunteer model to sit in a profile position for the class. Point out placement of features in relationship to each other, for example, the corner of the eye is in line with the top of the ear. Observe what happens to the face when seen in profile as compared to full face, using the student model to illustrate the point. For example, the eyes are seen as half-shapes in profile, instead of full almond shapes. Also notice the rounded proportion of the back of the head in side view. Student model may return to seat.

2. Distribute pencils, pens, and papers.

3. Using the reference material, develop a Renaissance profile in pencil. Consider the outside shape of the head to represent its contour. The drawing should depict a clear-cut profile with awareness of details such as hair style, jewelry, and costume. When a pleasing contour has been established, erase pencil line enough to leave faint outline. Draw over it with felt tip marker *only* if copier will be used.

3. Make duplicates of finished profile pen drawing on copier, allowing one copy for each student of his or her work. *If copy machine is unavailable,* carefully cut outside shape of profile and trace in felt pen—*two* times on two separate papers.

4. On one paper, create deep space. (See Activity 36.) The profile and the scene behind it will be done in crayon. Landscapes that include towns, cities, or rivers are ideal as backgrounds. To make space appear to be receding, objects—trees, houses, etc.— should be drawn smaller as they go farther back into the picture. Remember, darker colors and less detail also suggest distance. Blend crayons for a rich surface.

5. On the other paper, create flat space. A simple background of solid color will do it, or a flat, decorative pattern. Because this is less complex, students may want to spend some time on the qualities of their profile's hair, jewelry, and costume. Fuzzy surfaces represent hair and fur, spots of light color can be shown to reflect light from jewels, etc. In all pictures, use crayons as descriptively as possible.

6. Gather all completed pictures for students to review. Compare the various uses of space, watching for devices that make space appear far away or close up. Mount portraits on construction paper if desired; display as a Renaissance profile gallery. If Activity 35 has been completed, Florentines and Venetians may be displayed side by side!

FIGURE 108. A clearly drawn profile is seen against a deeper picture plane, depicted as a sixteenth-century town.

ACTIVITY 38
Things Are Looking Up!

DRAWING EXERCISE: "Ceiling" Painting

Things can look up or down depending on where you stand! In the case of the great painter and sculptor, Michelangelo, much of his art was above him, on the ceiling of the Sistine Chapel. He created the entire work while lying on a scaffold on his back, which was quite a feat indeed. Art can really change your point of view!

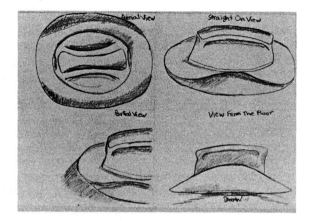

FIGURE 109. The phrase "from where I sit" takes on new meaning with this visual exercise. Notice how shading dramatizes various views.

SLIDE #15:   SISTINE CHAPEL CEILING

MATERIALS

- Drawing paper
- 3″ × 5″ cards
- Pencils
- Erasers
- Brown butcher wrap
- Markers
- Paint
- Brushes
- Tape, scissors

TEACHER PREPARATION

This is a two-part lesson. The first unit is a visual exercise that will help students with their observational skills. To accomplish the exercise, each student will need one everyday, dimensional object. This can be brought in by the students or provided by the teacher. Some suggestions are a coffee mug, a box of tissues, a hat (but not the soft, shapeless type)—even a radio will do. And what if students should forget their art assignment and the teacher runs out of objects? No problem! Students can simply remove a shoe from their foot and they'll be all set for the first part of the activity.

To be prepared for the second phase, which should take place in an art period that will follow Part One, you will need to cut lengths of butcher wrap. These will be taped *underneath* the desks. You might want to vary lessons by precutting paper in rounded contours, for example, such as ovals, circles, or cloud shapes. Five or six shapes might be good for the entire class, but you will need to estimate your own situation. Also, a reasonably clean floor is strongly suggested for Part Two of this activity.

Reproductions of Michelangelo's Sistine Chapel as well as other Renaissance ceiling painters should be made available.

FIGURE 110. Galaxies are certainly suitable subjects for ceiling painting.

DIRECTIONS

Part One: The Visual Exercise

1. Distribute drawing paper and pencils. Fold the drawing paper into quarters.

2. Place object on the desk in front of you. Draw what you see in the upper-right quarter. Shading may be added, but leave enough time to accomplish all four drawings.

3. When you have finished the straight-on view, move the object to the floor next to your chair. Draw the object as it appears below you in the upper-left quarter of your paper.

4. Replace the object on your desk as in Step 2. Get out of your seat, then sit on the floor in front of your desk. Using the seat of your chair as a drawing support surface, sketch the object above you in the lower right square. Return to your seat. Leave object in its place.

5. Distribute 3″ × 5″ cards and scissors. Fold 3″ × 5″ cards. Cut the keyhole shape out from the center of the card as shown in Figure 111.

6. Use the "keyhole" to view your object, which should be seen as partially obscured. Draw what you see in the last quarter of your paper.

7. Discuss students' work in a group review. Which views of the objects were most challenging? Which were most common? Was one view more or less dramatic than another? Which one? Are there other vantage points we might have used? Name some. Hints: Upside-down, rear-view (over the shoulder), and so on.

8. What have we learned? Even a single object can be seen in so many different ways! The next part of this activity applies our knowledge through concerted effort.

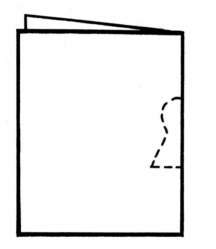

FIGURE 111. Fold a 3″ × 5″ card down the center. Cut half of a keyhole shape as shown here.

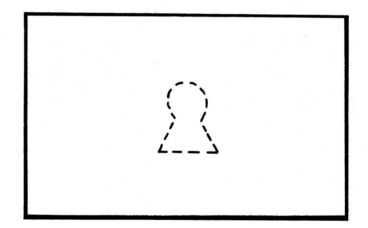

FIGURE 112. Open the card and it's ready to use for viewing.

Part Two: Ceiling Painting

1. As indicated in Teacher Preparation, tape undersides of several desks with precut brown butcher wrap. Distribute markers. (Keep paints aside for now).

2. Briefly discuss good subjects for a ceiling painting. The skies are a natural for this lesson. Also good are outer space, birds, aircraft, hot air balloons, and constellations. Consider perspectives shown in reproductions and their foreshortenings.

3. Students will form small groups that suit your classroom space and the amounts of brown paper you allocated for the lesson. They will need to get on their backs beneath the desk you assign to them with markers within reach.

4. Block in your determined choice of ceiling subject with markers. When compositions have been fairly well planned in marker, remove brown paper from under desks. Place on usual work surface and take out the paints! Work in same small groups.

5. Stars should twinkle, clouds float, birds soar—you get the picture! Make us forget this is brown paper. Cover all of it with bright paint! Let dry.

6. Can you suspend these ambitious works from the ceiling tiles? It would make a heavenly display!

ACTIVITY 39
A Panel of Experts

STUDIO PAINTING: Panels

Visit a museum and walk through a gallery of Renaissance Art. Notice how many different sizes and shapes of paintings are on the walls! From tiny to grand, to circular, oblong, horizontal—the list is quite long. Renaissance artists respected the shape their paintings were in, and they made sure their art fit those shapes just right.

FIGURE 113. Rolling hills and a waterfall make an ideal subject for horizontal panel painting.

MATERIALS

- Acrylic paints
- Palettes (see "Studio Painting in the Classroom" in Section One)
- Paintbrushes for oil painting
- Gesso (see Teacher Preparation)
- Masonite panels (see Teacher Preparation)
- Medium-grain sandpaper
- Mounting hooks

TEACHER PREPARATION

Masonite panels can be purchased at a lumberyard if they are not available through the school woodshop. Masonite isn't very expensive, and in the sizes you'll be using, you might even be able to get away with odd cuts and scraps. Ask for untempered masonite, ⅛″ to ¼″ is fine. The ideal sizes for this lesson may vary (a length of 12″ × 30″ is ideal), but most long and narrow boards will do fine. You can secure half the number of boards for your class size, since two students can work on one panel. Prepare panels according to the directions on the gesso label, after *lightly* sanding them. Mounting materials may be purchased at lumberyards or hardware stores.

If you are unable to get masonite panels and don't have acrylic paints in the supply closet, stay with us! Substitute the wood with posterboard in dimensions to those described above and use poster paint instead of acrylics.

Set up the room for a painting activity. Allow adequate class time for completion. Directions will not be broken into parts, for the procedure does not bear repetition.

DIRECTIONS

1. Have all materials ready: palettes arranged, paint rags (or paper towels) out, water containers filled, and so forth. Students should join with a partner. Distribute prepared panels.

2. Discuss appropriate subjects for the horizontal panels. What subjects lend themselves to such a space? Green, rolling hills, or the broad horizon of the sea, surrounded by ports-of-call? How about a parade, a marching band, a race—even a shelf of glass bottles and jars could do just as well!

3. Partners will reach an agreement on one of the many possibilities for their panels before they begin painting. NOTE: Students may ask if they can start their painting by drawing in pencil first. If they insist, use charcoal sticks instead; the use of pencil before painting can sometimes tighten student expression. Direct painting is recommended.

4. Begin to paint! Enjoy the process; don't worry about perfection. Acrylics air-dry quickly and can be painted over easily if corrections need to be made.

5. As in any composition, this horizontal painting will be complete when all elements work together. When finished, let dry.

6. Mount hanging hooks according to package instructions.

7. Exhibit your panels in a place of importance in the school. What conference room or office wouldn't be enhanced by these Renaissance masterpieces?

THE POST-RENAISSANCE

.....1500.....................	1600....................	1700....................	1800.....
Spain	Dutch School	France	England

Up until now, periods of art could be gathered in fairly manageable parcels: cave painting, the Ancient World, the Middle Ages, and the Renaissance. Then along comes the seventeenth century, and we have a bit of a dilemma on our hands! What do you call a period that encompasses so many divergent styles of art and artists? It can be quite unwieldy.

There was, however, no lack of effort to identify this time, with the hope of avoiding confusion. One of the big problems was the fact that various painting schools and individual painters were popping up all over Europe—from Holland, to Spain, and into France. Yet, out of sheer volume, proliferation, and extent of influence, the Dutch school had to be considered the most dominant of them all.

This was no coincidence, for at the helm of the Dutch tradition was Rembrandt, an artist whose enormous talent has rightfully earned the recognition he eventually received. He was a painter who could portray emotion without sentimentality, and play with light and shadow without melodrama. His portraits strongly conveyed dignity, even though the subjects were often everyday people, not kings and queens.

Interest in common people and subjects of daily life became an art movement in itself. It was called "genre," and was perhaps best depicted in the work of the artist, Vermeer. His paintings were of rich interiors filled with soft light and sensuous textures. Beyond Vermeer were numerous genre painters of all ranks, just as there were countless Dutch still-life painters as well. In fact, there were probably more Dutch still-life paintings than anyone could ever imagine! The seventeenth century was a prosperous, productive time.

Yet another extremely prodigious member of the Dutch school was the painter Peter Paul Rubens, although he was more closely associated with curvilinear Renaissance styles than with genre painting. Nonetheless, his output was awesome and his influence on later painters was rather impressive. Frans Hals was another prominent painter whose technique would tie into painters of other times—namely Manet—who also derived much from Velásquez.

114

Velásquez was a painter of the Spanish school, if indeed there was such a school at all. For you see, there were three remarkable Spanish painters—Velásquez, El Greco and Goya. But their styles were so completely their own, so highly original, it is hard to place them in any sort of group. In any case, the Spanish school is the most logical place for them since they were, after all, Spanish painters, although they were hard to pin down.

That is how this period of time in art history played out. Another example was Chardin, a first-rate eighteenth-century French painter, whose subject interest took him much closer to Dutch genre painting than to his own French roots. French painting was, in the main, considered light-hearted, lyrical, and delicate. Fragonard, Boucher, and Watteau typify French painting of this general period; they enjoyed painting the numerous pastimes of the life in the courts.

Claude Lorrain was a seventeenth-century French painter whose art concerned landscapes, minus the escapades. His art, like Poussin's, was more classical. In fact, many attribute the conceptualization of landscape, as an entity in itself, to Lorrain. His landscapes were—like England's Constable's and, to some extent, Turner's—substantial representations of real exterior space. It was a movement that preceded the Barbizon school.

So there you have it. Portraiture at its finest in the hands of Rembrandt. The advent of landscape in its own right. And, as we have noted, still-lifes galore. It all happened after the Renaissance, in a time of unequaled abundance of art.

ACTIVITY 40
A Portrait of the Artist

STUDIO PAINTING: Self-Portrait

Have you ever watched one of those quick-sketch artists—the ones who often work at seaside resorts—dash off a portrait? You may have noticed that they follow the same formula with every drawing. The results are pretty much guaranteed: a close resemblance to the sitter, who will then be pleased. Yet, in the end something seems to be missing. What is it, exactly, you wonder? The answer, although not easy to define, is art. It is the absence of art itself.

Art has the power to convey personality. It will allow you to know someone who lived hundreds of years ago by bringing you a very real sense of the individual on the canvas. Art breathes life into likeness and captures the sitter's spirit in paint. When a painter can go beyond the physical description of a person to extract the essence of their character, we call that painter an artist. Rembrandt was more than an artist. He was a Master.

FIGURE 114. There is a sense of self-confidence in this self-portrait by Michael, age 12. He even uses a spatial trick favored by many great painters—the "window device." By placing a painting, mirror or map behind the figure, the artist is able to suggest deeper space.

**SLIDE #16:   PORTRAIT OF THE ARTIST
                AT HIS EASEL**

MATERIALS

- Acrylic paints
- Palettes (see "Studio Painting in the Classroom" in Section One)
- Paintbrushes for oil painting
- Canvas boards (see Teacher Preparation)
- Mirrors (see Teacher Preparation)

TEACHER PREPARATION

Canvas boards are not extremely expensive, but you may want to ask students to furnish their own, or contribute to the art room budget. This request will, of course, depend on your own individual supply situation. Easels, too, would be ideal if available, but work tables will do instead. Drawing boards are fine to use if you have them.

Mirrors may be brought in by students if you don't keep them in supply. Make-up mirrors, or any others that can stand on a desk independently, are best.

Have all materials ready; the plan is to paint directly. No practice sketches will be called for in this activity, which may be completed in one class session.

DIRECTIONS

1. Observe the expressions on the faces of several Rembrandt portraits and self-portraits. What do they tell you about the sitter? Explain your reactions.

2. Now let's work with your own feelings. As in an acting exercise, ask students to think of something serious. This can be the day they moved from the old house or when an older sibling went off to college. Regard your expression in the mirror. What happens to your eyes? Your mouth? Keep looking.

3. Change your thoughts. Now concentrate on another experience. This one can be happy. You received a wonderful present for your birthday, or a brand new pet! Study your face in the mirror again.

4. What kind of personality do you think you have? Are you generally cheerful? Pensive? Moody? Serious? Consider this for a moment, then begin to paint.

5. Consult your mirror as often as you feel you should. It will help you with expression, but we are hoping to paint from "within." Do not be overly concerned with likeness. Sometimes the paintings that communicate the most effectively about the sitter look the least like that person!

6. Should you wish to add to or change the image in the mirror, feel free to do so. Paint background color or scheme in a way that you feel best complements your work.

7. The completed painting need not appear highly refined. It's the expressive quality that counts here. Let dry.

8. Perhaps you can enlist the assistance of a friendly industrial arts teacher in framing the paintings. Simple wood strips make fine frames. Students can paint or buff them in a selected color for a finished look.

9. Mount hooks on your self-portraits and hang with great self-assurance.

ACTIVITY 41
Behind Dutch Doors

MIXED MEDIA: Dutch Interiors and Exteriors

Interiors were important subjects in Dutch art. These were the settings in which the daily dramas of domestic life took place. Paintings offer us a peek inside homes where folks can be seen doing everyday things. Somehow, simple acts like putting on a sock or mending a torn garment can appear quite elegant when portrayed in paint.

SLIDE #17:   LADY READING AT AN OPEN WINDOW

MATERIALS

- Crayons
- Markers
- Watercolors
- Pencils
- Rulers
- 12″ × 18″ drawing paper
- Scissors
- Stapler or glue
- Self-stick labels (see Teacher Preparation)

FIGURE 115. What a lively little street scene! Why, there's even an artist at work at an easel in the "Swanson's" house. Also notice the "building materials." Crayon-resist techniques may be incorporated as in the roof at the right. Watercolor works well for larger surfaces and is perfect for colored glass window panes.

TEACHER PREPARATION

You'll need two drawing papers for each student, so double the number required for your class. Self-stick labels will be a treat for your students, but white paper, precut to the approximate size of labels, may be substituted (add glue to the list of supplies here).

Reproductions of *genre* painting, for example, scenes of daily Dutch life, as well as materials depicting Dutch house facades, are recommended.

DIRECTIONS

Part One

1. Observe reproductions that depict street scenes and house facades, as well as paintings that show everyday life. From what materials are these houses made—stone, brick, or wood? Note important features, particularly the style of the windows and doors. Don't overlook shutters.

FIGURE 116. Welcome!

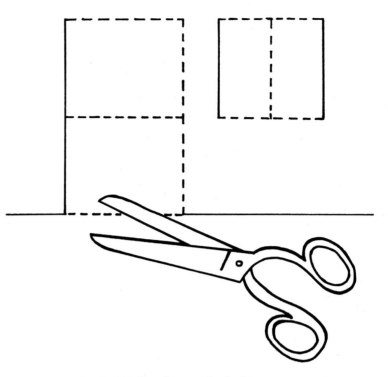

FIGURE 117. Cut door and windows as shown.

2. Distribute the first paper and pencils, rulers, markers, and scissors to students. Hold paper vertically. Measure windows and doors, spacing them apart appropriately. Pay attention to scale. Design Dutch doors and shutters. Be generous with dimensions.

3. Draw the building style contour along the outside edge. Cut the shape of the house. Distribute all other media and mix for effects. Pay attention to the "building materials" your house will be made from; apply markers, paint, crayons, etc., to make it convincing!

4. Add design details to window shutters and doors and any other touches of realism you like, such as nesting birds or clinging vines. Watercolor can help with covering not only the larger surfaces, but in suggesting stained or tinted glass window panes.

5. Penetrate the shutters and door with the point of the scissors, carefully, along the cutting edge. (See Figure 117.) Cut open and fold back. You may want to decorate both the front *and* back of your windows.

   Part Two

6. Distribute the second drawing paper and all art materials. Place the first paper of the building facade on top of the blank paper. Trace the outside contour and cut.

7. Keep both papers lined up evenly with one another. Holding in place, trace the apertures of the door and the windows. Remove the facade. Go over the rectangles you just traced, with the assistance of the ruler, for further definition of the rectangular shapes. This is where all the action will take place.

8. What daily activities and tasks might you find the people in this house doing? Here are a few possibilities:

   - Petting a cat or dog
   - Playing a musical instrument
   - Writing a letter
   - Feeding a baby
   - Painting a picture
   - Threading a needle
   - Pouring milk

All of these little scenes are played out in Dutch paintings, yet they are acts we have all experienced either directly or indirectly. Choose some of the above and come up with a few of your own!

9. Show people in the rectangles, which will now become our windows into the interior rooms. Think about the purpose of the task in relationship to the particular room (for example, pouring milk in the kitchen, writing a letter in the living room or den, and so forth).

10. Can we see beyond the room in which the action is occurring? Dutch artists liked to peek into interior space extensively, which was accomplished by showing additional doors slightly ajar. Slivers of other rooms suggest deeper space and add interest. So try adding pictures and maps hanging on the walls.

11. Staple or glue the facade over the house's interior. Make any necessary adjustments to shutters. Have you made good use of that double Dutch door? Have you put out the cat? Swept the front step? Shook out the welcome mat with your name on it? Put down the label, turn it into a front door mat or mailbox—a perfect place for your signature!

12. Display houses in a row, thus recreating a lively street and offering an active slice of Dutch life!

ACTIVITY 42
Miles of Tiles

PAPER AND CLAY: Tiles

Tiles seemed to be everywhere in Holland during the seventeenth century! Rooms were lined with them, whether the house was in the country or in town. From the tulip designs of simple picture tiles to entire walls composed of grand scale hunting scenes, tiles of every description abounded. Booming industry and burgeoning art form were one and the same in the ever-popular ceramic Dutch tile!

FIGURE 118. Paper tiles can be quite convincing!

MATERIALS

- Illustration boards
  (see Teacher Preparation)
- Markers
- Colored pencils
- Glue
- Manila paper
- Pencils
- Posterboard
- Clay (optional; see Teacher Preparation)
- Masonite boards (for clay tiles only)
- Double-faced foam tape (optional)

TEACHER PREPARATION

This lesson can be presented as a clay slab activity (see "The Clay Studio" in Section One) or tiles may be successfully fashioned from illustration board as indicated in the directions. Should you elect to make clay tiles, you'll still find that this plan will assist with the implementation of Dutch tile design. Whether you choose tiles of paper boards or clay, or favor markers over ceramic glazes, you will want students to grasp the idea behind tile imagery and its direct, decorative applications.

To prepare paper tiles, precut illustration boards into four-inch squares. Plan on each student making *at least* two tiles. Have posterboards in quantities to accommodate the mounting of the tiles.

NOTE: There's an in-between alternative for tile production you might want to pursue. Instead of making clay tiles from scratch or paper board tiles which, admittedly, don't impart the same sensorial quality of the ceramic tile, consider the ready-made glazed tile. White four-inch square glazed tiles can be quite inexpensively purchased from tile and floor covering centers. These real tiles may be painted with acrylic paints, yielding impressive results. Just be careful with finished products; the applied paint tends to chip off tiles easily.

Ceramic tiles, either preglazed or slab-produced, make outstanding gifts. You can display tiles on small stands made especially for that purpose, or hang on the wall with picture-mounting materials. To make a partial wall of tile, described in this activity, you'll need masonite boards or wood boards of a similar type.

This activity, presented either in clay or in paper, will require several class sessions.

FIGURE 119. Plain, store-bought ceramic tiles may be painted directly with acrylic paint. Remember: paint tends to chip off easily with this method, so handle carefully!

DIRECTIONS

1. Discuss the use of tiles with your class. Where in your own home or in other familiar buildings might tiles be found? Cite both decorative and utilitarian examples.

2. Before we practice designs for our tiles, let's consider some of the plentiful subjects enjoyed by the Dutch. Here's an incomplete list:

- Flowers, such as tulips
- Fruit; fruit bowls
- Vegetables
- Animals
- Ships; harbors

- Mermaids; dolphins
- Children's games
- Wooden shoes, windmills, and other objects and scenes from daily life

Perhaps your class will want to compile their own categorical subject list on the chalkboard.

3. Distribute manila paper, pencils, and other materials needed for practice work. Fold paper to produce four-inch squares. Students can now experiment with a variety of tile formats and pictorial ideas. Advise students in advance that corners will contain a specific motif, determined by group selection.

4. You may now want to draw some sample motifs on the chalkboard. (See Figure 120.) Simple designs, such as hearts, fans, and fleur-de-lis derivatives usually work best. Assign students to groups.

5. Each group will agree on one motif, say, hearts. Students would then be required to place a heart, or one half of a heart (this takes a little planning) in the corners of their tile. The rest of the tile design can be entirely individual.

6. Offer precut tile squares. Draw selected design and group's corner pattern in markers and colored pencils. Pay attention to color—blue and white Delft combinations are effective. Often tan and orange were used with the blue along with other subtle colorations.

FIGURE 120. Some suggested corner motifs.

FIGURE 121. These tiles have departed from our suggested unifying border motif, but are charming nonetheless. Made from "scratch," which is ambitious and rewarding, our fired and glazed ceramic tiles are mounted on masonite with strong double-faced foam tape.

7. You might want to impart further surface interest by suggesting a ceramic tile glaze. For example, sketch in hairline cracks, chips and shading (called "flashing" in tile language) to fool the eye for fun.

8. Initial your tiles. Gather all group tiles together and affix to posterboards with glue or double-faced foam tape. You may want to leave a little breathing space between the lines of tiles to suggest a grout line. What's the payoff for your group efforts? The corner motifs will visually unify all the tiles.

9. A dull wall? A dreary corner? Not any more! Mount your tile boards where they can cover unsightly areas, enliven the decor, and draw admiration. Such clever interior decorating surely won't get you in Dutch!

ACTIVITY 43
Still Life: A Dutch Treat

MIXED MEDIA, COLLAGE: Still Life

Dutch still lifes can include any number of objects, from fancy goblets and silver trays to baked breads and pretzels. Sometimes the still life was arranged in an orderly, formal way, but more often it would topple over with fruits and finery. Frequently, items like letters, pens, and books would hint at something about the world from which the still life was borrowed.

Dutch still-life painters loved to trick the eye by making the painting look like the real article. Realistic objects set against a dark background are trademarks of Dutch still-life painting.

FIGURE 122. The teapot whistles while the pocketwatch ticks and a bee flies out the window. A still life that is anything but still!

**SLIDE #18:   STILL LIFE WITH CRABS
                AND FRUIT**

MATERIALS

- 12″ × 18″ or larger black construction paper
- Colored paper
- Colored tissue
- White glue
- Watercolor cup
- Medium to wide paintbrush
- Pencil
- Crayons
- Scissors
- Collage scraps (see Teacher Preparation)
- Fruit (see Teacher Preparation)

TEACHER PREPARATION

You will want to have reproductions that represent Dutch still lifes with a range of different contents. Using one or more visual references as a guide, gather items that would be at home in a Dutch still life. Ask students to lend contributions and suggestions, too. A trip to the market should provide appropriate food and fruit. Bring in a paring knife for peeling the fruit.

Gather materials for the collage that match the items in the still life as closely as possible. For example: paper doilies for lace tablecloths, foil papers for silver and copper, fabric swatches for napkins and curtains, woodgrain self-stick vinyl Contact© paper, for wooden objects, and so on. In some cases, as in envelopes and old book covers, you may even use the actual object right in the collage.

DIRECTIONS

1. Using Dutch still-life reproductions as a suggestion for arranging objects, plan the setup with the class. Get students' input on what should go where! HINT: Dutch still lifes often show water in glasses, have items turned on their sides, and show fruit peeled with curly skin coiling down.

2. Study the still life and plan the order in which shapes will be applied. Talk about what must be glued first so that other items can be placed on the paper later. "What's closest to you? What's farthest away?" This should also be discussed, as well as the relative sizes of items.

3. Decide what materials will be used to represent the elements in the still life. After considering the special collage scraps, note that colored tissue may be used for the translucent qualities of liquids and glass. Colored paper is good for solid items and adds local color.

4. Scissors are used in direct response to the still life. Avoid drawing first—the scissors are the drawing tool. Paper curling is accomplished by simply pulling one inside blade of the open scissors along a cut paper strip. Cut out the other shapes needed for composition.

5. Arrange elements on paper in their proper order; glue down. For colored tissue, mix half water and half white glue in cup. Brush misture on cut colored tissue and apply. Again, think about what goes inside bowls and glasses and what stays on the outside.

6. Use crayons and pencil to indicate patterns and textures. Complete your still life by adding realistic touches, like a fly with tissue wings sitting on a piece of fruit.

ACTIVITY 44
Group Dynamics

DRAWING, COLOR: "Tableau Vivant"

FIGURE 123. Our very own "Dutch Masters." Left to right: Victor, Jennifer, Robin, Yaroni (standing), Robert and Kenny.

There are many reasons why artists paint people in groups. Figures can be used in paintings much like actors on a stage—to portray the action of a scene. On the other hand, the artist may wish to concentrate mainly on the movements of the figures as well as the interaction between them. Gestures reveal thoughts and inner feelings. Paintings of this sort are among the most candid, for the people in them appear to be quite unaware of the artist's attention.

Group portraits are just the opposite. The sitters pose especially for the artist and are indeed concerned about how they will be interpreted. When painting several people at the same time, the artist must capture many different personalities, while emphasizing any individuals who might be considered more important than the rest. This is what you might call a real artistic challenge, but it is one that many a Dutch painter managed to master!

FIGURE 124. Kenny elevates his status by stacking things in his favor.

SLIDE #19: THE ARTIST AND HIS FAMILY

MATERIALS

- Pencils
- Erasers
- Rulers
- 8″ × 10″ white paper
- Colored pencils or markers
- Black construction paper

- Glue
- White crayon
- Instant camera (see Teacher Preparation)
- Clear self-stick vinyl (optional; see Teacher Preparation)
- Large paper fasteners or three looseleaf rings

TEACHER PREPARATION

An instant camera, because of the immediate feedback it provides, is recommended for this activity. You can, however, substitute it with another available camera. Just be sure to do your picture-taking and developing in advance of the lesson.

Clear self-stick vinyl will enhance the last step of the lesson as well as preserve the work, but it is not essential by any means.

You will want to have reproductions of Dutch figure groups on hand as described in step 1 in the directions.

DIRECTIONS

1. Study several paintings of figure groups by Dutch masters. These may include family portraits, military groups, doctors, guilds, and scenes from everyday life. Discuss the different feelings and moods suggested in these reproductions. Are they light-hearted, somber, hard-working, sincere? Use your own words to describe them. For what purpose do you suppose the painting was intended; for example, is it in the same category as a photographic "record" shot?

2. Examine the action between the figures in the groups. Can you identify the dominant characters—either through their gestures, which might be "grander" than the others (e.g., arms outstretched)—or by their position in the picture? How else has the artist established the importance of certain models? Through use of light or relative size? If all sitters look like equals, explain how you think that was accomplished.

3. Students will be assigned in groups. Using a Dutch figure group painting as an example, students will physically replicate a portion of the pose for the instant camera. The teacher will take the picture of the students in their "tableau vivant." (This term describes the dramatization of a scene or painting by persons who pose motionless to enact it.)

4. Distribute 8″ × 10″ papers, rulers, pencils, and markers or colored pencils. Students will share the photograph, which they will use for direct drawing reference.

5. Students will measure and draw a half-inch border around their papers, which will represent the standard photo format. After studying the group photo, the figure composition should be blocked into the rectangle.

6. Now, for the problem. How can you draw attention to yourself within this group? What will make *you* the dominant figure? Pencil and eraser work together here. Try changing positions and gestures; experiment with costume effects. A flamboyant hat can work wonders!

7. Use some tricks of perspective and color. (See Activity 36.) Remember, bright colors and lighting make figures move forward.

8. After your outstanding position has been attained, and the others in your group recede, you've done the job. The teacher will retrieve the work for a class "picture"— shown together, the results should prove amusing.

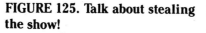

FIGURE 125. Talk about stealing the show!

9. As a matter of record, all "8 × 10 color glossies" may be gathered in a class album with their accompanying group photos. Arrange images on black construction paper as in a photo album and glue down. Identify photos with white pencil or crayons. Decorate the cover page if you wish with "Class of _____."

10. Laminate pages with plastic according to the instructions on the roll. Bind all pages together with either paper fasteners or looseleaf rings. This will be quite a conversation piece for such school events as Parents' Night. It's what you call a photo finish!

ACTIVITY 45
What's Cooking in the Dutch Oven?

MIXED MEDIA: Home Design

The more homey the scene, the more inspired the Dutch painter, or so one might conclude. The home seemed to provide endless sources of inspiration. Artists who most often responded to these cozy subjects were sometimes called genre painters. They reveled in the sensuous qualities of domestic life. The textures of various foods, the gleam of copper pots, the smoky patina of an iron stove—these could not be artistically ignored, thus placing kitchen and hearth as a clear favorite.

FIGURE 126. A well-equipped kitchen if ever there was one! When the refrigerator door closes, a shopping list appears, held on with a magnet, as one might expect.

**SLIDE #20: BACK FROM THE MARKET
(OR THE PROVIDER)**

MATERIALS

- Pencils
- Rulers
- Crayons
- Poster paints in assorted colors
- Acrylic paints in metallic tones of silver, bronze, and so forth (optional, but recommended)
- 12″ × 15″ white paper
- Scissors
- Glue
- Masking tape or cellophane tape
- Wallpaper sample book (see Teacher Preparation)
- Magazine and coupons (optional; see Teacher Preparation)

TEACHER PREPARATION

Because this is a mixed media activity, all materials should be offered together. Acrylic metallic paints usually come in tubes; therefore, meat styrofoam trays will make good palettes for their distribution.

Magazines of the homemaker's variety, as well as food coupons, will help to fill the cupboard and fill in details! Wallpaper books representing discontinued patterns can be easily acquired from paint and wallpaper stores for this activity. We are interested in kitchen wallpaper patterns in particular, but country prints will do just fine. Have extra pieces of white paper on hand to provide "back-up" for insides of cabinets, ovens, etc.

Photographs and reproductions, such as old-fashioned kitchens and examples of modern kitchen design, would be helpful for reference.

DIRECTIONS

1. The seventeenth-century hearth, which so captivated the eye of many a European painter, had certain characteristics that are similar to kitchens of today. What *has not* changed? What *has* changed? Compare similarities and discuss contrasts between old-fashioned and modern kitchens. Some points for review: kitchen equipment and appliances, furniture and room design, food preparation and service. Name some modern conveniences, then identify items that might be the same as those used hundreds of years ago.

2. Make all art materials available. Students can design a kitchen they would like to have built for their very own home, or depict an old-fashioned kitchen in the seventeenth-century style. Time-tested materials, as well as labor-saving devices, should be considered, from butter churns to ice cube makers.

3. Encourage students to block in their plans in pencil and rulers without becoming too concerned about demonstrating perfect drawing skills. Include kitchen cabinets, storage closets, a refrigerator, and a dishwasher, if so desired. Stoves and sinks are necessary, but microwaves, food processors, and coffee makers fall under the category of personal choice. Leave wall space for the decorator touch—real wallpaper.

4. Use color with thought given to its visual effects, and for the mood it creates. Do you want a cheery kitchen, or a formal arrangement, or an ultra-modern scheme? Color and design decisions will help determine the end result.

5. Crayon and paint will be applied as suggested by the specific requirements of certain objects. For example, large appliances may lend themselves to silver paint and baked goods might be best expressed by blending crayon colors. Various textures, such as wood grain and shiny plastic or enamel, should be texturally defined. Decorate your walls with wallcovering samples and don't be shy about using them for kitchen curtains or tablecloths.

6. So you think you're finished? Surprise! Pierce kitchen cabinets, refrigerator doors, or any other panel that could open (microwave oven door, storage closets) with the pointed end of your scissors. Carefully cut them completely open. (See Figure 117, Activity 41.)

7. Tape white paper in appropriate sizes behind the openings. Draw shelves and racks. Stock them with your favorite foods. Now's the time to "go shopping" with your coupons. Cut out images of suitable size and paste them in. Draw some in, too. Show what's in store for the next meal, what's cooking right now in the microwave, and what's in the freezer.

8. Some things never change, and never fail to please us, like good food in friendly surroundings. It's one of life's great pleasures. Share it by displaying your works in a suitable place. How about the teachers' lunchroom or school cafeteria? Bon appétit!

FIGURE 127. A very inviting table suggests that the turkey in the oven, as well as the fixings cooking on the stove, will soon satisfy hungry tummies! But don't overlook details—like pots and pans inside cabinets and even pipes under sinks—for additional visual interest.

ACTIVITY 46
Dutch Uncles

PAPER CRAFT: Pop-up Costume

The Dutch had style! They were acknowledged as trend-setters in European society during the seventeenth century, ushering in the cavalier look of the musketeers. Those notable Flemish collars, wide and dramatic, were not only fashion statements—they were, above all, unmistakably Dutch!

FIGURE 128. It's a good idea to move around the picture parts and join the elements of the figures themselves before gluing them onto paper. You will need to plan ahead and consider the background in advance of the foreground. Your pop-up Dutch aunts and uncles will be the last word!

MATERIALS

- Black construction paper (see Teacher Preparation)
- Colored paper including peach, tan, brown, and ochre for skin tones (see Teacher Preparation)
- 12″ × 18″ white paper
- Manila paper
- Pencils

- Scissors
- Glue
- Markers
- Foil paper
- Foam of ¼″ to ½″ thickness (see Teacher Preparation)
- Doilies, lace trim, buttons (see Teacher Preparation)

TEACHER PREPARATION

The peach, ochre, brown, and tan colored paper are recommended for flesh tones. If these shades are not available, use manila paper instead. White paper will be fine for collars cuffs, and gloves—but doilies, lace, and buttons are simply wonderful for costume effects.

Foam should be cut into small squares for mounting selected picture parts. Should foam not be readily available, you can purchase inexpensive household sponges.

To avoid wasting paper for the activity, cut the construction paper and manila paper into 5″ × 7″ squares ahead of class time. Foil paper may be cut into even smaller pieces to be used for buckles and other metallic accessories.

Reproductions used in Activity 44 may also be presented here for reference.

DIRECTIONS

1. Observe reproductions of portraits and other paintings of people in finery by Dutch masters. Note the contrast of costume elements, such as white collars, against fields of darker color. Also pay attention to placement of figure arrangements on the page as well as compositional details.

2. Distribute all materials. You will use the white paper to arrange your cut-out picture, but draw the outline of your composition first. Plan in advance as much as possible.

3. Pick up the scissors and begin. Experiment. Try cutting lace using the "snowflake" approach of folding and snipping. (See Activity 22, Figure 57 for some cutting techniques.) Press pleats into the paper to make it appear more like fabric. Don't forget your hats!

4. Consider the drama of white against black, as in those oversized collars, particularly. Markers will help with faces and with other specifics.

5. Determine which parts of your picture will stand out from the rest. Glue down background elements. Attach foam to the backs of the foreground figures. Make sure figures are joined before affixing foam squares and gluing on to manila paper.

6. Add all buttons, hooks, and other embellishments.

7. Has your picture been developed to its fullest potential? You're finished! They're flying Dutchmen, and they're absolutely outstanding!

ACTIVITY 47
Say It with Flowers

BOOK ILLUSTRATION: "Herbals"

Around the time the Dutch school of art was flourishing, a special form of floral pictures and prints was coming into vogue. Detailed botanical illustrations were available in flower books which bore close resemblance to the particular style of many Dutch still life and floral painters. It would almost seem that scientific drawings furnished handy references for most floral Dutch paintings.

While botanical studies and natural history books of this period were understandably realistic, they were quite exquisitely drawn. They appear to be related to the *herbals,* which were printed books depicting plants and their medicinal uses. Whatever the case, it turned out to be artful science and scientific art!

FIGURE 129. Flower books are not too far afield from Dutch still life arrangement. Students may use real floral and herbal sources for their illustrations or invent their own!

MATERIALS

- 9″ × 12″ white paper
- Watercolors or colored pencils
- Black fine-tip markers
- Pencils
- Rulers
- Erasers
- Ribbon (see Teacher Preparation)
- Scissors
- Hole puncher

TEACHER PREPARATION

Each student will need two white papers, which will comprise their flower book. This will include a front and back cover, along with six "plates" (pages). Ribbon will be a good means for binding books, but roving (yarn) may be substituted. Precut ribbon or yarn into suitable lengths.

"Say It with Flowers" will unite botany and horticulture with art and illustration. Students will need advance time to find library reference books on flowers and plants.

Garden and field guides that illustrate, identify, and classify flora are ideal. Photographic books are satisfactory, but line drawing illustrations are preferred. The categories you can scout are numerous: flowering plants, vegetable gardens, fruits and trees, herbals—even mushrooms and weeds! A couple of books on butterflies, birds, and insects will provide proper details for your botanical studies. If you can also find some examples of the older natural history books, this is excellent!

Let's not forget the Dutch still life, the progenitor of this lesson. Reproductions of Dutch floral arrangement paintings should be available for reference and later discussion. You may also wish to keep fresh and/or dry flowers in a vase for the duration of this activity, to remind students of the characteristics of the real articles.

This lesson will take several class sessions.

DIRECTIONS

1. Exchange and share all reference materials. Discuss botanical illustrations. What do they and the Dutch floral paintings have in common? They are realistic, detailed, and finely drawn. What is the primary difference? The botanical studies are for a specific purpose, to give information, yet they are still artistic.

2. Distribute all materials. Fold papers in half, establishing the book's pagination (the front and back cover, pages one through six). Number them lightly in pencil. The inside front cover is *page one*.

3. Select categories you want to illustrate. This will require some research, for there are many attractive possibilities. You might want to do all flowers, all herbals, or mix plants, weeds, and ferns. Whatever the combination or theme you decide upon, some information will be required about each one.

4. Design your first page in pencil. Do you want a border? Now's the time to include it. Be sure to leave room for a blurb about your plant, such as name, habitat, and any other vital statistics you wish to submit. Some names are metaphorical and poetic, like the Toadflax, a.k.a. Butter-and-Eggs, or the Lady's Slipper! You can also give Latin terms, medicinal uses, dangers and precautions—and salad recipes would be interesting, too. Use your fine-tipped marker for hand lettering.

5. Follow the same page planning procedure throughout the book. Line or contour drawing will be perfect. Students can either apply all color at the same time, or work from plate to plate—this depends on personal preference. Add bugs, beetles, and so forth.

6. The cover remains for your design. Choose a border motif based on an inside illustration, such as berries, thistles, and so forth, if you wish. Hand-letter an appropriate title for front cover, for instance, "Book of Herbs and Spices." Make sure you credit both the author and illustrator!

7. The back cover may also carry the front cover border motif, although an illustration isn't necessary here. However, a little poem or description might be just the ticket. Do state the "publisher's" name at the bottom!

8. Punch two holes in the centerfold, spacing them a few inches apart. Draw the ribbon or yarn through. Tie in a bow on the outside spine.

9. Gather all your finished flower books. It might be fun to see if they (along with reference materials) can help you identify some of the flora in the Dutch floral paintings!

10. Well, there you have it—a garden of delights! Place books in an area where others may enjoy their bouquet. They are, after all, rare editions.

FIGURE 130. Can you find the brazen little bug? Insects often enter these pictures.

ACTIVITY 48
Time Out for Play

PAINTING WITH SPONGES: "Parkscapes"

People at play delighted the French painter Fragonard. His canvases followed them as they pranced through meadows and parks filled with billowing trees, while great, puffy clouds hung in the sky. The atmosphere was light and happy. Even the sculpture in the garden seemed to watch the carefree games with much amusement! A good time, as they say, was had by all.

SLIDE #21:   THE SWING

FIGURE 131. Even Fragonard himself would have to agree that our young artist did indeed capture the carefree spirit of this park scene.

MATERIALS

- 11″ × 18″ white paper
- Roving (thick yarn)
- Poster paint (see Teacher Preparation)
- Scissors
- Glue
- Sponges (see Teacher Preparation)
- Jump rope (see Teacher Preparation)

TEACHER PREPARATION

Cut the roving ahead of class time so that each student will have two to three pieces.

Cut the sponges into small sections. Wedged shapes, if you can manage them, will work best.

Tempera paints are a good substitute for poster paint from jars. However, if you do use poster paint you'll want to set the colors out in shallow containers, such as watercolor cups, so that the sponges may be easily dipped into them.

NOTE: You'll still need the usual paintbrushes. You may also want students to experiment with dry brush techniques. As the name implies, this is simply the application of paint to paper without the lubrication of the water. Dry brushes may be gently dabbed or scumbled onto paper for interesting foliage effects. In addition to preparing your classroom for a painting activity, clear some space for an introductory movement exercise. For this, you will need a jump rope on the day of the lesson presentation.

DIRECTIONS

1. Engage in a brief opening discussion on where you go when you want to play outdoors. Is it a playground? A park? A tree house? Think of some of your favorite games and activities. Have you ever played leap frog? Swung inside a rubber tire? Chased a butterfly?

2. Time for the jump rope. Ask for student volunteers to jump rope either alone or with another student, depending on the rope's size. Class will be asked to observe what happens to expressions on the jumper's face; watch the movement of hair and clothing. Students can take turns modeling this most active pose.

3. Return desks to regular room arrangement. Distribute all materials. Ask students to place the yarn on their papers and consider what they will do with it. Move it around your paper for ideas. Name some ideas for how it may be used, such as for double-dutch ropes, tug-or-war, and of course, swings!

4. Glue down the roving as desired and build the rest of your playful scene. Keep it active! Show movement. Hats and shoes can fly off, swings can soar high over mountains and rooftops! You can even suggest "off stage" action, as Fragonard did, by showing figures looking out of the picture with anticipation.

5. Paint your sky and landscape with the brightness and exuberance this pictures deserves! Sponges and brush techniques enliven your foliage and shrubbery.

6. Fun and games is what all of this is about. If the games are over, your picture is done. This play is definitely made for display!

ACTIVITY 49
Landscape Sketchbook: The Faces of Nature

SKETCHBOOKS: Landscapes

Landscapes, not unlike people, have their moods. They can express joy, sorrow, tranquility, even anger and violence. Artists have several means to convey the characteristics of their landscapes. Weather is one way—showing clear or stormy skies—as well as movement in the trees and elsewhere in the composition. Yet the landscape's personality is derived mainly from light and color, the reasons why a picture is somber or bright. Have you ever been blue? Or is life simply rosy? No one knows the full meaning of these colorful phrases better than the landscape artist.

FIGURE 132. A brilliant sunset is recorded in glowing terms!

SLIDE #22:   THE FORD (IL GUADO)

MATERIALS

- Watercolors (see Teacher Preparation)
- Markers (optional)
- Colored pencils (optional)
- Oaktag
- Scissors
- Stapler
- Glue
- Sketchbooks (see Teacher Preparation)
- Colored plastic in red, yellow, blue (see Teacher Preparation)

TEACHER PREPARATION

This lesson has two phases. The first phase asks students to construct colored "glasses" from oaktag and tinted plastic, which is available in sheets from art supply and paper goods stores. To construct your "sun and moon glasses," refer to the instructions and diagram in Figure 133. This part of the activity should be completed prior to the sketchbook experience as outlined under the directions.

Also, secure sketchbooks in advance of lesson presentation. If budget or other constraints represent a problem, substitute the standard spiral sketchpads with several sheets of drawing paper. Bind the pages together by any method available to you, perhaps with plastic binding spines or paper fasteners. Provide boards or other hard surfaces to support papers.

This lesson will be based on direct observation of nature, the availability of which will vary with your own circumstances. If nature is right outside your classroom windows, you need only open them wide and gather student desks in front of them. Or better yet, step right outside! Should this not be possible, a nature walk or field trip, even a small one to a nearby park, will do just fine. At the very least, get to a patch of greenery with a tree or two and a slice of the sky in full view (lakes are lovely, too, but optional). Houses, buildings and people; however, are secondary to this particular activity.

A note on trip preparation regarding selection of media: watercolor is recommended, but not exclusive to other choices. Markers or colored pencils may be used, too. Do bring all the necessary supplies, for example, paint boxes, paper towels, and water cups. Water can be carried in an empty plastic gallon-sized milk container if no outside water source is anticipated. Pick a good day for this outside activity and check the weather forecast.

FIGURE 133. DIRECTIONS FOR SUN AND MOON GLASSES: (1) Cut a wide band of oaktag that is proportionate to size of eyeglasses. Fold in center. (2) Trace the frame shape as shown. Cut out the contour and lens opening. Open. (3) Cut acetate or plastic to lens size. Glue in place, then wear. Glasses may be folded back to original flat position for placing neatly into pockets for sketchbook traveling.

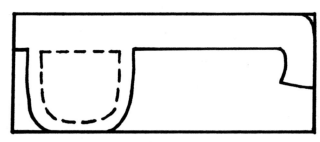

DIRECTIONS

1. Our starting point will follow the construction of paper sunglasses which we'll be folding into our pockets. Then pack up sketching and painting materials and head for the great outdoors.

2. Locate students in spots where they can directly respond to the scenery, but keep them in close earshot of the teacher. Talk a moment about the landscape that unfolds before our eyes. Is it a wild, natural setting, or an orderly, trimmed one? A full sweep of space, like a rolling field or a cozy corner of the world? Each landscape has its own distinctive characteristics.

3. Set up your materials. Take a good look at the sky. What does it tell you? Now put on those glasses and look again! How has it all changed? Take off glasses and prepare to paint.

4. Select your dominant color, the one that best matches your glasses. First try some pencil sketches of your selected view of the landscape. Wash the selected color over the drawing. Switch glasses with fellow students, noting the contrasts between cool and warm colors, and the effects that different colors have on the mood of the landscape. After experimenting with little colored studies, flip to a new page and begin your "good" painting.

5. Feel free to alter what is before you and decide on a specific mood. Your painted scene can express qualities that differ from the real one, which will be accomplished by adding or removing people, objects, clouds, or whatever. *Use that dominant color.* It will determine the "temperature" of your painting and give it a special quality.

6. Is your painting calm or lively? Stormy or sunny? Have you used the elements of nature—the color of the sky, the movement of the clouds, and the posture of the trees—to establish the mood? Close the sketchpads; it's time to return to class.

7. Ongoing sketchbooks should be kept by students, who will continue to work in them independently. Some suggested assignments might include:

> • Vacation sketches, especially trips to foreign countries or other new surroundings
> • Imaginary landscapes, based on your own fantasies of places you'd like to be
> • Family outing sketches, like visits to the zoo, the country, and so forth

8. Completed sketchbooks are wonderful to share, talk about, and save. Students may want to select the more successful sketches for mounting or framing.

ACTIVITY 50
Ladies of Spain

PAINTING: Fans, Costume

The Spanish painter Goya passionately painted the horrors of war, while his other canvases portrayed the picturesque ladies and gentlemen of Spain with charm and delicacy. The brush that had a deep political conscience could also lovingly record the gentle flutter of a fan. This was not a contradiction of terms. Goya, like any artist, responded to that which he most cared about by painting it.

SLIDE #23:   MAJAS ON A BALCONY

MATERIALS

> • Bristol board
> • White paper
> • Poster paint
> • Assorted brushes
> • Markers
> • Scissors
> • Paper fasteners
> • Glue

FIGURE 134. Do you speak the language of the fan? These lovely Majas do. The fan on the left says, "We will be friends," while the fan on the right says, "I will speak about it with you!" Sondra and Patricia, two third graders who are also friends, painted this extraordinary balcony scene. They have also learned a little more about the importance of gesture.

TEACHER PREPARATION

This activity can open the door to other areas of study. Foremost, the charm of Spanish costume—mantillas, tiaras, toreador outfits, and the look of Spanish gypsies—do invite further exploration. Books on the history of European costume will provide reference materials for "The Ladies of Spain," while you may find some good ideas for other lessons.

The accessory to pay attention to here is the fan. Books are available specifically on this topic, too. You'll be making a fan, and will use it to dramatize gesture in the students' paintings.

You may also want to present books and photographs on decorative iron work. This is an interesting and appealing topic that will aid students in the design of the balcony in their interpretation of the Goya painting.

Finally, be sure to have a full selection of poster paint colors on hand. Students will select their paints based on the colors used in "Majas on a Balcony." Part One of this activity will require that paints and accompanying supplies be set up for lesson presentation.

This is a two-part activity.

DIRECTIONS

Part One: Painting

1. Study the slide of "Majas on the Balcony." What colors did Goya use for his painting? Choose your poster paint based on his color scheme. Notice, too, the placement of the women's hands. We will change their positions to suit our own purposes.

2. Write selections from *The Language of the Fan* on the chalkboard. Students will decide on what they want their ladies to "say" through their fans:

   a. At one time, women communicated with their fans. Twirling the fan in the left hand meant, "We are watched," while drawing the fan across the forehead stated, "You have changed!" Fans could reveal marital status, requests for acquaintance, and show feelings. They could make accusations— "You are cruel!"—or, by drawing the fan across the cheek, simply state "I love you."

   b. If your interest in fans has now increased, you might seek out further information on the subject, such as in *The Language of the Fan,* published by the London Fan House of Duvelleroy.

3. Block in painting composition on bristol board, based on the slide. Imagine that either or both women are "talking," with their fans. Position their hands accordingly. You won't need to paint in the fans themselves, but an outline of where it will be placed is helpful. Hands should be painted in a pose that anticipates holding a fan handle.

4. Using Goya's colors and compositional sense, paint your version of "Majas." You might even include the dramatically cloaked gentlemen in the rear who act as foils for the lovely ladies. Facial expressions should agree with the message of the fan.

5. Paint in your various details (lace, iron grill work) with appropriately sized brushes. Cover large areas, too. Let dry.

Part Two: The Fan

6. Distribute markers, white paper, glue, scissors, and paper fasteners. Give out tongue depressors if you are planning a more elaborate fan. (Fans may be stapled to tongue depressors, then slipped into slits in the posterboard that have been cut for them. Position accordingly.)

7. Again, use your reference materials (costume books, *The Language of the Fan,* and so forth). Based on Figures 135 through 138, determine the style of fan you want to make.

8. Work flat on fan with marker. What will you illustrate? Imitation lace, combined with a simple motif? A scene of the Spanish countryside? A bullfight?

9. Fold and/or assemble finished fans. Place in hand(s) of Spanish ladies in the intended position. Affix with glue and paper fasteners.

10. Can you "read" the fan and its gesture? Have a class review to see how effectively meanings have been conveyed. Display all work after the discussion. Your Majas should bring Goya many new fans!

FIGURES 135–138. Sample fans.

ACTIVITY 51
Another View of Toledo

DRAWING: Wet Chalk

A painter may see a certain quality of light, an unusual perspective, or even recognize a new way of expressing the human form. Yet the real test is in the artist's ability to communicate his ideas. Otherwise, he cannot possibly pass them along. To have not only originality, but the talent to make it understood, is the rare combination we find in El Greco. His was a unique vision, one where the mystical often emerged from the commonplace. In sharing his particular reality, El Greco allows us to discover the world through the artist's eyes. This broadens our own view, and helps us to see what we might otherwise overlooked. It is the special gift an artist can give through his or her art.

FIGURE 139. An everyday scene can appear "other worldly" when viewed with some of El Greco's sensibilities.

SLIDE #24:   VIEW OF TOLEDO

MATERIALS

- Colored chalks or pastels, including white
- Shallow water cups
- Black paper
- Charcoal
- Manila paper
- Chamois or tissues
- Glass carafe bottles or reasonable facsimiles (see Teacher Preparation)
- Fluorescent chalk (optional)

TEACHER PREPARATION

Long stretched-out figures and multi-layered landscapes flashed with lightning have become the trademarks of El Greco. We will experiment with different ways of seeing, an exercise for which we'll need glass bottles. Carafe bottles (or bottles of similar shapes, such as those with a narrow neck) will work best. Glass with natural irregularities, or imported beverage bottles, can also prove quite interesting. So you will need to collect a variety of tall bottles (no plastic ones, please) in advance of class. Be sure to handle these with care.

Because we'll be doing a wet chalk drawing, you will want to prepare the classroom for a "wet" activity, so cover desks and have clean-up towels available.

Finally, this lesson is most effective when done in front of a window with a view. You might want to arrange desks so that students have access to a window space. If your classroom is deficient in this regard, plan to have some photographs or magazine pages on hand that represent landscapes, cityscapes, or other outdoor scenes.

DIRECTIONS

1. Distribute manila paper, charcoal, and chamois. Have glass bottles ready.

2. Show and discuss the slide of "View of Toledo" and any other El Greco reproductions you may have. How did the artist achieve this extraordinary look? What's different from the world as we know it? Did he not twist, pull, and exaggerate material forms? Let's try an exercise that will give us another view. Bring glass bottles forward.

3. Hold bottle in front of your eyes and, looking through it, study either the outside landscape or the visuals provided. What happens to the shape of things? Adjust your glass and exchange bottles.

4. When you've had enough variety, as well as idea stimulation, you may then jot down what you've seen in several charcoal sketches. These will be your "notes."

5. Now that we've bent some naturally straight lines, let's reconsider perspective and lighting effects. Again, show slide as indicated in Step 2. The question: how did the light create this other worldly atmosphere? What makes it so spooky? Can you recall a similar scene? (Hint: the flash of lightning on buildings and trees.) To a lesser extent, reflections of a full moon, or artificial, fluorescent light on interior objects and faces.

6. Distribute water cups, water, colored chalks, and black paper. Materials from Step 1 may be retained for further use.

7. Based on what you observed "through a glass wavily," along with your own experiences of stormy night light, begin to think about your own picture. One more thing: you'll want an interesting perspective. You can create several levels, or layers of landscape, by including hills, mountains, valleys, winding roads, and so on.

8. Start your composition by dipping the chalk (working end only) into the water. You may want to compose your entire picture with a chalk line drawing or build it up as you go; it's up to you.

9. Consider the El Greco color scheme. He did not use pastel blues and pinks, but favored acid greens, yellows, reds, and blues. Your white chalk will create the important lighting effects and a dramatic sky. Black charcoal will intensify contrasts.

10. Don't be afraid to be extreme. Distort, elongate and bend! This is your chance to make wierdness work for you.

11. Utilize your chamois cloth or tissues to blend and accent. Try different techniques. If you have fluorescent chalk, apply highlights with it.

12. Completed pictures will encourage group discussion. Students may want to identify specific experiences, such as thunder storms, that inspired their pictures or describe how they used their personal sense of fantasy and imagination. Note individual interpretations of subject matter. Display.

ACTIVITY 52
Go for Baroque!

FURNITURE DESIGN

When is the leg of an armchair not an armchair leg at all? That's easy—when the leg is a dolphin whose fishy mouth meets the floor! Well, we know we're in the Baroque period when furniture acts more like sculpture...or tables, and chests of drawers have mermaids, scrolls, leaves, and seashells climbing all over them.

There is no other style that managed to get as carried away as Baroque, but that's the fun of it! Where else could you find gold gilded horses rearing on the base of a chair? Tangled vines and dragons wrapping around a love seat? It was overdone, heavy-handed, skillfully carved, outrageous—all of those things and more. But best of all, Baroque had an unparalleled and irrepressible sense of fantasy.

FIGURE 140. The chair that "baroque" all the rules. Hard to imagine that this outrageously attractive furnishing is, underneath it all, only a common classroom chair.

MATERIALS

- Brown butcher wrap
- Charcoal
- Acrylic paint (poster paint may be substituted)
- Wide and flat to regular paintbrushes
- Newspapers
- Felt (or similar fabric)
- Scissors
- Thumbtacks
- Masking tape
- Yardstick for cutting brown paper
- Gold paint (optional)
- Camera (optional, but recommended)
- Black paper for mounting photographs or a commercial photo album (optional)

TEACHER PREPARATION

You and your students will love this project; it's sure to tickle the imagination. We are about to turn your classroom into a grand Baroque palace. All you'll need for this amazing metamorphosis are the supplies listed here. Lengths of brown paper from a roll will supply your chair or desk facade. Felt or similar fabric (even brocade remnants) will lend further reality to furniture. Newspaper will provide the arms as well as the fanciful Baroque curves.

Since we plan to cover a number of classroom desks and chairs with our elaborate Baroque designs, you'll need to assign certain numbers of students to specific pieces of furniture. Two to three students per desk or chair is a good team. The size of furniture will help determine the number of students needed. For example, a teacher's desk may require more students than a single chair. Remember, desks may become anything you wish—a chest of drawers, a dresser, even a much fancier style of desk.

Gold paint is great because it represents highlights and mocks gilding—but it's not critical. A camera, however, will record this event and allow you to produce your very own Baroque furniture catalogue.

You will, of course, want to have reference materials or reproductions that illustrate the Baroque style in furniture. Books on the history of European furniture should yield good examples from this period. But do not confuse it with Rococo, which is somewhat similar but from a later period — and is actually more delicate and far less robust than Baroque. (NOTE: Baroque is often used as a term to identify the period of art that follows the Renaissance in Europe. In this book, we refer to this era broadly as "Post-Renaissance." This is done to avoid confusion, for the word "baroque" is also used to describe a specific style, as in baroque architecture or music. Usually, this means heavily carved, or flamboyant, or irregular. It is a meaning that chiefly encompasses certain baroque characteristics, not an entire period of art necessarily. The descriptive meaning of baroque style is what this activity, "Go for Baroque," teaches.)

This activity will require more than one class session.

DIRECTIONS

1. Look over the pictorial examples of Baroque furniture. What do you see? Name some of the motifs you can find in the carvings. Also consider the curvy lines. It's impossible to find a straight edge anywhere.

2. Discuss various styles of furniture and the materials they are made from. Name names! If you can find some dominant patterns, note the designs. What are some objects or designs you could dream up for your Baroque fantasies?

3. Students should now join the groups assigned to specific furniture items. Distribute materials.

4. Measure paper to cover desk fronts, chairs, etc. Cut. *Wrap around* your furniture and tape from behind. Groups should refer to reproductions and decide on style of furniture and division of labor. Motifs and designs should also be determined. Let imagination flow! Sketch ideas in charcoal.

5. Begin your task. It's easier to remove paper "upholstery" and to work on a flat surface, but return papers to intended furniture portions frequently to check your progress. Paint your scrolls, grape clusters, claw feet, and whatever you fancy.

6. Paint generously! Thick paint will look more substantive. Don't be afraid to mix divergent objects together, such as conch shells, watermelons, skate boards, sneakers, and scrolls. That's what Baroque is all about!

7. Cover furniture with your advanced versions of Baroque furniture veneers by simply wrapping lengths of painted butcher wrap around the object. A stapler, as well as tape, may be used to close seams and hold facades in place.

8. Twist several sheets of newspaper together to create the curvy, Baroque look. Attach to paper with stapler (stapler gun may be used directly if you are working with wooden chairs that would not be harmed by this approach). Manipulate newspaper and enlist tape and/or glue as needed. Make it all convincing.

9. Paint newspaper (use a wide brush for an overall covering and a smaller brush for getting inside folds). Let dry. NOTE: Some newspaper furniture parts might benefit from further support, like the insertion of a flexible wire core. Add finishing touches, such as gold gilded highlights.

10. Measure parts you wish to upholster with fabric, like the seats of chairs. Cut to size and mount with thumbtacks.

11. Before you return your resplendent surroundings back to normal, record the Baroque wonders with a camera.

12. After displaying photos for all to see (they'll never believe it's your classroom!), gather photos for your very own furniture catalog. Be sure to credit the furniture makers!

PRE- THROUGH POST-IMPRESSIONISM

.....1800............. 1850............. 1880............. 1890............. 1900.....		
Realism	Impressionism	Post-Impressionism

A new art form was about to be launched. Was it completely unexpected?

Not really. Even though Impressionism is viewed as a monumental event in art history, it must be seen within its context. It was the logical outcome of the art that preceded it. Impressionism was a highly innovative recasting of the painting traditions of the past.

The exotic art of Delacroix and the realism of Courbet seemed to ease the transition. But it was by the brush of Manet that a new art form appeared. Modern art soon came to mean Impressionism, and the thread of Manet was picked up by Monet, Pissarro, Sisley, Renoir, and other painters of the period. Light and color were treated as they had never been treated before—and nature itself was seen in a new light.

Care must be taken, however, to not tuck all the Impressionists away into the same basket. Each Impressionist interpreted art in a novel, original way. To over-summarize their accomplishments, and hence, their characteristic strengths: Manet's simplicity and economy of means; Renoir's mastery of paint and pearly color; Monet's perception of light and its effects; Sisley's atmospheric clarity; Seurat's ingenious pointillistic system; Degas' superior pastels. All of them are unique and individual, but not without their influences.

Many Impressionists recalled the Venetian school in their art, Renoir's composition and volume in particular. But there are as many influences as there are painters, which also applies to the period following Impressionism, known as Post-Impressionism. Even one who appears to be as lonely a figure as Van Gogh drew upon outside sources. Van Gogh and also Gauguin, like so many others, borrowed from each other as well! Non-western art forms, such as the Japanese print in particular, were major inspirations. And although it may not have been conspicuous at the time, Cézanne's art even managed to anticipate cubism.

What is the conclusion? Look into the work of one artist and you will find the seeds of another.

ACTIVITY 53
Down to the Sea in Ships

MARITIME PAINTING: "Salty" Watercolor

Over the rolling waves, past castles and towns and into the fiery horizon of the painting sailed these graceful ships. Spanish galleons, clippers, and even modest fishing boats lent a needed reality to many a seascape. The romance of ships has long intrigued artists, just as surely as sailors are drawn to the sea!

FIGURE 141. The motion of the ocean!
A seascape that expresses stormy seas.

SLIDE #25: KEELMEN HEAVING IN COALS BY MOONLIGHT

MATERIALS

- Watercolors
- Sponges
- Watercolor paper (see Teacher Preparation)
- Kosher salt (optional)

- Tissue paper
- India ink (optional)
- Pens for drawing (optional)

TEACHER PREPARATION

In order to insure the success of the kosher salt technique, it is best to use *watercolor* paper. Kosher salt is used rather than regular table salt because of its coarseness. It will create an interesting, grainy texture that works particularly well for creating watery effects. However, this lesson can be presented without the salt, as directed.

We will be "working wet," which means that sponges need to be kept close at hand to prevent water from evaporating. Sponges can be used to rework areas, too. All regular painting materials should be prepared as usual, with water sources nearby.

Materials that illustrate various styles of ships from different countries or eras should be made available. Encyclopedias are a ready reference. Three-dimensional models of ships as well as any nautical memorabilia you might have would be perfect!

Should you wish to use pen and ink, be sure to supervise students. Spilled ink is messy and it stains! Younger children should not work with it—it requires a certain kind of control they may not yet have. However, for those students old enough to handle it, pen and ink will delineate the shapes in their pictures nicely.

DIRECTIONS

1. Consider our subject—seaworthy vessels. Ships are as unique as the many species of fish in the sea. Examine the features of the crafts that give them their own special appearance. Have you ever sailed in a boat? What kind? Students may have favorites that they can identify.

2. All materials should be made available. Before you begin, you should have some plan for what you want to paint. Pirate ships sailing the high seas or a boat you sailed in on your trip to Maine—whatever your pleasure. With the wet method, you'll also be working against time.

3. Wet down your paper with a water-soaked sponge. Paint the areas broadly, running colors into each other. Bunch up tissues, press into freshly painted sections for selected printed effects. Experiment, but don't overdo it. Create your picture.

4. Whenever you wish, you may "salt" the sea or sky with kosher sea salt. The area must be good and wet with paint, then toss in a pinch of salt. Brush off *after* paint is dry.

5. If you are using pen and ink, you can try it on both wet and dry painted paper for different techniques. It also adds finishing touches.

6. Details will steer your ship away from dull stereotypes. Figureheads, portholes, rigging, signal flags, and the like establish the ship's identity. Other specifics, like a calm or a choppy sea, will also advance your picture's theme.

7. If the pictorial elements balance with your "special effects," then you are afloat! But don't just throw away your signature; use it on the side of your ship. Take the poetic license of the old salts by adding a little descriptive motto, such as Betty's Birthday Present, Tom's Good Luck Charm, etc.

8. See if you can name the kind of boat you've painted and perhaps place some identification discretely on the page. Display all works. It's your very own boat show, and you sure have something worth showing. Anchors away!

FIGURE 142. A seascape so calm that there's nary a wave. The depiction of the ship is reminiscent of a maritime print.

ACTIVITY 54
Be Realistic!

MONTAGE, DRAWING: "Photographic" Realism

Realistic painters took their art literally enough. In order to paint a given subject, it was believed that one had to be there, or at least know things first-hand. For realists, you see, drew their material directly from real life. Day-to-day events, such as laborers going about their duties, were ideal topics because they were readily available and familiar. Much like journalists, realist painters reported their themes with accuracy and clarity, but they did not resist giving it their own personal touch.

FIGURE 143. Jennifer faces her fate with aplomb! A visit to the orthodontist is realistically—if not courageously—reported.

SLIDE #26:   THE GLEANERS

MATERIALS

- Markers (or colored pencils)
- Drawing paper
- Scissors
- Glue
- 3″ × 5″ cards
- Shoebox (or brown bag)
- Photographs (see Teacher Preparation)

TEACHER PREPARATION

We will recreate a "Day in Our Lives" with the help of a photograph. Students will need to bring in a photograph of themselves. Photos will not be returned in the same shape, so no heirloom photos, please! Students can make a photocopy of their chosen snapshot for this lesson. Full-scale poses, not portraits, will work best. The teacher may want to keep an instant camera handy on the day of the lesson for the students who arrive without a photo. (NOTE: You may want to make photocopies of snapshots the students bring in for this lesson in order to use for future activities, specifically Activity 66. Or, you might ask students to bring in an extra photograph of themselves that you can keep on file for future activities.)

Cut 3″ × 5″ cards into strips the size of paper fortune cookie slips. Write a single common event on each one using any number of ideas. Some suggestions are

- A birthday party
- A visit to the dentist
- Babysitting
- A day at camp (also a day at the seashore, recreational park, mountains, vacation, etc.)
- A job I do (raking leaves, helping to wallpaper or paint, fixing a broken bike)

You can add to the list but don't hesitate to repeat topics, just have enough slips for each student in your class. Select themes we've all experienced. Be specific! Fold the written idea slips and put them into a shoebox or brown paper bag (a hat would be fine, too). Have all this together prior to class presentation.

DIRECTIONS

1. Students will have brought to class their photos of themselves (or a photocopy of same). Distribute all materials, keeping mystery box (or bag) aside.

2. Ask students to cut themselves out of their photo, along their contour. In other words, tell them the cut-out photo should be in the shape of themselves! Now for the dramatic presentation.

3. Pass the box (or bag) around the room. Students should shut their eyes, select one slip, and accept their fate like good little sports—even if this means a visit to the dentist! This slip will be the theme of their picture, based on their own experience.

4. Glue the photo down in a strategic spot, after some thought as to how you will present your topic. Pay attention to scale! For example, if the photo is three inches tall, your hypothetical dentist should not be proportionally much taller than in real life. You may also wish to change your posture in the photo which can be accomplished by altering it with scissors and markers.

5. Develop your picture. In realism, details are important; they lend "autobiographical" touches as well as establishing the particulars. Remember, too, that dark and light contrasts, shadows, tend to look more photographic, hence, more realistic. Photography was a major influence on Realism.

6. When you've finished, you have, in effect, told us about a day in your life. Assemble work in a group review and display. These are perfect vehicles for editorial comments by the young realists who recreated them as well as by other class members.

ACTIVITY 55
Manet, the Father of Modern Art

STUDIO PAINTING: "Palette Knife Painting"

It was Edouard Manet who ushered painting into the twentieth century. His work hooked up past art traditions with a new movement known as Impressionism. If this movement had a founder, it was surely Manet.

Never before Manet had anyone painted so directly and achieved such results. He managed to paint rich and colorful paintings with a minimum of surface detail and not very many colors at all. His art was simplicity itself with a brilliance and immediacy that set him apart from his predecessors. Even today, you might almost expect to see a FRESH PAINT sign hanging under much of his work. But the only tag you'll find under these remarkable paintings will spell the name Manet!

FIGURE 144. Wouldn't Manet be proud of this remarkable work by a sixth-grade artist? The model for it was our student teacher, Omar, who posed in a jaunty bowler.

SLIDE #27:   GEORGES CLÉMENCEAU

MATERIALS

- Canvas boards or illustration boards (see Teacher Preparation)
- Acrylic paints (see Teacher Preparation for specific colors)
- Paintbrushes for oil painting in assorted sizes
- Palettes
- Plastic butter knives or tongue depressors (see Teacher Preparation)
- Costume props (see Teacher Preparation)

TEACHER PREPARATION

Set up for this activity as you would for any studio painting lesson (see "Studio Painting in the Classroom" in Section One). The difference here is that we will not put out full palettes; we'll be painting, instead, from "limited palettes." The colors suggested are white, black, blue, tan, red, and green. The shades that you use will depend upon your own paint inventory, but the idea is to restrict colors to resemble Manet's palette, while encouraging students to develop "more from less." (NOTE: Manet's palette, that is, range of colors, became lighter with his later works. His early works were more restricted to earth tones. Colors extended to the pastel range as Manet continued into Impressionism. Generally, painters' palettes do change with the growth of artistic expression.)

Also, this is a palette knife painting. Our palette knives will be supplied by the plastic knives you'll find in disposable flatware, or by tongue depressors. They may be more safely and practically utilized by children than professional palette knives would be.

You'll need a student—or a free teacher—to model. Maybe a student from another class could pitch in so no one has to miss the painting part of the activity. Recommended props are simple: clothing in black and white (or other dark/light) contrasts, such as overcoat, cloak, jacket over light shirt. Other details like a pair of gloves, a hat, and a bright red scarf are desirable. An umbrella, either open or closed, makes a wonderful addition to any of the above outfits. If you happen to have some garments from grandma's trunk, by all means, bring them forward!

This lesson should *not* run too long in order to maintain the direct painting quality so be sure your model and materials are ready at the beginning of the lesson presentation.

DIRECTIONS

1. Study the Manet slide and any other Manet reproductions you may have. Notice the way he lays paint on his canvases. It is applied in slashes and dabs—small details are unimportant. He reduces the various features into punctuation mark-type abbreviations. A slash may represent a mouth; a shadow may equal a nose!

2. Your supplies should be distributed, and your model in place. Ask the model to assume a comfortable pose. This need only be an ordinary and natural pose, such as pulling off a glove, holding a book, etc.

3. Observe the way light falls, breaking shapes into shadows. Begin painting with your palette knife.

4. Use your brushes to assist and to stretch out paint expression, but try to stick mainly with the palette knife method (see Figure 145). Use bright colors, such as red, sparingly. It will be your dash of hot sauce! Mix and blend colors as needed.

5. Don't overwork any areas. Once you have something down, move on. This is how to keep it spontaneous.

6. Think about completing your whole painting, background included. Again, this should be a simple sheet of solid color. Indicate shadows. Don't be afraid to "invent" shadows if it lends solidity to your picture.

7. By all means *stop* if you think you're finished! This is one painting activity we don't want to draw out—thank the model, put down your painting tools, and you're finished!

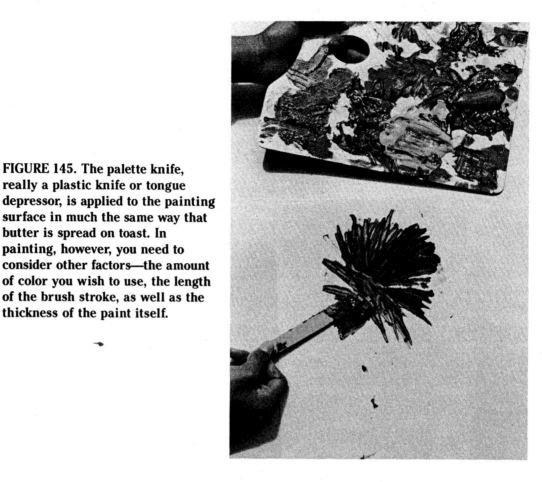

FIGURE 145. The palette knife, really a plastic knife or tongue depressor, is applied to the painting surface in much the same way that butter is spread on toast. In painting, however, you need to consider other factors—the amount of color you wish to use, the length of the brush stroke, as well as the thickness of the paint itself.

SUGGESTIONS FOR FURTHER DEVELOPMENT

Limited palette paintings are excellent exercises for learning economy of color. You can use the same principles with poster paints as in the Manet lesson—restrict the students to select colors. This is also a good way to encourage mixing and color experimentation.

ACTIVITY 56
Strokes of the Genius

PAINTING LAB, STUDIOS: "Brushstrokes"

Brushstokes are the bricks from which a painting is constructed. Without them, no painting could ever exist. Many artists in the past, such as the early Flemish, preferred that their painted surfaces appear quite smooth, to the extent that you could barely see the brushwork at all. Not so with the Impressionists, who valued brushstrokes for their own sake. Theirs were strong and structural and the Impressionists were not afraid to show them off! Impressionists' brushstrokes were as recognizable as each artist's signature and every bit as unique.

FIGURE 146. Brushstroke cards not only provide handy reference, they direct attention to the very stuff from which paintings are made. Students also learn recognizable styles of great Impressionists and Post-Impressionists. Can you find Van Gogh's postman's beard? (Answer: Third from the left.)

MATERIALS

- Acrylic paints
- Pastels or colored chalks
- Paintbrushes for oil painting in assorted sizes
- 3″ × 5″ cards
- Scissors
- Glue
- Hole puncher
- Looseleaf ring (see Teacher Preparation)
- Sandpaper (see Teacher Preparation)
- Oaktag or illustration board
- Postcard reproductions (see Teacher Preparation)
- Magnifying glasses
- Black markers

TEACHER PREPARATION

This is a two-phase activity. In the first phase, we'll be producing a "swatch book" of Impressionists and Post-Impressionist brush strokes. Our observation of postcards (readily available at museum bookstores) or book reproductions will assist us. This swatch book will be kept as a reference chart for other student painting and studio activities.

Examples of the artists' works that you'll want to have handy:

Manet   Seurat

Monet   Degas (the pastels,

Renoir   any of the dancer series)

Sisley   Cézanne

Van Gogh

Any other artist you'll find in this section of the text may be included.

A magnifying glass will be useful here. Also needed for assembling the 3″ × 5″ cards is a looseleaf ring but other available materials, like yarn, may be substituted.

Sandpaper, medium to rough, should be cut into 3″ × 5″ sections. A sandpaper rectangle may also be glued to a corner of the oaktag, which is the application (second phase) of the activity, as well as to 3″ × 5″ cards for sturdier inclusion in swatch books.

Prepare your room for a painting workshop. (See "Studio Painting in the Classroom" in Section One.)

DIRECTIONS

1. You may need to set up several palettes as in any studio painting presentation. Make all materials available. Bring your postcards and reproductions forward along with magnifying glasses.

2. Let's examine the various brushstroke styles under the magnifying glass. Using your own words describe what you see. Swirly, whirly, squiggly—whatever best expresses your observations.

FIGURE 147. One tree—seen six different ways!

3. Compare one style of brushstrokes to another. Does one appear shorter and quicker? Does another painter dab more than dash? Can you tell pastel work (Degas) from oil paint? Please explain how.

4. Select your brushes and your artists. We'll be replicating brushstrokes on the 3″ × 5″ cards. *Use only one artist per card!* Refer to reproductions as often as necessary.

5. Use pastels on sandpaper in response to Degas' technique. Watch out for chalk dust!

6. Let all painted cards dry. Take out the oaktag.

7. Select a simple, single subject—a *tree* is an excellent choice. Utilizing the many techniques with which you just experimented, paint the same tree several different times: plan to leave space on the paper for each interpretation. The sandpaper corner will be used for your pastel rendering. Again, reference materials, including your own swatches, may be used.

8. Are the 3″ × 5″ cards dry? Turn them over and identify the artist on the back with marker and sign your name. Perforate a corner through cards and join with looseleaf ring.

9. Display all tree painting studies in a group review. Using the swatch books, ask students to match brushstroke techniques with specific artists. Don't cheat by matching your own cards with your own painting. Try to guess the other students' renditions!

10. Did you say we're young and impressionable? Young and impressionistic is more like it—and our swatchbooks should prove the point. Put the books in a place where they are accessible for future reference.

ACTIVITY 57
First Impressions

WET CHALK DRAWINGS: Waterscapes

When Impressionism began, it was as though great curtains were pulled back to let light flood into the world of painting! The Impressionist's paintbrush introduced the use of vibrant color. Light was woven into the paintings through the dots, dabs, and slashes of sparkling pastel paint.

Impressionists were especially interested in the way that sunlight affected the color of outdoor scenes. Trees, gardens, and grassy landscapes were the frequent subject of Impressionist canvases. But perhaps nowhere was the quality of light more spectacular than when it was shining on water. The water itself scattered color and light in shimmering reflections, challenging the Impressionists to capture its natural brillance.

FIGURE 148. A bridge spans this "impressive" pastel drawing.

MATERIALS

- 12″ × 18″ or larger manila paper
- Chalk in pastel colors
- Watercolor cups
- Paper towels
- Sketch pad (see Teacher Preparation)

TEACHER PREPARATION

The ideal introduction to this lesson is to go on a class trip to a park where a lake, stream, or river may be found. If this *is* possible, students should make visual notes in a sketch pad with colored pencils, observing the way the water reflects objects, people, and sunlight. Should this not prove feasible, simply allow students time to expound on their own personal experiences with the topic at the start of the lesson. (See step 1 of the directions.)

There are also many good examples of Impressionist paintings dealing with water as a subject. Try to provide several reproductions for your students. Monet has done famous works, such as "The Frog Pond" ("La Grenouillère") and many others, that feature water and its qualities. Other inspirations for the lesson may be found in the paintings of Sisley, Renoir, Seurat, and Pissarro.

DIRECTIONS

1. Discuss the way that water reflects the landscape, people, animals, and structures above it. Does it return an exact mirror image—or will it distort according to movement of waves, ripples, and so on? What about the effect of the sky and the sun's light on the water below?

2. Distribute all materials.

3. Fold paper in half horizontally. Open. Dip the working end of the chalk into the water.

4. Begin drawing the scene as an outline *above* the fold, using the fold line as the boundary between the water below, and the landscape upon it.

5. While images are still wet, fold paper over and rub the back of the paper with the blade of the hand, or press and rub with chalk box top. Fold paper back open again. This process may be done several times as the top picture is being drawn, or may be done only once when the outline is completed—provided it is still wet.

6. When paper is folded and pressed, the picture above the fold will "print" on the bottom half of the page. After the basic composition has been established above and transferred upside-down into the "water," the entire picture may then be developed.

7. Remember to treat the solid objects, such as houses and bridges, with appropriate chalk applications, and to let the chalk suggest the lighter, fragmented characteristics of the water.

8. Build the surface with wet chalk until desired effects are achieved. When picture is "impressive," it's finished.

ACTIVITY 58
In a New Light

TIMED PASTEL STUDIOS: Still Lifes

Light is the all-powerful source that gives color and definition to earthly objects. It was the single element that most captivated the Impressionists, who chased its ever-changing properties with their palettes. In a sense, the interpretation of light was a puzzle that Impressionists felt compelled to solve. The chief detective on the case? Claude Monet!

From the soft haze of the morning fog, to the glare of the setting sun, Monet was there to track down the many qualities of light. His art measured and recorded its every phase. In the end, Monet broke down and arrested light's fleeting effects with his brush. These now-familiar dashes and dabs were the very marks of Impressionism—and specifically, the original brush strokes of the all-time catcher of light—Claude Monet.

FIGURE 149. The indoor natural light still life is expressed in soft hues. It sometimes helps to select ahead of time the pastel colors you think best express the given situation.

SLIDE #28:   THE CATHEDRAL OF ROUEN
             IN FULL SUNLIGHT

MATERIALS

- Chalk in pastel colors (see Teacher Preparation)
- Spotlight or high-intensity lamp (see Teacher Preparation)
- Bowl of fruit
- Sketchbooks (see Teacher Preparation)
- Fluorescent chalk (optional)

TEACHER PREPARATION

You'll need to gather fruit for a still life. Even though fruit will require refrigeration (this activity takes more than one session), select fruits that won't spoil easily. A bowl will also be needed to hold the fruit—try for a glass receptacle, particularly one which has some irregularity, such as fluting, cut glass, and the like. Set still life up near a natural light source before class begins.

The larger the variety of chalks and pastels you have, the better. Some color groups of specific boxes may even lend themselves more readily to specific lighting situations. For example, fluorescent chalk can be handy for interpreting artificial light.

Sketchbooks are best to use here, but manila (or construction) paper may be substituted. We're going to try to go outdoors, so loose paper should be clipped to drawing boards.

You'll also want to have a spotlight or floodlight for this activity. The kind that photographers use are fairly inexpensive and come with clip-on attachments. They're available through camera stores and home supply centers. A high-intensity or gooseneck desk lamp will suit your purposes, too. Have an extension cord available in the event that it's needed.

This lesson may require several sessions. You may want to divide the lesson into "indoor" and "outdoor" drawing experiences, or use any other plan that works for your own schedule.

FIGURE 150. Your artificial light still life would surely be more stark and contrasted than the others. You might even want to use fluorescent pastels if you have them.

DIRECTIONS

1. Set up still life where it will be illuminated by *natural light* and seen by all students, who may want to position their chairs and desks accordingly.

2. Discuss the quality of the light—is it soft? harsh? dazzling? If your particular circumstances lend themselves, turn off overhead light briefly. Now analyze the difference between the lighting of the two situations.

3. Distribute materials. If you have completed Activity 57, take out swatch book for reference on Monet's brushstrokes. Try to incorporate Impressionistic technique in your chalk application.

4. Use as many colors as you deem necessary to acquire lighting effects, and register the source of light (for example, from a nearby window, hitting fruit from behind). Attend to what the glass bowl does to the light and color of the fruit. Show it!

5. When students seem to have accomplished their natural light still lifes, it's time to turn the page of the sketchbook (or give out the second piece of paper).

6. Access your *artificial* light source, either a lamp or spotlight. Pull down your shades or decrease the light in the room by adjusting room dimmers. Do not make the contrast overly dramatic—just enough to make the difference between real and artificial light obvious.

7. How would you now describe the light? Do this in words first, but convince us with your picture!

8. Now, take the bowl of fruit *outdoors.* Find a convenient place to set up. A grassy patch on school grounds is good. Students will do as they have been doing in other phases of the lesson— first (briefly) discuss the way the sunlight acts on the fruit, then sketch in on a new page.

9. Discuss *all* studies in group review of students' work back in the studio, a.k.a. art room. See if students can identify the light sources and specific lighting situations in the various depictions.

FIGURE 151. Outdoor lighting is diffused and less focused than indoor light in this still life. Maybe even more "impressionistic," one might say.

SUGGESTIONS FOR FURTHER DEVELOPMENT

Time-lapse studies are difficult to do within the time frame of school schedules. However, students could have a weekend assignment in their sketchbooks that is something like this: "Do three pastel studies at different times of the day (morning, noon, and dusk), using the same outdoor object for your subject. The tree in front of your house or the building across the street would be fine. Bring the three completed sketches to class for discussion." The truly ambitious student may wish to photograph the chosen outdoor object at the times set aside for sketching. Photos are interesting for the lighting effects they record as well as for the opportunity to compare the photographically lit atmosphere with the artistically sketched one.

ACTIVITY 59
Greetings from the Frog Pond!

POSTCARDS

What drew Monet to the Frog Pond? What attracted Cézanne to the mountain St. Victoire? Why did Degas visit the ballet studios again and again? These artists never seemed to tire of painting their special themes. Yet the reason why one artist prefers flower gardens over snowy Paris street scenes is hard to understand. One thing for sure, artists cannot keep their favorite places to themselves. You can count on their paintings to give away their secrets every time.

FIGURE 152. "Wish you were here" says the landscape of this student's favorite vacation getaway.

MATERIALS

- Markers
- Bristol board (see Teacher Preparation)
- White paper
- Postcards, assorted Impressionist art reproductions and travel posters (see Teacher Preparation)
- Scissors
- Glue (see Teacher Preparation)
- Rulers
- Black ballpoint pen or fine-tip black marker

TEACHER PREPARATION

Postcards are needed first and foremost. Ask students to bring in postcards they've saved from special trips, or ones they have received and kept. The teacher will provide postcard *backs,* so get yourself a blank postcard that has the address and stamp spaces clearly defined. The recommendation is to photocopy the postcard's blank back (the writing side) for the number of students in your class. Correction fluid will rid your sample card's reverse side of any unnecessary information. You can ask each student to cut the photocopied card's back or simply precut them along with the bristol board in generous postcard sizes.

Regular white glue could cause the paper backs of the postcards to pucker when later attached. Students may want to use the popular glue sticks (nontoxic, for paper use only) instead. If, in fact, you do not have access to a photocopy machine, postcard backs may be recreated with markers directly on the reverse side of their postcards. Use a blank postcard as a sample for replications. Skip step 6 if using this alternative.

DIRECTIONS

1. Bring all postcards forward. This is an ideal opportunity for students to share their experiences with the group in a friendly atmosphere.

2. Compare the actual designs of postcard illustrations with one another. Most of the travel cards will be photos, while your art postcards are reproductions of paintings. Yet there are design decisions even in the photographed cards. For example, some cards may show several views or sightseeing highlights of a given place.

3. Decide what designs and graphics you think are most effective. Bring out the paint swatch reference materials you produced in Activity 56. Distribute all materials.

4. Wish you were here? Where? What favorite place would you like to show? It can be a place where you've vacationed or one you have always wanted to visit. It can be across the world, in your own city, or in your own backyard. Plan the most effective way of presenting it in the small picture space allowed by your card.

5. Use the brushstroke references to give it the Impressionistic touch. You might want to combine several techniques. Include graphics if you wish, such as "Bonjour from Paris." Specifics, such as weather, time of year, and *exactly* where you are (town, city, or resort, as opposed to the entire country) seem to work best.

6. Glue the cut postcard message backs onto bristol board cards when front picture is complete. Let dry.

7. Using the pen, identify your scenes in small print in the upper-left hand corner on the backs of the cards.

8. Tack up these extraordinary cards on the bulletin board for all to see. When they are returned to students, they most certainly may be sent through the mail with the usual proper postage. Wouldn't these original postcards delight a friend, a cousin, or a pen pal? They are indeed collectors' items!

FIGURE 153. Loose and splashy brushwork is "reflected" in this postcard designed by a seventh-grade boy.

ACTIVITY 60
Straw Hats and Bonnets: The Joyful Art of Renoir

STUDIO PAINTING: Acrylic on "Glass"

Long ago in Limoges—a French town famous for the china of the same name—lived a young procelain painter named Renoir who lost his job to automation. Renoir soon landed on his feet—right in front of an easel! He was to produce some of the most colorful, luminous canvases the world has ever known.

Renoir seemed to find beauty everywhere—in the city parks, the sidewalk cafés, and even in his own backyard. A touch of his creamy paint, and a rose on a bonnet became rosier, a peach fuzzier, a young girl's eyes more radiant. Such was the extraordinary talent of the artist who once painted Limoges china, a small beginning that he was to leave far behind. But the dazzling quality of porcelain never quite left the artist. His painting was among the best and the brightest in Impressionism and in the entire history of art.

FIGURE 154. The lower right window pane is graced by a youngster's interpretation of Renoir's brushwork on clear acetate.

SLIDE #29:   AT THE GRENOUILLÈRE

MATERIALS

- Acrylic paints
- Palettes
- Small to medium paintbrushes for oil painting
- Clear plastic (see Teacher Preparation)
- Scissors
- Cellophane tape and masking tape
- White paper
- Magnifying glasses (optional)
- Hat, scarf, real and/or artificial flowers (see Teacher Preparation)
- Paint swatchbooks from Activity 56 (optional; see Teacher Preparation)

FIGURE 155. Robin looks like she just stepped out of a Renoir canvas with her straw hat and fetching pose.

TEACHER PREPARATION

This is essentially a studio activity on Renoir that has a twist—students paint directly onto a clear surface. Painting on glass is very exciting, but impractical for the classroom. Fortunately, there is clear plastic. Of course, you may use plexiglass squares and remnants if they are available to you. Clear plastic on a roll is generally more accessible and is therefore recommended. Select a gauge that feels heavy enough to remain stable for paint application (plastic kitchen food wraps are not suitable). Plastic may be purchased on rolls in art supply or hardware stores. It is also available in sketchpad form for "wet media"— but this may be less economical for classroom use.

You will want to precut plastic into manageable "canvas board" sizes, about 12″ × 15″. It would be ideal if students could work with plastic sheets taped to windows. But if this is not possible in your art room, simply work on a flat surface with a sheet of white paper of a corresponding size beneath the plastic.

Set up your room for a studio painting experience (see "Studio Painting in the Classroom" in Section One). You will need plenty of white paint for mixing pastels. Small brushes will also be helpful in this lesson, as indicated in step 1 under the directions.

Have reproductions of Renoir's paintings on hand for study, along with brushstroke sample packs, if available. Props for your students will include a hat—preferably a straw or felt type and—a soft, silky scarf, and a flower, which really does the trick. This lesson may be accomplished in one full session, particularly if all materials and directions are in place at the onset. Have the area set aside for model and supplies. You may find it convenient to arrange plastic sheets in their positions on either windows or tables prior to the arrival of the class.

DIRECTIONS

1. Look over the Renoir reproductions. If you use the magnifying glass you'll see that he favored smaller brushstrokes, even though he painted in generous volumes. Refer to brushstroke reference card (from Activity 56, if available, to compare and contrast Renoir's painting style with that of other Impressionists).

2. You may choose one or two models on the basis of the poses in a selected Renoir reproduction. For example, "Two Sisters Drawing" would require two young ladies to model or you can simply invent a suitable pose. Use props accordingly. Flowers may be held or placed on a hat. Perhaps they can be installed as a boutonniere in a boy model's lapel.

3. All materials should be made available. Paint directly from models on to clear plastic sheets, a la Renoir! The surface will naturally be slicker than paper or canvas, but should be quite workable and novel. Adjust paint viscosity with water as needed. (NOTE: Use the surface to your advantage—a little water on your painting will wipe out areas you don't want to retain. It will keep the painting light.)

4. Ample mixing of white paint with lively color choices will provide the pastel ranges required. Small brushstrokes will best recall Renoir's style. Little dashes and dabs of bright color—red and orange and white—can accent an area, even suggest a fuller volume. But don't overdo it, as a speck of orange near an eye or pupil, or a dash of white on a satin bow is enough!

5. If you are not working at a window, hold plastic paintings up from time to time to see how light is affecting the picture. Return to applying your paint until you feel the play between subject, paint, and light is harmonious.

6. These paintings are like flowers; they will need sunlight to survive. Mount them with clear tape in a sunny window for a brilliant display!

ACTIVITY 61
What's the Point?

MOSAICS: "Cotton Swab" Pointillism

Seurat developed a system for painting that was at once creative and scientific. His original method, called *pointillism,* was based on one small but indispensable element—the dot! By using multitudinous numbers of bright dots to convey colors and volume, Seurat could paint an impressive picture. The result of the dot-filled canvas was not unlike that of a mosaic—all the bright little parts add up to a sparkling whole. So don't think that Seurat went completely dotty, for his plan for painting in colorful particles worked out mighty well!

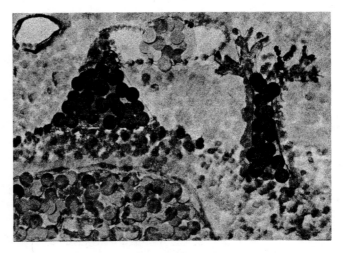

FIGURE 156. Pointillism is a challenge that this youngster met enthusiastically. It sometimes helps, though, to pencil in your composition before the advent of the dots.

SLIDE #30:   SEASCAPE AT PORT-EN-BESSIN, NORMANDY

MATERIALS

- 4″ × 6″ white drawing paper
- Watercolors
- Hole puncher (see Teacher Preparation)
- Glue
- Cotton swabs (see Teacher Preparation)
- Paint chips (see Teacher Preparation)
- Magnifying glass and reproductions (see Teacher Preparation)
- Tweezers (optional)

TEACHER PREPARATION

There is more than one way to produce a pointillistic painting, as you shall see. You will need a hole puncher with a good-sized aperture. The paper dots will be provided by punching holes in the paint chips, available free in all paint stores. These swatches come in every delicious color and shade imaginable, so secure what you wish. The circles that fall from the hole punch will be yours for the mosaic aspect of this lesson. Other paper circles may be found in stationery stores as self-stick dots. Also, small multicolored paper circles are often used for teaching shapes on the primary grades. These may be punched up, too.

The painting part of the activity will be done with cotton swabs. These are sold in economy-sized packages in most health and beauty aid stores.

You will need some Seurat reproductions (color plates, postcards, etc.) to examine under the magnifying glass.

Set the room up for painting and workshop activity. This lesson may extend beyond one class period.

DIRECTIONS

1. Put the reproductions under the magnifying glass and study the dot system. It is best to focus on a detail, such as a hat, glove, or ball. How does the artist achieve volume? In what way are light and dark dots arranged?

2. Punch out dots from paint swatches. Distribute all other materials. Decide on the picture you wish to represent. Perhaps a vignette from the circus, such as a juggler or a clown? How about a small scene from an afternoon outing, like a picnic basket on a blanket? Keep it uncomplicated.

3. Take the brush out of your paintbox and put it aside for now—you won't need it immediately. Paint by dipping the cotton swabs into the water and then into the selected paint. Start with light colors, like yellow, to create a "dotted line" outline for your planned picture (NOTE: You may want to use the paint reference materials from Activity 56 here.) Some students may want to assign colors to areas of the picture before it is applied.

4. Using a combination of paint and paper dots, flesh out your composition in dots only. Take particular notice of how the darker shades of the dots will suggest volume. Unlike many mosaics, this painting should not appear to be flat. Seurat achieved space and mass with dots—so can we! Tweezers can help with paper dot application.

5. How do you know when you have pasted or painted your finishing dot? When you've gotten your point across! Sign your name—in dots, of course—and display.

ACTIVITY 62
Post No Bills

POSTER ART: Graphic Design

Toulouse-Lautrec found the circus, the busy sidewalk cafés, and the theatre—complete with their casts of characters—to be irresistible! He often painted scenes from places like the Moulin Rouge, a Parisian music hall, which not only pleased him, but contributed to the success of that establishment, too. His posters, advertising various events, were plastered all over town. The lively singers and dancers from Montmartre, as well as the signature of the artist himself, would long be remembered because of the famous high-spirited posters by Toulouse-Lautrec!

SLIDE #31:   MOULIN ROUGE

FIGURE 157. Move over, Toulouse...here's a smashing poster from "L'Atelier Dana," a fourth grader. Ooh la la!

MATERIALS

- Full-size posterboards or 18″ × 24″ paper
- Poster paint
- Wide and flat paintbrushes in assorted sizes
- Manila paper
- Magnifying glasses
- Brown butcher wrap (optional)

TEACHER PREPARATION

Posters that you may have collected—particularly posters that mark a major art exhibit—should be brought to class as reference material. Also, there are books available that identify artists' signatures as well as books that list the autographs of famous people. Consult the librarian for these materials and include them for reference purposes in "Post No Bills." You will want reproductions of Impressionists' paintings handy as well to further augment the observation of artists' signatures.

DIRECTIONS

1. Study the design of Lautrec's poster art along with any other posters you may have brought in for reference. What makes the poster effective? Squint your eyes. You will see that large flat areas of color play against each other to create strong visuals.

2. Notice how the graphics are done—they don't look "stuck on"—they are an important part of the overall design. Get out the magnifying glass to examine the way the artist signs the work. Sometimes there's a seal or symbol that represents the artist's studio along with the name. Many artists have distinctive signatures, not unlike their unique art.

3. What subject would you like to paint as a poster? Maybe you like landscapes, or still lifes. Perhaps the circus or the theatre appeals to you, too. Whatever most reflects your tastes is the right choice.

4. Make a small "thumbnail" sketch in paint on manila paper before you begin your poster. Understand that this will not be a painting as such, but a *poster*, which means that details should be kept to a minimum. Plan large areas of color and think about a heading and a signature!

5. Practice your "autograph" before you begin. Use reference materials, comparing the characteristics of various signatures. Some are wide and expansive; others are tight and controlled. It's almost like handwriting analysis. Now, for your heading—the poster will announce *you* as an artist. How about:

   THE EARLY WORKS OF (YOUR NAME)

   THE YEARS AT P.S. (YOUR SCHOOL)

   (YOUR NAME): PAINTINGS AND DRAWINGS

   Use your imagination. You may include dates and years.

6. Begin your poster. Larger, flatter brushes are good for large areas of color; smaller brushes should be used for lettering. The hand-lettered look is not only acceptable here; it's desirable. You can even create a sign for your studio, like "L'atelier."

7. Fill your big paper with bright color, but don't shy away from black outlines; this can give definition. Keep it simple. Use your graphics wisely and voilà!

8. If the teacher is really involved with this activity, *kiosk* shapes (based on European display stands and newstands) may be cut from brown paper for mounting the posters. Your posters are sure to be the toast of the school!

ACTIVITY 63
Once Upon a Starry Night

WATERCOLOR RESIST: Painting with "Stars"

Vincent Van Gogh worked on his art night and day. His paintings were bursts of radiating patterns—of blazing suns and of star-studded skies in inky swirls. Feverishly, the artist painted his whirling canvases, indoors and out, from morning until night. Whether the subject was spiky sunflowers or wheat fields, Van Gogh's interpretation was always intense. Things that would otherwise appear quite calm became dramatic, even frantic, when Van Gogh painted them. It was a restless art that could change a quiet night sky into an explosion of comets and burning stars. But it was also an art that abounded with feelings, spirit, and life.

SLIDE #32:   THE STARRY NIGHT

FIGURE 158. Stick-on stars and swirly paint are the stuff of starry nights!

FIGURE 159. Brushstrokes, whether in oil, acrylic, watercolor, or ink, can say a great deal. Can't you just feel the wind blow in this painting?

MATERIALS

- Watercolors
- 12″ × 18″ white paper
- Self-stick foil paper stars (see Teacher Preparation)
- White oil pastels

TEACHER PREPARATION

Stationery and paper goods stores sell foil stick-on stars in gold, silver, and other colors. The ones with stick-on backs are recommended, but if the only sort you can find require water for sticking, have students use a sponge or damp paper towel on them before applying.

Reference materials may include pen-and-ink drawings by Van Gogh, which are closer in medium to the watercolor paints we'll be using. They also show his technique quite clearly. Just for an added footnote of interest, you might want to acquire some books on astronomy and astrology for this lesson. Students may be interested in the positions of stars and other heavenly bodies. This sort of material might give them some more good ideas for their compositions.

Set up the classroom for watercolor painting.

DIRECTIONS

1. Discuss the quality of Van Gogh's brushwork. It always has definite direction, does it not? Trace his brushstrokes in the air with your finger when you're looking at the slide or the reproductions. Your movements will be quick, choppy, and swirly.

2. Briefly discuss some places you've been to at night that stay in your mind. An amusement park or a pier at the seashore with a lighthouse nearby? How about the city at night, with its tall buildings, bridges, and bright lights? A fireworks celebration? An outdoor evening sports event? The airport at night? There are plenty of ideas for your nighttime picture.

3. One more thought. Do you recall ever *really* seeing the night sky, like in the country, where the view is clear? Remember what all those twinkling stars looked like? Now get out the paints and the stars and begin.

4. You may want to initially block in your composition or your may wish to work spontaneously; there's no "correct" method here. However, if you wish to arrange your stars in an intriguing yet systematic way, look to the illustrative materials. Maybe you want to actually follow the path of a constellation. Oil sticks may be applied here at this point and later on, too. They can be applied under and over paint.

5. Make sure that the paper surface is dry where you place your stick-on stars. Brushstrokes should be expressive and directional. Refer to your brushstroke swatchbook from Activity 56, if desired.

6. Someone said that the night has a thousand eyes, but our nights are filled with countless dazzling lights. Flash your sparkling art!

ACTIVITY 64
Cézanne: Painting on a Higher Plane

ACRYLIC PAINT ON PAPER: Paper Folds

Cézanne used his paintbrush like a chisel, carving planes from solid mass. Whether he painted Mt. St. Victoire or a pear suspended over the edge of a tablecloth, Cézanne's highly original art revealed many facets and planes. His hatching brushstrokes created a surface energy and rhythm that might even be called abstract! Yet Cézanne is considered a Post-Impressionist. Whatever you wish to call him, this vigorous nonconformist was certainly a powerhouse.

SLIDE #33:   STILL LIFE WITH PEPPERMINT BOTTLE

FIGURE 160. Cézanne is certainly remembered here!

MATERIALS

- Acrylic paint
- Stiff-bristle paintbrushes
- Bristol board
- White paper
- Practice paper
- Pencils
- Scissors
- Brushstroke reference cards from Activity 56 (optional)
- Masking tape

TEACHER PREPARATION

This is both a painting and paper-folding activity. Students will need extra paper on hand to experiment with cutting shapes. You may want to precut bristol board into various sizes, for paper formats (12″ × 15″), as well as into smaller squares and rectangles for cutting picture parts.

Reproductions of Cézanne's work should be used for reference. Utilize brushstoke cards if available.

You may also want to bring in anatomy books that illustrate division of planes within the human body, for example, facial structure of the head. Other materials that demonstrate projections of planes or facets, like geometry, gemology, or architecture books, may be introduced for additional interest.

DIRECTIONS

1. Study reference materials on Cézanne's painting. Describe what you think the surfaces of the objects he paints might feel like if you touched them. Do they remind you of other substances or materials? Present any illustrations you may have on minerals or architectural elements and their elevations.

2. Distribute all supplies. Students will begin by selecting *one* item from a Cézanne, such as a bottle. Sketch it in pencil on practice paper. Use the brushstroke reference card and study the direction of Cézanne's paint. Using the side of the pencil, hatch out your own drawing in this style. Indicate planes by delineating them in your drawing. Cut out the object.

3. Score the paper (see Activity 10, Figure 27) along the edges of the lines that indicate planes. Fold paper to suggest dimensionality. Try other objects in the same manner. Experiment.

4. When ready, switch over to white paper. Cut and score paper as directed above, but *include an additional border approximately ½" to ¾" on either side* for attaching to larger paper surface. These objects will be scored and folded, then glued to the bristol board to form the composition.

5. Decide which objects you want to include in your painting, then cut and score them (include borders). Sketch in your overall composition, marking the places where paper-folded objects will go. Begin painting the objects with the directional strokes of the great Cézanne. Let dry; then paint the bristol board in a corresponding fashion.

6. When ready for application of cut picture parts, fold them on their scored edges and glue in predetermined places on bristol board. Tape may be used over glued edge to further secure it.

7. Before your painting is declared complete, use paint to blend and touch up entire composition.

8. These still lifes are stand-outs! An exhibit of your multi-dimensional Cézanne interpretations is in order.

MODERN ART

When we refer to Modern Art, we are usually speaking of art of the twentieth century. As one period merged with another, the era of Post-Impressionism found its way out of the preceding century in several different directions. Much of the activity to come was stimulated by a single artist who was an entire art movement in himself—Picasso!

Pablo Picasso came into the art world at about the same time that the incomparable Matisse was painting and cutting his bold shapes. There was already a new feeling in the wind. Picasso eventually reached his own departure from accepted forms but first, like the history of art itself, he went through several stages. The early work was sensitive and creatively distorted—the Blue and Rose periods. But if there is one period for which Picasso will be remembered, it will be Cubism.

Coming under the auspices of Abstract Art, Cubism represented the most radical break with the classical ideals that had ever occurred. Along with his sidekick Braque, Picasso dissected and divided volumes into planes and fragments, and thereby exposed an entirely new sense of the object. Thus, Cubism was hatched.

As noted earlier, no artist is without a debt, and Picasso's was to the sculpture of Africa, where natural planes had been successfully manipulated for centuries. Nonetheless, it took some daring and a great deal of pluck for a European artist to pursue this route—something which Picasso did not lack.

Pluck seemed to prevail throughout the time period in general. Frivolous, but amusing in a literary sort of way, the movement of Dada appeared with its unlikely assemblages. It was a form not far from Surrealism, another school that encouraged absurdities. De Chirico elevated the level of surrealism, however, in his masterful other-worldly, dreamlike art.

Things went a little haywire. Painters slashed canvases with their brushes, even threw around buckets of paint! You can only guess the reaction this behavior first received, but, in the end, Jackson Pollock's name went into the history books. His abstract work, dubbed Action Painting, made the way for the next nontraditional art movement. It was called Pop Art—short for *popular art*. Appropriately named, this art form took its inspiration from the immediate commercial world of advertising and product graphics—even comic books. Op Art, the cousin of Pop Art, appeared on the art scene as visual optics and vibrating patterns. Where would all this lead?

Many feel that art is essentially a mirror to be held up to our technological age. Others, however, would like originality of view, combined with mastery of traditional techniques, to remain as important as ever to art and artists.

Undoubtedly, much confusion surrounds the identity of art today. It is a puzzle that will likely be solved when it is viewed through the critical lens of history.

ACTIVITY 65
The Call of the Wild

MIXED MONTAGE: Photographic "Primitive" Art

Rousseau loved green tropical jungles and other faraway lands. Although it is not clear if the artist ever really traveled very far from home, one can always dream! His fantastic setttings are so vivid, so very colorful, they could make you long for wild, exotic places, too.

SLIDE #34:   THE EQUATORIAL JUNGLE

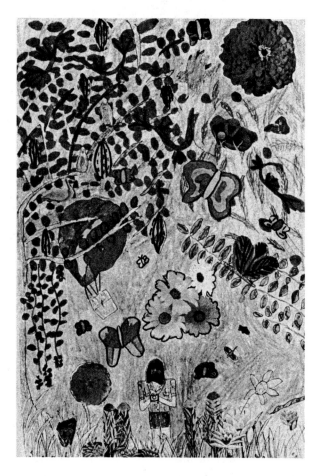

FIGURE 161. What to do when your hot air balloon is snagged by a vine? Amanda gets out her trusty camera, for there is much to photograph in this lush place.

MATERIALS

- Markers or crayons
- Scissors
- Glue
- 12″ × 15″ white paper
- Manila paper (see Teacher Preparation)
- Garden and seed catalogs (see Teacher Preparation)
- Empty seed packs (see Teacher Preparation)
- Photographs (or photocopies of photographs) of students (see Teacher Preparation)

TEACHER PREPARATION

Save garden catalogs. If you're on such a mailing list, then you're in good shape. Other sources for photographic illustrations of flowers, plants, and vegetables are empty seed packs, as well as house and garden magazines. Students can bring in materials of this nature from home for the lesson.

Don't miss the golden opportunity to put yourself in the picture. Students should bring in photos of themselves (or photocopies of the photographs) as explained in Activity 54.

Have manila scraps on hand for costume details (see step 4 under the directions).

DIRECTIONS

1. What's your idea of a jungle? Big, gorgeous flowers? Monkeys swinging on vines? Palm trees? Bright tropical birds? And, of course, the burning sun.

2. Discuss your thoughts and fantasies about jungle environments. Think about the way nature changes with the climate. How do people dress in such hot weather? Name some different costumes or uniforms people might wear in the tropics.

3. Distribute all materials. Students should have photos of themselves. Cut along the contours of all photographs, your own photo, as well as the pictures of the plants and flowers you select. It is important that the shapes have clarity.

4. If you were to visit a jungle, how would you like to do it? On a safari (*photographic safari*, please), or as an explorer? Or would you rather be even more scientific and go as a zoologist, a botanist, or a bird watcher? Archaeologist? Adventurer? Decide, then consider what wardrobe and accessories you'll need for your trip, such as camera, pith helmet, binoculars, etc. Cut out appropriate shapes from manila paper for your selection.

5. Cut up the photograph of yourself to fit your outfit and determined pose. Glue down the garden clips. Remember, flowers grow big in the jungle, so don't be afraid to exaggerate the scale of the flora and fauna. Use your drawing skills, too.

6. Are there tigers in the tall grass? Crocodiles in the swamp? Add all the jungle dwellers you wish—even the smaller ones, like snakes and butterflies. Draw the picture to completion in bright, tropical colors.

7. Now you can see why Rousseau let his imagination run wild. Display these lush works. It's a jungle out there!

FIGURE 162. Gena has the command of a Jungle Queen! She even keeps a pet tiger on the line. The monkeys, it is clear, would do anything she asks!

ACTIVITY 66
Cut It Out!

PATTERNS: "Wallpaper"

Bold, bright colors. Striking patterns, playing off one another. Matisse. Just as one-two-three, they go together, for Matisse's influence on design everywhere can almost be taken for granted. Yet the artist had a few influences of his own. The art of the Middle East and Morocco was a great source of inspiration for Matisse. Later, when he exchanged his brush for scissors, these important design elements were distilled into pure, organic forms. What power they had in their simple shapes! What a colorful punch! Once again, Henri Matisse shocked and delighted the world with his new modern art style in the highly unique paper-cut!

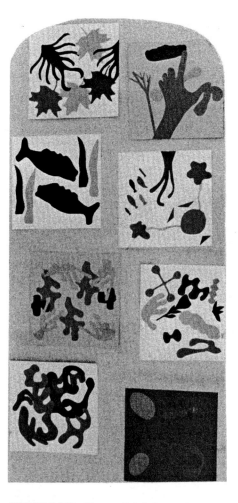

FIGURE 163. If you didn't know better, you might think you landed in Nice, along the Cote d'Azur—smack in the middle of the Matisse Museum!

SLIDE #35:   BEASTS OF THE SEA

MATERIALS

- White paper from a roll (see Teacher Preparation)
- 9″ × 12″ or 12″ × 15″ white drawing paper
- Poster paints in bright colors, such as yellow, turquoise, and magenta
- Wide and flat paintbrushes in assorted sizes
- Scissors
- Glue
- Construction paper in assorted colors (see Teacher Preparation)
- Practice paper
- Tape for mounting

TEACHER PREPARATION

This lesson has two parts. The first part is introduced with a color exercise, for which you'll cut some three-inch squares of colored construction paper. Have some colored construction sheets intact for this activity, too. You will also be *hand-coloring the white drawing paper,* so set up the room for painting.

The second part of the activity will ask students to make *papercuts* of their hand-painted color papers. These shapes will be assembled on lengths of white paper from a roll. Cut several pieces in manageable sizes. (NOTE: The colors of cut shapes will be complemented by white, not brown, paper. If you have only brown butcher wrap, it may be gessoed beforehand.) If you wish to fit the "wallpaper" into a niche (as Matisse often did), precut the paper to fit the intended space. This aspect of the lesson will yield your large, paper-cut wallpaper. A big wall would be perfect for installation with push pins, tape, or whatever you would normally use to mount large papers.

For reference, you will want to have some Oriental (Islamic) design motif materials on hand. Also suggested are science books on natural elements, e.g., shapes of cacti, coral, sea forms, and plants—even amoeba. Books that offer examples from these various categories are excellent.

NOTE: Scissors should be in smooth working order. Dull or stubborn scissors will sabotage all your efforts.

DIRECTIONS

Part One

1. To demonstrate the direct effect that one color has on another, place colored squares on the various colored backgrounds, provided by the larger sheets of construction paper.

2. Which colors vibrate? Identify combinations that intensify each other. Move components around to discover the ones that work together well. Use Matisse's color choices as a guide.

3. Either glue down the successful color relationships for future reference, or simply remove the experimental materials, noting the color information for painting purposes.

4. Distribute white paper and painting supplies. Colors should be mixed to create richer, bolder shapes. Pastels such as shocking pink and lavender are desirable. Give your own color names as you go along—outrageous orange, screaming green—invent and experiment.

5. Let dry flat.

Part Two

6. Consider your reference materials on Matisse's Moroccan motifs as well as books on natural forms. Practice your cutting skills with scrap paper. Do *not* use pencil first! You are responding *directly* to the subjects with your scissors. *This is your drawing tool.*

7. Try free-form cutting—looping movements, undercuts, jagged edges, and the like. When you are reasonably comfortable with the scissors, begin cutting shapes from the hand-painted papers. Share colors, don't try to use only your own creations.

8. Bring precut sheets of paper from the roll forward. You may treat every sheet as a separate format for a new design, or treat each as a continuation of a single design motif. Students will contribute their paper cuts to each piece, helping to decide on overall design, with the guidance of the teacher. Additional shapes and clips of colored paper may be needed to unify the arrangements. Glue all parts required for overall designs as determined.

9. Mount your finished sheets on the appropriate wall or space. It's wallpaper heaven—à la Matisse!

ACTIVITY 67
South Sea Paradise

PAPER, FABRIC, MIXED MEDIA: Appliqué

Have you ever seen a brilliant sunset or passed by a snow-covered bridge and felt an overwhelming urge to record it in some artistic way? Call it inspiration, it is often this very impulse that causes artists to pick up their brushes, too! It was the South Seas islands that inspired the artist Gauguin, who was irresistibly drawn to the place. The extraordinary appeal of the Tahitian people, their colorful sarongs, the lush countryside—even their language and their ancient beliefs—completely enchanted him. The famous paintings he created while he lived there reflected his strong attachment for this exotic island. Indeed, Gauguin captured the spirit of Tahiti, just as surely as Tahiti captured Gauguin.

FIGURE 164. The South Sea maiden plucks a luscious tropical fruit from a bush. Does the snake in her basket expect a bite? Drawn by Robin, age 13.

SLIDE #36:   WOMEN OF TAHITI
             (OR ON THE BEACH)

MATERIALS

- Manila paper
- Fabric (see Teacher Preparation)
- Scissors
- Glue pastels
- Oil pastels
- Pinking shears (optional)

FIGURE 165. Wrap a sarong with complete confidence! Drape fabric around yourself so that it is across your chest and back and is clearing your underarms. Gather fabric, front and back, over one shoulder and tie both ends in a big knot. Boys may knot shorter (or folded) lengths of cloth at the side of their waists.

TEACHER PREPARATION

Swatch books of discounted fabric from upholstery stores or home decorating centers can easily provide the necessary element of this lesson. However, if you can get ahold of a few yards of splashy floral remnants, you're in business. Fabric lengths can be used to introduce the lesson as students can learn to wrap a sarong. Should you then wish, the same material may be divided (with pinking shears, if possible) for the project as directed. Either way, students will have swatches of brightly patterned fabric.

Construction paper should be made available in a variety of colors. Flesh tones will have full range: tan, peach, black, brown, rose, etc. Encourage students to use variety. Construction paper will also come in handy for details like flowers or fruits, so you may want to provide colorful paper scraps or small precut pieces.

Just for an added touch, travel brochures and guidebooks of the South Sea Islands—Tahiti, Bora Bora, the Marquesas—might be included as motivational materials. If you enjoy musical accompaniment for your lesson, here's your chance to bring out such albums as "South Pacific," or any tropical themes you consider appropriate.

DIRECTIONS

1. Distribute all materials, including examples of various fabric. Allow time for students to respond to prints they find attractive. Browse through the travel brochures, noting the features of the climate and characteristics of this particular part of the world.

2. Let's briefly pretend that we are there. Ask if any students, male or female, would like to learn to wrap a sarong. (See Figure 165.) If you are working with swatch books only, proceed to the next step.

3. Cut and paste, using Gauguin as a guide for planning and composition. Try to show the fabric over the form.

4. Think about action and interaction. What might be happening in your picture? A man bringing in a fishing boat? A woman pinning a flower in her hair? A boy chopping wood?

5. Use your oil sticks to achieve rich and bright color. White is especially good for highlights, such as whites of the eyes, foam on the waves and clouds, and so forth. Don't be shy about trying unusual colors, such as pink for grass or lavender for the sky. Add such details as flowers and jewelry.

6. Finished? Title your work and be descriptive. The travel brochures and Gauguin reproductions can help with that.

7. Ah, the lure of the South Seas! Now you know why Gauguin said, "Au revoir Paris." Display your windows on paradise!

ACTIVITY 68
Abstract Thinking

DRAWING: Montage

FIGURE 166. Does your closet ever look like this?

Humpty Dumpty sat on the wall. Humpty Dumpty had a great fall. Well, if all the king's men had been abstract artists, they would have easily put Humpty back together again! Shuffle, scramble, and rearrange in the abstract process known as Cubism, and you have new meaning for your object. The head honcho of this art form was Picasso, who fractured the subjects of his paintings to give several views at once. When Cubists wanted to know more about something through their art, they simply broke it apart, whether the topic was eggs, chairs, or three lively musicians.

**SLIDE #37:   STILL LIFE WITH
                CHAIR CANING**

MATERIALS

- Crayons or colored pencils
- White paper
- Scissors
- Glue
- One paper clip per student
- Magazines (see Teacher Preparation)
- Mirrors with special requirements (see Teacher Preparation)

TEACHER PREPARATION

The magazines you'll want to have ready for this lesson should vary: fashion, home decorating, food, and special interests such as cars, nature, sports, and so forth. Students may supply their personal favorites from home subscriptions.

If you have a mirror (in a frame) that has been broken, but remains intact, you will have a device to dramatize Cubism. It is essential, however, that the mirror does not leave the teacher's hands and is reinforced with tape along the crack lines. Bring the mirror into the lesson as directed *only* if you judge it to be quite safe. Another (uncracked) mirror should be ready for image comparisons.

This may be a two-part lesson.

DIRECTIONS

Part One

1. To start the activity we'll need a working definition for Cubism, which embodies abstract art. Bring out the mirrors and let students see their reflections in the regular glass first, withholding the broken mirror. Let them observe themselves from several different angles. Now retrieve the broken mirror.

2. The teacher will show students the broken mirror. How many different "views" can you see at once? The fractured reflection makes the point. Distribute materials.

3. Students will select a specific topic in the magazine, such as shoes, cars, or furniture. Pages that contain the selected theme will be removed from the magazine then placed aside. Pick clear, good-sized pictures.

4. Plan an environment to go with your selection. This will be drawn on the paper. For example, if your choice is shoes, then you might draw a bedroom closet, complete with shoe bag and shelves, or you might draw a shoe store. Other suggestions include: cars/ white line highway; sports/arena (or ski slope, basketball court, etc.); furniture/living room; and so forth. In other words, you will draw a picture that is analogous with your topic.

5. Use crayons (or colored pencils) to create an environment for the chosen topic on your paper. Do not think of this page as a picture necessarily; it's more like a *"back drop"* to which we will add other elements.

6. Cover your paper with the drawing and details and finish it. If the art period is over, attach magazine illustrations with paper clip, and hand in papers.

Part Two

7. Return finished papers with magazine illustrations attached. Remove paper clip. Distribute materials once again.

8. Cut magazine photos into sharp geometric shapes, such as shards and fragments. Avoid cutting tiny pieces that are more like splinters than sections of the photo.

9. Here's the fun part. Ask each student to sweep the cut photos from the desk into their hands, then cup their hands closed. At the count of three, students will toss the cut photos onto their drawings. Ask them to aim for their *own* papers—not across the room!

10. Let the chips fall where they may. Shapes may be adjusted to create a well-balanced arrangement, but the spontaneous, explosive look should remain. Glue parts in place.

11. Use crayons/colored pencils to further unify cut parts with the background through design. Gather all art for class review.

12. Can students "read" the original objects in their present abstract shapes? Give it a try. Display these multiple images with gusto!

ACTIVITY 69
The House That Color and Design Built

3-D CONSTRUCTION: Architecture and Interior Design

Take red, yellow, and blue. Add black, gray, and white. Apply to simple geometric shapes, mostly rectangles. Mix in straight lines. What do you have? Mondrian and also De Stijl! Mondrian, a painter, belonged to De Stijl—a group of artists and architects with specific principles about art. Their ideals? Clean-cut lines; flat, uncluttered space; and pure color. Whether it was painting, architecture, or interior design, these artistic beliefs were upheld. You could say it was a case of art imitating life, but as far as the De Stijl were concerned, there was little difference between the two at all.

FIGURE 167. The interior is pure De Stijl—clean cut and uncluttered. Designed by a ninth grader.

SLIDE #38:   NEW YORK CITY

MATERIALS

- Unlined 3″ × 5″ cards
- White paper
- Bristol boards (see Teacher Preparation)
- Scrap paper for sketching
- Pencils
- Rulers
- Scissors
- Markers
- Colored tissue paper scraps (optional)
- Foil paper scraps (optional)
- Gesso or white poster paint
- Glue
- Tape
- Shoeboxes (see Teacher Preparation)
- Colored graphic arts tapes, such as Chartpak® (optional; see Teacher Preparation)

FIGURE 168. Another first-rate structure inside and out.

TEACHER PREPARATION

We will first be replicating a Mondrian painting on a 3″ × 5″ card. Precut bristol board into small sections for construction of other parts, such as furniture bases and additional supportive elements.

Shoeboxes, preferably larger sizes, as from men's shoes, are needed for the construction. Lids may be utilized for assembly, too.

Graphic arts tapes (particularly in black) will help define areas and actually aid in design. They are, however, *not* essential to the activity.

Illustrations of De Stijl furniture by Gerrit Rietveld, for example, as well as other interior design reference materials from this period, are strongly recommended.

This lesson will require several class sessions to complete.

FIGURE 169. Here is tribute to modern furnishings as well.

DIRECTIONS

1. How would you describe Mondrian's art? Use your own words: geometric, straight, clean, organized, and orderly. It's hard to find anything that isn't at a right-angle, isn't it?

2. Distribute 3″ × 5″ cards, rulers, markers, pencils, and graphic arts tape. Using a reproduction as a guide, recreate a Mondrian or two! Alter as desired, but stay with the basic idea.

3. Once you're satisfied with your replication, put the drawing aside momentarily. Distribute the rest of the materials.

4. Paint the shoebox white, inside and out. Let dry.

5. Retrieve the 3″ × 5″ Mondrian imitations; these may be used for decorative purposes or as architectural elements, such as partitions, doors, cabinets, and furniture. Include them in your planning. Sketch out ideas for interior design of overall structure on practice paper. Experiment with furniture, as shown in Figures 170 through 174.

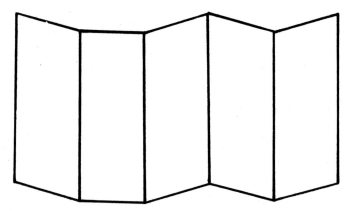

FIGURE 170. Step one: fold paper.

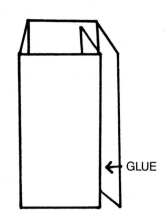

FIGURE 171. Step two: glue.

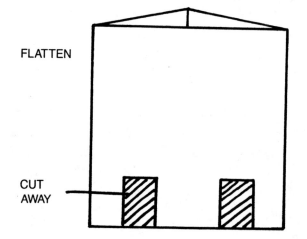

FIGURE 172. Steps three and four: flatten and cut away.

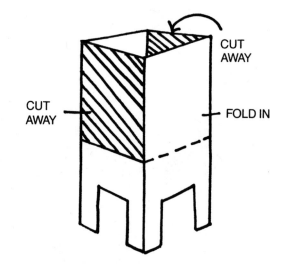

FIGURE 173. Steps five and six: cut away and fold in.

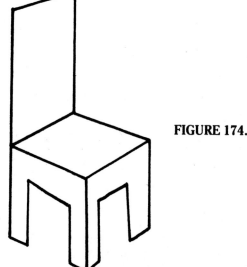

FIGURE 174. A chair!

6. Cutting and pasting may begin whenever you feel ready. Consider windows. Colored tissue will make "stained glass." Foil suggests reflective surfaces, like mirrored panels. You'll need some sense of an overall floor plan to decide where elements will eventually fit.

7. Assemble parts in any order that suits your own working arrangement. Determine interior space. Is it bi-level or otherwise? Do you need stairs? What about the exterior of your building? Do you want terraces? Add, along with any other "extras" you desire.

8. Now it's time to decorate! Furniture may be constructed, and Mondrian painting parts incorporated. Ceiling and floors should be brightly and simply colored, and may easily be drawn to resemble tiles.

9. If time permits, hang a few paintings! Design some in the De Stijl style to go with the rest of the theme. Throw in a few rugs.

10. Your thoroughly modern-looking home is ready for an open-house inspection! Line up all building models on what one could rightly name "De Stijl Street." A first-class neighborhood—and the last word in design!

ACTIVITY 70
Upwardly Mobile

MOBILES

They could well be on a collision course, the shapes that whirl and swirl past each other in constant motion. Alexander Calder perfected that magical form of sculpture known as the mobile. Its many moving parts are balanced to rotate indefinitely. With every turn, a new design appears. If it's art that can change itself constantly, and art that plays with the space that surrounds it—if it's art that's always on the move—then you can be sure that it's a mobile!

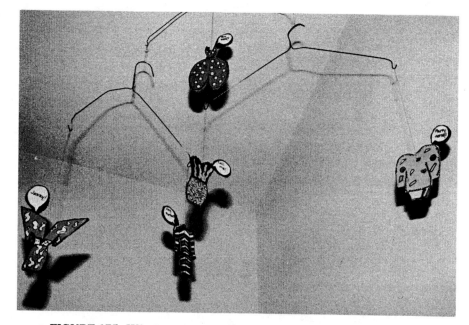

FIGURE 175. What goes around, comes around. This mobile not only has moving parts, it has speaking parts, too! The dress on the left says "Jazzy," while another outfit declares "party time."

MATERIALS

- Pencils
- Scissors
- Glue
- Markers
- Bristol board
- Corrugated cardboard (see Teacher Preparation)
- Nylon string (see Teacher Preparation)
- Pliers (see Teacher Preparation)
- Wire clothes hangers (see Teacher Preparation)
- Clothesline or thick roving
- Nail or other sharp object

TEACHER PREPARATION

We'll be constructing our mobiles from corrugated paper, the type from which cardboard boxes are made. Boxes can be broken down to provide the cardboard shapes for this lesson. You may want to precut bristol board into manageable sizes. The students will be sandwiching the corrugated cardboard to form sturdy mobile elements.

The kind of hangers recommended for our mobiles are those with the paper tube crossbar. The cardboard tube may be removed, leaving the wire frames for the mobile's structural base. Three hangers per student makes a respectable mobile.

Fishing leader line is a nylon thread that will be good for the mobile's hanging parts. If "invisible" line is not available, substitute with string—but the illusion of free floating elements can be quite enchanting. Pliers will be needed to manipulate the wire. Needle-nose pliers are best for the task.

This lesson will require several sessions.

DIRECTIONS

1. Discuss the basic nature of mobiles. They are art objects in space defined by the interrelated motion of their components. Many are made of simple shapes, but we'll be more detailed.

2. Think about situations in which people must interact, as in teams, dance troops, and circus acts. It's an exciting list—you can also include scuba divers and astronauts. Interacting with fish, and the moon and stars, will be acceptable, too!

3. Distribute all materials. After picking a theme, draw your figures. Try to show motion and expression. Try drawing talking (or thinking) "balloons"—the kind used in cartoons. (The mobile in Figure 175 shows talking balloons that have been cut out as part of each mobile element contour.) Imagine what your characters have on their minds or what sort of conversations they might be having with each other.

4. Cut elements from bristol board. You'll need to cut all shapes in doubles. Repeat the same contours and cut from the corrugated cardboard.

5. Glue all corresponding parts together, sandwich-style. Block in bright colors and patterns, front and back. Write "lines" into talking balloons, if desired.

6. Pierce holes for hanging with care (and teacher assistance) at the tops of various shapes. String fishing line through holes and tie one end.

7. Assemble mobile as shown in Figure 176. Balance may need adjustment. Weigh down elements with small handy items (paper clips, pennies) until desired symmetry (or assymmetry) is achieved.

8. Test "flight paths" to make sure that parts work together without interfering with one another. Manipulate with pliers—bend, stretch, or retract as needed.

9. Hang mobile elements on the coat hangers as shown. Mobiles may be hung from a clothesline that you may string up in the classroom.

10. Mobiles that not only display motion but exhibit conversational skills, too, are hard to beat, especially ones with lines like these!

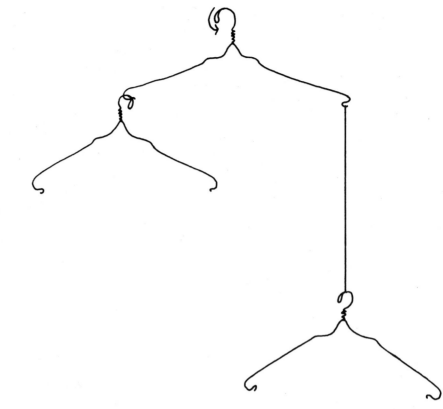

FIGURE 176. Hangers should be joined as indicated to form mobile.

ACTIVITY 71
Wired Up!

DRAWING EXERCISE: Wire Sculpture

Line and wire are like first cousins. The family resemblance is undeniable. Both are able to show volume very simply with just a curve or a twist. When you build up wire, it becomes more massive. It is dimensional and occupies space. Therefore, it is considered sculpture, while line in drawing stays within the two-dimensional plane. But both have their magic, making us believe in the shapes they define mostly by their expressive movement. A wiry line can say so much!

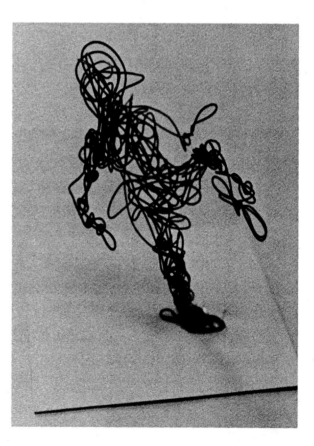

FIGURE 177. There is drawing in sculpture, just as there is sculpture in drawing. This lively figure attests to both!

FIGURE 178. Quick spiral sketches help capture the immediate movement of the pose.

MATERIALS

- Soft wire (see Teacher Preparation)
- Wire cutters
- Pencils
- Practice paper
- Staple gun
- Steel wool (optional; see Teacher Preparation)

TEACHER PREPARATION

You'll need a soft, flexible wire. It must be malleable for this lesson. If you don't have any in your art room supply closet, the local hardware store is a ready source. Spools of either copper, brass, or soft steel will do the trick. Should you have access to the wire used for telephone installations, you are in luck, also. (NOTE: Copper phone wire may be a bit soft. Double it if you use it, and build the figure's legs up heavier for greater support. Do not use solder with lead in it at all!) Wire cutters, or pliers with a wire cutting edge, are needed to cut the wire into sections. Prepare to let each student have several pieces.

Corrugated cardboard will make the bases for our wire sculpture. Two- or three-ply is fine, but you may need a mat knife for cutting through it by teacher only. You may want to glue cardboard layers together for thickness, but it is not required. Single-ply is quite suitable.

Steel wool (no soap pads, please) may be torn into tufts and used for hair if desired. Watch out for metal splinters.

DIRECTIONS

1. Start with your drawing materials. We'll move from two-dimensional to three-dimensional expression, swinging over from pencil line to wire sculpture. Two student volunteers should be drafted to model for each action sketch.

2. Student models will assume a pose that requires activity, such as shaking hands, dancing, and so on. Poses should be timed by teacher with a watch (preferably with a second hand) to about three minutes. At that time, direct student models to change into another action pose. Models should stand where they can be seen by the rest of the class. The models can interact together or stand separately.

3. Demonstrate to students how to draw using the coiling line, as shown in Figure 178. Try to draw quick, spring-like sketches in response to poses. Spirals are reminiscent of wire and make for an easy transition. Students may draw one or both models.

4. Drawing may end after about ten minutes. This is essential as a means for "warm-up." Turn your attention to the wire now. Several lengths should be provided for each student.

5. Student models are no longer necessary although you may prefer to let them continue. Your sketches are your frame of reference. Pick a pose for interpretation in wire.

6. Those familiar stick men can be used for starting your wire sculpture. You will be bending active stick figures—show points of stress. Don't be afraid to exaggerate.

7. Build mass by wrapping wire around the stick men. It is not unlike the spiral lines in the drawings. You may need to hook wire ends to core figure in order to begin building up your forms.

8. Add steel wool. Use it to accentuate the direction of the figures' action. Steel wool hair, if it is used, should appear to be in movement, so adjust accordingly.

9. Tape figures to cardboard base. Use a staple gun to fix the figures in place.

10. Do you have a showcase? Exhibit these wiry guys in twos, threes, or groups. Figures should appear to interact and will surely elicit attention.

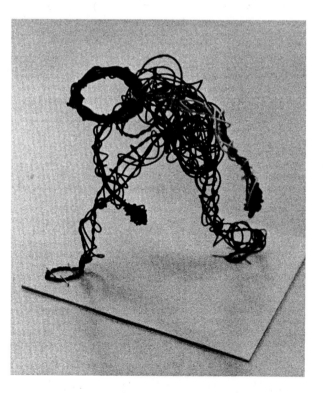

FIGURE 179. Talk about affirmative action!

ACTIVITY 72
Absurd Assemblages

3-D CONSTRUCTION: Found Object Sculpture

Dada was the name given to a group of artists who seemed to enjoy tickling imaginations. Their art was whimsical, even silly. Dadaists produced questionable, nonetheless amusing, objects of art. They were zany, but not without their charm, these outrageous assemblages of Dada art!

FIGURE 180. Art that tickles more than the imagination! A feathered scale would cheer even the most determined dieter.

MATERIALS

- Acrylic paints or poster paints
- Markers
- Cardboard paper odds and ends
- Scissors
- Hammer and nails
- Glue
- Scrap materials of all kinds (see Teacher Preparation)
- 3″ × 5″ cards
- Pens

TEACHER PREPARATION

The form of found object sculpture we'll be making will be as nonsensical as the infamous Dada fur-lined teacup—and just as much fun! Students and teacher will have to save no-longer-working household objects before they get discarded, such as broken clocks, old shoes, empty product containers, small desk lamps (that are ready for retirement), umbrellas that don't open anymore, broken toy trucks—all things of this sort. In other words, assorted junk. A selective junk drive within your school to furnish objects for this activity might also be considered.

Scrap fabrics, feathers, shoeboxes, papers, and other materials you have stocked in your classroom will also be useful. *But please note:* because of the serendipitous nature of this activity, needs for specific items or supplies may occur as ideas develop. It is difficult to predict exactly what will be needed in each case. Try to plan the lesson presentation with an allowance for response time to individual supply requirements.

DIRECTIONS

1. Gather all the glorious junk that has been donated to the cause. Review the array with students, asking for identification of each item's normal function. Follow with the question of how could we reverse or change uses of items to render them entirely absurd? Here are some concepts that might give you something to think about:
   —A clock with many hands and a different sort of face (with numbers in no particular sequence)
   —A lamp that sits upside down with a light bulb glued on the wrong end
   —An umbrella that has cut-outs through its fabric
   —Sunglasses with miniature shutters or window shades

   The list goes on. Also, consider making smaller models for the larger-scaled ideas. For example, a house made of feathers might be fashioned from a shoebox, or a model of a chair without a seat and back could be constructed as a model from cardboard.

2. Begin construction. Use objects for spare parts, trading off with one another. Share, alter, and add. Attach wheels from broken toys; hook up cords that don't logically connect anything; stick on handles where they don't belong—go to it!

3. All art supplies should be available for assembly purposes. Teacher should offer technical assistance as indicated, particularly with hammer and nails. Apply paint and glue to all parts. Let dry.

4. Fold 3″ × 5″ cards in half to use in identifying your wacky assemblages. Give an appropriate title, like Swiss Cheese Umbrella, The House That Tickles (feather house model), A Clock That's Right No Times a Day, etc. Use your poetic license here. Sign your name.

5. Want to have some fun with the display? Besides the showcase, place the assemblages (with I.D. tags) where they are least expected. For instance, a niche in the teacher's lounge, a dull corner in the school office, or a shelf in the library. Take advantage of the element of surprise, which is the operative behind these lovable, nutty Dada-esque works!

ACTIVITY 73
Lights! Camera! Action!

ACTION PAINTING: Gift Wrap, Bookcovers

It has been observed that the patterns on Jackson Pollock's canvases look much like a house painter's drop cloth. The resemblance is not entirely coincidental. Both are, in fact, the result of action. Drips, splotches, and splats were the badges of the action painter. This was Instant Art—fling the paint! Wherever the colors land, that's the painting!

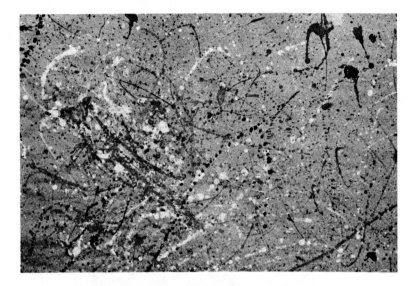

FIGURE 181. A call to action answered by a flick of the wrist and by blowing paint through a drinking straw.

MATERIALS

- Butcher paper
- Poster paints
- Paintbrushes
- Rulers
- Pencils
- Scissors
- One drinking straw per student

TEACHER PREPARATION

Precut butcher paper to cover several desks. Because of the nature of this lesson, it's advisable to cover the floor and move back the extra furniture. Smocks should be worn, of course. But most important, be clear on behavioral expectations. Students will flip paint from their brushes and onto the paper in front of them—not anywhere else. Blatant disregard should suggest the end of the lesson. However, the freedom to move about might be granted if cooperative behavior is demonstrated.

Painting by blowing through straws is fun, but should *not* be overdone to the point where children get winded. Be aware of any students with respiratory conditions, such as asthma, and regulate the use of straws accordingly.

Poster paint should be in accessible containers, within students' reach. Paint should not be too thick. NOTE: the last step of this activity, which yields the final product, will take place after the paint dries. Also, leave *plenty* of time for clean-up.

DIRECTIONS

1. Spread paper over desks. All supplies are in place. Load your brushes with paint. Students will probably do better to paint standing up. Ready, aim, fire!

2. Fling paint onto paper. A simple flick of the wrist will do it. Aim for a specific spot near you. Blow through straws directly onto paint to further manipulate it.

3. Sure you're painting spontaneously, but you can still make decisions. Where does the pattern lack a spot of paint? What color? Respond!

4. When paper is covered with your remarkable blobs, initial your area. Let paper dry to the touch.

5. Measure a sizable section of paper, equitable to others on your action painting panel. Cut out a liberal rectangle.

6. There you have it—original gift wrap! May also be used for a snappy book cover. Such is the gift of your art!

FIGURE 182. That wraps it!

ACTIVITY 74
I Must Be Dreaming!

MIXED MEDIA: Drawing

Surrealism loves to change the rules. Gravity is defied; perspective and proportions are altered. Places and things are not where they should be, and the unexpected happens! Even time itself takes on new meaning. It is the Art of the Impossible and the Incredible. Reality does not exist as we know it in the outrageous world of surrealism.

FIGURE 183. If you've ever seen a purple cow or a parachute like this one, then you've seen surrealism.

MATERIALS

- 12″ × 15″ white paper
- Colored pencils or crayons
- Fine-tip markers
- Magazines (optional; see Teacher Preparation)
- Glue (if magazines are used)
- Scissors (if magazines are used)

TEACHER'S PREPARATION

Any popular magazines will work for this activity if you wish to use them. They must contain clear photographic images. Home decorating, fashion, sports, car, and truck magazines are all suggested, but, again, use of magazines is optional.

Some good examples of surrealism may be found among the works of René Magritte. Have these reproductions and others on hand.

If your art room does not include a chalkboard, plan to include a large sketchpad or poster-sized paper to display the list as shown in the directions.

This lesson will require more than one class session to complete.

DIRECTIONS

1. Observe the examples of surrealism you have on hand. What is it about these pictures that makes them so strange? The objects in surrealism have a basis in reality, and may even be ordinary. But the artist has changed their definitions somehow—either through manipulating their size, dimension, basic characteristics—or through an unlikely combining of elements. Surrealistic imagery often resembles the atmosphere of dreams.

2. It's time for demonstrating the sensibility of surrealism on the chalkboard. In one column, create a list of places and locations. Right next to it, a list of common objects or animals. Teacher may start lists and students will contribute suggestions. It may look something like this:

Outer Space	Elephant
Desert	Typewriter
Seashore	Bedroom slipper
Mountain top	Hot dog
Sky	Toothbrush
Frozen lake	Eyeball
Highway	Sofa

   Draw random connecting lines between the two columns. Can you imagine these objects together? How would you illustrate such a picture?

3. Distribute all materials. Ideas on the chalkboard should help with themes; mainly, the lists dramatize the meaning of surrealism and stimulate imaginations. Images culled from magazines may be used as the major component of surrealistic compositions, but are not essential. Students may find that cutting out their own drawn images, then pasting them down on their pictures, can work out just as well.

4. Consider where items would *not* be found. Use clear, precise imagery if possible. If you are cutting photographs or drawings, cut along contour and glue in place. Remember, upside-down is all right.

5. Compositions may be illogical, but drawing should be sharp and "readable." Students' own dreams—particularly vivid ones they can recall in detail—may be used as personal reference.

6. Finished pictures might be displayed by students or teacher in novel ways. Perhaps upside-down, on pieces of classroom furniture, or where they might be least expected. This is, after all, surrealism. Surprise us!

ACTIVITY 75
The Sky's the Limit

DESIGN: Architecture

They can strain the neck as well as the imagination, these steel giants that reach high into the clouds. Gleaming with pride, towering skyscrapers form the familiar skylines of major cities around the world. But never take these structures for granted, for they are true wonders of design. Tons of metal, holding steadfast, yet soaring to incredible heights! Their very existence bears hard evidence to the accomplishment of human endeavor. Skyscrapers are the bright, shining monuments to the art and science of architecture itself.

FIGURE 184. Men and women at work! The grillage is the structure on which that amazing architectural wonder, called a skyscraper, is built. The core, or center of the building, is the central source of all support.

FIGURE 185. The occupied building is buzzing with activity! Finishing touches are being applied to the interior, as your can see on the scaffold.

FIGURE 186. Believe it or not, the outside of the skyscraper offers virtually no support at all! Called the "curtain wall," the facade is essentially decorative—and of course separates the interior from the elements of weather. Fancy that!

FIGURE 187. Fait accompli. The skyscraper is standing because all its "layers" are so carefully planned. Well done!

MATERIALS

- Pencils
- Yardsticks
- Brown butcher wrap (see Teacher Preparation)
- Markers
- Poster paints
- Acrylic paints in metallic colors
- Flat and wide paintbrushes in assorted sizes
- Scissors
- Stapler

TEACHER PREPARATION

We will be creating three-layered skyscrapers. The first panel will represent the framework, e.g., the building core, the grillage (criss-crossed beams), girders, etc. The second panel will reveal the occupied building, a kind of "see-through" to the everyday activities going on inside. The third panel, the façade, (also called the curtain wall) will reflect the style of the skyscraper, as well as the materials from which it was constructed. Students will then work in teams of six to fabricate it; two students to each panel, six students to each team. Cut number of vertical panels in quantities needed. Adjust your room arrangement to this team project accordingly. Lengths of panels should match in threes—their predetermined yardage is discretionary.

Reference materials on architectural styles of skyscrapers should be furnished along with illustrations of tall city buildings under construction. The children's library is a suggested source for picture books on this topic.

Several class sections will be required for the completion of this activity.

DIRECTIONS

1. Discuss skyscrapers and their construction. Have you ever watched a building going up? What happens on the inside and the outside? Explain.

2. Look over reference materials. Consider the use of building materials, architectural styles, and function of various elements.

3. Distribute all art supplies. Assign panels to teams (two partners on each panel, three panels to a team). Divide the labor. Decide who will do which one of the panels. Consult each other on your plans. You may wish to cut contours of the buildings. Be sure they conform with corresponding panels. Paint when ready.

4. Partners on the structural framework panel will want to depict building core, girders, beams, and so forth. You can show workers and equipment too—this is a hard hat area!

5. Partners on the inside occupied building will reveal what goes on in those busy offices. Determine how many floors you'd like to *reasonably* include. Basements and boiler rooms are great, but be sure that everything will line up when layers are attached.

6. Partners on the facade will need to think mainly about materials and style, and about matching windows with inside activity. Remember proportion and scale.

7. Flesh it out, add telling details. Let dry.

8. Sandwich all three layers together. Cut out windows if desired. Join with staples to form the world's tallest book. It tells the story of the skyscrapers, inside-out. Display in a dazzling line-up. It's your class's own original skyline!

ART OF THE AMERICAS

America is heir to many states-of-art. We may claim the furniture and crafts of the colonial period, or outstanding individual artists, such as Mary Cassatt, Maurice Prendergast, Horace Pippin, or William Glackens; there's a long line, right up to Georgia O'Keefe. And we may rightly be proud of the many charming American folk arts as well.

Yet among the most powerful of the American arts is that of a nation within a nation—the art of the Native American Indian. The ancient history and spiritual imagery of the many tribes that comprise American Indian art is rich indeed. Pottery, sand painting, decorative crafts, and artifacts bear the powerful design motifs of this compelling art form.

The scope of Indian art goes beyond our borders. We have the striking totemic carvings of the Northwestern Indians and Eskimos to the North, and the vibrant and varied textures of Mexican and Guatemalan crafts to the South.

When it comes to first-rate native crafts, we are positioned most advantageously!

ACTIVITY 76
Made in the U.S.A.

PAPER CRAFTS: Colonial Design

Unlike mass-produced goods today, colonial crafts were carefully honed by an artisan's hands. Such labors were realized in exquisitely turned woodwork and meticulous detail. There is much interest today in Early American decorative arts, as witnessed in our love of antiques. Furniture reproductions of the colonial period are among our most popular. It is clear that Americans like their furnishings to have a sense of history.

FIGURE 188. A cozy Colonial home in Philadelphia. How do we know? Independence Hall is right outside the window!

MATERIALS

- 12″ × 18″ oaktag
- Drawing paper
- Glue
- Scissors
- Crayons
- Fabric and paper scraps (see Teacher Preparation)
- Sewing supplies (optional)
- Wallpaper books (see Teacher Preparation)
- Paper doilies (see Teacher Preparation)
- Furniture catalogs (see Teacher Preparation)
- Wood-grain self-stick vinyl (optional)

TEACHER PREPARATION

Wallpaper books containing small country prints will be of great value in this activity. Wrapping paper may also be used. Paper and fabric scraps in old-fashioned patterns and fabrics such as calico, velvet, and brocade will be needed. Sewing supplies aren't necessary, but may be requested by ambitious students. Paper doilies, cut into small sections for picture accents, are recommended. Wood-grain self-stick vinyl such as Contact® paper is fun to use, but not required.

Furniture catalogs that illustrate colonial-style pieces are desirable—they'll be cut up by students for their pictures. Reference books on colonial furniture and crafts are helpful. Students may also wish to bring in miniature models of furnishings from doll houses for further reinforcement and fun. Reproductions of paintings by American primitive painters and early American artists are suggested. Much later, Horace Pippin's paintings are fine examples of American decorative design in art.

This lesson will require a few class sessions.

DIRECTIONS

1. Look over reproductions of colonial art, including doll house furnishings, if available. Also note furniture styles and the qualities of folk art. Colonial furniture has the graceful flowing lines of European influence, while folk arts are rustically charming. Consider paintings of the era, too.

2. Distribute all materials. Students will plan a two-dimensional Early American interior—not unlike a dollhouse room in concept. First consider the wall coverings and floors. "Install" wallpaper and floor. Draw floor planks or use wood-grain self-stick-vinyl.

3. Cut furniture from catalogs. Plan your room as you proceed. Fixtures not found in catalogs may be drawn in crayon on paper, cut out, and glued on. Utilize fabric scraps. Add people in appropriate costumes.

4. Accessories may be included, such as fireplaces, spinning wheels, and grandfather clocks. Pets could be included, too! Be sure furniture and people are in proper scale. NOTE: furniture may be drawn first on wrong side of self-stick vinyl, then cut and applied.

5. Is there Colonial art on the walls? You should have samples as a reference. Create some "paintings" to hang in your cozy room. A hooked rug on the floor or a set of silver teapots and cups all lend warmth.

6. An all-American room is what you have in the end. It's as American as apple pie, and every bit as delightful. Display.

SUGGESTIONS FOR FURTHER DEVELOPMENT

Ambitious teachers may wish to retrieve cardboard cartons that are similar in scale to the drawing paper. These may be cut to match the size of the drawings, which can be glued inside the box. Students, working as teams, would then decorate the front side(s) of the carton in construction paper and poster paint—treating the facade as a colonial style house. Carpet remnants or wood-grain self-stick vinyl may be installed on the "floor." Architectural elements—such as a roof and chimney—may be fashioned as desired; windows and doors cut out with a mat knife (by the teacher only!) to reveal interiors. Result? A doll of a house!

ACTIVITY 77
All Along the American Highway

SIGN MAKING: Weather vanes

Signs offer quick directions and deliver messages. True or false? Both, actually—for that narrow definition does not begin to tell of the rich legacy of American sign making! The outstanding American sign was at once purposeful and artistic—even poetic. It announced the personality of a shop or an inn even before one entered—bidding the customer welcome, or the weary traveler rest. All was made clear through picturesque words and images that inspired imaginations and whetted appetites.

Not all signs were swinging over doors. Carved, painted figures—such as the infamous wooden Indian chief at the tobacco shop—alerted passersby to a merchant's wares. Weather vanes, too, reported information through the movement of their evocative silhouettes.

There have indeed been many signs along the American road, and they've had a great deal more to say than "No Left Turn!"

FIGURE 189. "The Cat in the Bag" is a student's original interpretation of an old saw. Try some popular sayings or proverbs for your sign.

MATERIALS

- Cardboard (see Teacher Preparation)
- Poster paints or acrylic paints
- Glue
- Dowels (see Teacher Preparation)
- Mat knife (for use by teacher only)
- Practice paper
- Pencils
- Scissors
- Markers (optional)
- Hinges (see Teacher Preparation)
- Butcher wrap paper (optional)

TEACHER PREPARATION

Cardboard from appliance cartons may be used for more substantial signs, but heavy posterboard will also do. If you are planning to make a weather vane (see Part Two of the activity), dowels will authenticate the form. Cardboard that does not yield to the scissors may require your intervention with a mat knife.

NOTE: Weather vanes are generally made of copper. You may want to stick closer to this traditional material by fashioning your weather vanes from copper foil. Of course, cardboard may be painted entirely in copper acrylic paint, but students may not find this to be as colorful as nontraditional painted silhouettes. Copper acrylic may still be included in your colorful weather vane painting, nonetheless. You may want to paint selected areas in copper color, or "glaze" your (dry) weather vane figure with a mixture of copper paint and water to create light iridescence.

Reference materials may include books on American folk arts and crafts as well as guidebooks to country inns that include examples of signs.

This lesson has two distinct parts. Part One is a sign-making activity. Part Two is intended for weather vane production.

DIRECTIONS

Part One: Signs

1. Discuss the uses for signs in general and their function in early American society. Might signs have been designed to attract attention and ensure clarity with pictures for people who could not read? Were they not also a means of simple advertisement? Discuss.

2. Often signs that swung above inns and taverns had colorful names. Do you know of any that are descriptive in this way? For example, there are country inns today that bear names like "Inn of the Raven" or "The Black Bass Hotel." In old Philadelphia, there still stands "The Man Full of Troubles Tavern"!

3. Distribute practice paper, pencil, and scissors. Study reference material for lettering styles, pictorial images, and sign shapes of the period. Try some ideas for trade signs or

FIGURE 190. Warm summer
evenings on the veranda...these
flamingos say it all!

FIGURE 191. There are signs that
advertise services, such as shoe
repair, that are still popular today.
Shaped signs are always pleasing!

FIGURE 192. Tacos, you say?
Mexican food is all the rage!

inn signs. What if you need a sign for *your* store or hotel? Practice your name as part of the sign design and decide what product or service you might have been providing. What were some colonial trades?

4. When a sign image and shape is settled upon, students may begin to cut cardboard. Outlining the shape before you cut may help with execution. NOTE: Symmetrical sign styles, such as Chippendale, may first be cut from (folded) butcher paper, then traced and cut from paperboards.

5. Paint the symbols and pictures on your sign simply and directly. Lettering and numbers may be done with markers if desired.

6. Consider the surface treatment. Is it supposed to be a wooden sign? Most old signs were made of wood. Add "knotty" touches and distress lines to affect realism.

7. Hang out your shingle!

Part Two: Weather Vanes

1. Weather vanes conveyed messages about weather through the figures and symbols that best suited the region in which they were crafted. For instance, farm animals are common in country weather vanes; sea creatures, such as dolphins and mermaids, along the seacoasts. Figures from mythology were popular, too, like Diana, the huntress, with her bow and arrow. Study examples should be provided in reference materials—angels with trumpets, racing horses, and crowing roosters, too!

2. Students will practice ideas on scratch paper. Old-fashioned images, based on traditional material in reference books, or "new-fangled" vanes that express the student's own environment, may be used.

3. Transfer idea onto cardboard. Keep fingers at a *manageable* size: 2½ feet is a fine length. Cut out.

4. Paint. Details are desirable even though vanes are of a silhouette dimension.

5. Completed vanes may be mounted on dowels. Hardware hinges may be utilized to ease mounting and to allow movement:

   a. Push dowel (with approximate diameter of ⅜″) *between* layers of corrugated board—far enough for figure* to sit securely upon it, but *not* all the way through the other end. NOTE: Glue should not be used at juncture if movement of vane is desired.
   b. If directional attachment has been produced, also push it through the corrugated board at N/S/E/W intersection. Reinforce with glue at joints.
   c. Top should be free to rotate. However, cardboard weather vanes should not be exposed to the elements.

6. Vanes should be displayed where they can respond to wind, yet are protected from the elements (unless you have used wood for fabrication). A patch of grass under a shelter would be an ideal place to stake the vanes into the ground and let them loose. They are mostly decorative—but if they have a chance to tell you which way the wind blows, you can be sure they will!

---

* Keep figure smaller, rather than larger, for better support (e.g., 2½ feet).

FIGURE 193. Does the mermaid
weather vane hear the sea in her shell?

ACTIVITY 78
Quilts That Won't Quit

PAPER CRAFTS: Paper Quilts

You can't get much more American than a good old-fashioned quilt. With lyrical names like Star of Bethlehem, Log Cabin, and Bee on a Bear's Nose, quilts surely possess the American pioneeer spirit. Their patchwork may be presented in squares of symmetrical bouquets or in a happy hodge-podge of appliques, scattered over an aptly named crazy quilt. Whatever format it took, the quilt was, in the end, a kind of cloth history book, incorporating bits and snatches of peoples' lives. It would not be an exaggeration to say that quilts greatly contributed to the very fabric of American folk art!

FIGURE 194. Many happy memories have gone into the making of this cheerful quilt. Students brought in scraps of wrapping paper from birthday presents received, friendly notes and cards sent to them, even the candy wrappers from favorite sweets!

MATERIALS

- Brown butcher wrap (see Teacher Preparation)
- Pencils
- Yardstick
- Colored paper (see Teacher Preparation)
- Assorted paper scraps (see Teacher Preparation)
- Scissors
- Glue
- Oil pastels

TEACHER PREPARATION

Teacher will precut butcher wrap to accommodate six to eight students. Each length will represent a "quilt." The easiest way to establish butcher wrap section sizes is to allocate one quilt per seating, for example, one per desk cluster or worktable. Cut as needed.

You will find that providing a grid on the butcher paper for the paper quilt "patches" is an efficient approach to this lesson. (See Figure 195.) Measure squares or diamonds in pencil to match the colored paper squares students will be "quilting." Six inches is a good size for squares; leave at least a three-inch border on the butcher wrap between the squares along the outside edge. Precutting construction paper squares also saves time.

FIGURE 195. Mapping out a grid like this one expedites quilt production. Students simply glue completed quilt squares into matching squares, then flesh out borders. Make the squares six inches and leave three inches between the squares.

Students will have to be told in advance of this lesson to begin saving and retrieving bits of particular scrap papers. The papers may include gift wrap, greeting cards or postcards, favorite candy wrappers, ticket stubs, and otherwise appealing design paper, such as the wrapper of a special soap. The greater the personal meaning, the better for the quilting bee. Teacher may contribute with back-up scraps of all kinds.

Reference materials on American textiles and quiltmaking may be provided. If you have a real handmade quilt, bring it in.

This lesson will take several sessions to complete and is presented in two parts.

DIRECTIONS

Part One

1. Show students illustrations of American quilt designs or any examples of actual fabric quilts you might have. Point out that saving of fabric from garments long since worn out was the basis for quilts—an early form of what we now call "recycling." How were quilts made? Some combined patchwork and appliqué. Try to analyze sewing techniques based on your samples and references.

2. Consider quilt patterns and subjects as well as the meanings some might have to the artisan. Also note the social nature of quilting, which included the opportunity for folks to get together and share experiences and news. Ask students to show some of the papers they brought in and to tell of their significance.

3. Distribute precut squares, scissors, glue, and oil pastels. Cut scrap papers into desired patterns. These may be representational or straightforward designs. Glue into place.

4. Do as many "patches" as class time will allow. Just be sure "quilting" looks complete. Construction paper scraps may be used as "filler."

5. Oil pastels may be used to indicate "stitches." Work your signature or initials onto the patch.

Part Two

6. Distribute butcher wrap, oil pastels, and glue. Return completed squares. Keep paper nearby.

7. Glue patches into spaces provided by premeasured grid of brown paper. The area of one's immediate workspace is the fairest way to define "territory." If any squares come up short, students may fill in with extra scrap paper.

8. Each quilt will have a motif that will be drawn into the borders to unify all diverse patchwork. The group of students working on their quilt will agree on one common motif, for example, hearts, stripes, snowflakes, stars, daisies, etc. Each student will be responsible for the borders in his/her work area and will interpret the agreed-upon motif in his or her own way.

9. Completed quilts should look full and rich, just like the fabric counterpart does. The finished product should make us forget that we are looking at paper.

10. How many special memories have been "stitched" into these classic quilts? Well, time sure flies when you're making history. Preserve your artistry on the wall and display.

ACTIVITY 79
Old-Fashioned Fun and Games

FOLK ART TOYS: Jumping Jacks

You can almost hear the bouncy tune of a banjo when handmade toys hop and dance. Whirligigs, cornhusk and applecore dolls, mechanical banks—the engaging playthings from yesterday—have won many a youngster's heart. Grown-ups, too, delight in the craft and charm of our all-American toys.

FIGURE 196. "We're off to see the wizard...and Alice in Wonderland, too," the Tin Man and Tweedledee seem to be saying.

FIGURE 197. Uncle Sam, and his sweetie "Samantha," are clearly American folk heroes!

MATERIALS

- Manila paper
- Pencil
- Oaktag
- Markers
- Scissors
- Paper fasteners
- String
- Hole puncher

TEACHER PREPARATION

We'll be making our jumping jacks from oaktag, but there's no reason why you can't use wood construction as long as appropriate materials and means are available (lightweight wood, a jigsaw for cutting toy body parts, and cutters for holes to be drilled into joints). Either way, follow steps as directed.

Jumping jacks have traditionally been fashioned after popular or familiar personalities. In the South, "Seed Salesmen" have appeared as animated toys! Our jumping jacks will be based on favorite book characters or folk heroes. Students will need to visit the library prior to class presentation in order to make their selections. More than one choice is advised, so provide enough illustrations for students to use as reference.

You may want to make a basic demonstration model to better understand the construction. Students will also appreciate seeing the entire toy in advance.

You might cut the string for pulleys in lengths ahead of time to save time and confusion. You should be prepared to assist students in assembling the jumping jacks.

This activity will require more than one class session.

DIRECTIONS

1. Who are your favorite book characters? Snow White? Peter Pan? Puss 'n Boots? Here's your chance to bring literary personalities to life and make them dance. Choices may be culled from Mother Goose, Hans Christian Anderson, Aesop, Disney, the classic novels such as *Bluebeard, Robinson Crusoe,* and so forth.

2. After discussing possibilities, sketch out ideas in pencil on practice paper. Draw the entire figure, head to toe.

3. Pay attention to the costume when planning characters. What are some particulars that identify your choice? A musketeer's plumed hat? A basket of red apples? A parrot on the shoulder? Include the telling details.

4. Distribute oaktag, markers, and other materials. When you do decide on a character, outline body parts on oaktag, using the jumping jack demonstration model as a guide. (See Figures 198 and 199.) Cut the body parts you'll need for your jumping jack. Shapes (and details incorporated) may vary from the examples shown but keep it fairly simple. Skirts, for instance, are *not* recommended.

5. Flesh out the jumping jacks. Use markers for features, hair, etc.

6. Punch or pierce holes where indicated. Assemble with paper fasteners and attach pulleys as shown.

7. You bet they're jumpy! They're animated and cheerful, too. The library is an ideal place to showcase your folksy and literary luminaries.

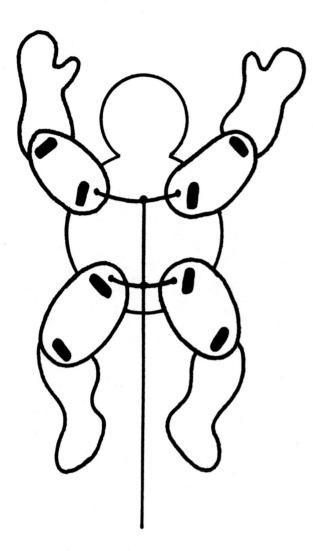

FIGURE 198. You will need three pieces of string—one long and two short. Thread through the holes as shown and knot inside the arms and legs.

FIGURE 199. Articulate by pulling the string.

SUGGESTIONS FOR FURTHER DEVELOPMENT

If you're often seeking projects with instant appeal for children, toys are the ticket. Antique American toys and games will yield scores of great ideas. Banks, for instance, may be fashioned easily from cigar boxes or shoeboxes. Pull toys can be simply constructed from corrugated cardboard; farm animals are always adorable. Wheels made from the same cardboard material—or added from discarded toys—make them even more irresistible. Puzzles, paper dolls, card or board games are educational and artistically sound. Reference material on American folk arts provide excellent prototypes.

Recommended: The Smithsonian Illustrated Library of Antiques: *Toys and Games* by William C. Ketchum, Smithsonian Institute, 1981, Cooper Hewitt Museum.

ACTIVITY 80
The Spirit of the Eagle:
Ceremonial Dance Masks

PAPER PLATE MASKS: Dance Masks

The powerful geometrics and dramatic color contrasts in American Indian art set it apart and establish its fiercely individual appearance. The earth elements—clouds, rain, fire, sun—combine with the spirit world in this compelling art form. Punctuated with feathers, fringe, and beads, Indian folk art delivers charm and magic!

FIGURE 200. It's difficult to believe that a common paper plate can be transformed into this compelling dance mask.

MATERIALS

- Markers
- Colorful felt scraps and strips
- Scissors
- Glue
- Paper plates
- String or yarn
- Staples

TEACHER PREPARATION

It's hard to believe that paper plates are behind this lesson, but they are very effective for mask construction. Be sure to have extra paper plates set aside for building mask forms.

Feathers are often available in hobby shops and in actual feather supply stores in many metropolitan areas. If you are unable to find feathers, you can cut feather shapes from colored paper and fringe them. But nothing beats dyed turkey feathers for this lesson!

You may want to precut felt into manageable sections instead of offering it to students in large pieces.

NOTE: The ceremonial dance mask lends itself to the discussion of American Indian life and the part that craft played in it. You may want to examine symbols and their meanings further. For beautiful illustrations of Indian art and accompanying information to share with students, try this excellent reference:

Dockstader, Frederick, J., *Indian Art in America,*
Promotory Press, New York.

Should this particular text not be available, you'll want to have some good examples of Southwest Indian design on hand.

DIRECTIONS

1. Discuss the distinctive motifs of Native American design. How do they achieve their visual impact? Consider the power in their simplification of shapes: eyes may be narrow rectangles, mouths might be slits or crescents. All this gives Indian art much visual appeal.

2. Distribute materials. Extra paper plates may be used to develop the ceremonial headdresses that are often extensions of the dance mask form.

3. Apply markers and felt in strong geometric patterns. Remember, facial features are represented in the same way as the rest of the symbols in the design—symmetrically and thoughtfully placed.

4. Pierce, then cut open the spaces for eyes and the insertion of string. Add all decorative touches—use feathers to accentuate. Stapler may be employed for reinforcement.

5. String yarn through holes. These magical masks may be worn and most certainly displayed!

ACTIVITY 81
Hopi Kachina: A Real Doll

3-D CRAFTS: Dolls

They can be friendly, comic, or downright menacing—they are the remarkable Kachina dolls! To the Zuñi and Hopi tribes, Kachinas are not merely toys. They are the embodiments of the legendary Kachina spirits who were believed to bring the rain. Children now receive the dolls as gifts at dances that celebrate Kachina. They are indeed a treat for young Native Americans, and a delightful way to keep the Kachina spirit alive!

FIGURE 201. Kachina dolls are both playful and powerful. Note the details of this figure—the Zūni belt, for instance.

FIGURE 202. Design elements and details carry from front to back.

MATERIALS

- Drawing or manila paper
- Acrylic paints
- Paintbrushes
- Yarn
- Feathers
- Scissors
- Masking tape
- Glue
- Fabric and paper, including foil (see Teacher Preparation)
- Beads (optional)
- Shoebox lids (see Teacher Preparation)
- Stapler
- Soft wire
- Applicator sticks (see Teacher Preparation)

TEACHER PREPARATION

Cardboard rolls will provide the basic form for our Kachina dolls. (See Figures 203, 204, and 205.) Ask students to save the rolls from bathroom paper or kitchen wrap. Soft wire may be cut with wire cutters—use these as cores for arms and legs. Fabric and felt scraps,

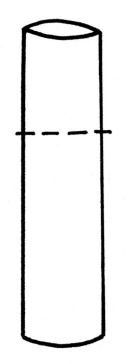

FIGURE 203. Cut the top off for the head.

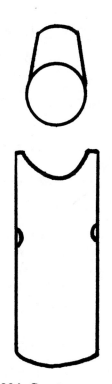

FIGURE 204. Create a scoop for the head rest. The pierce the sides for wire core or pipe cleaner arms.

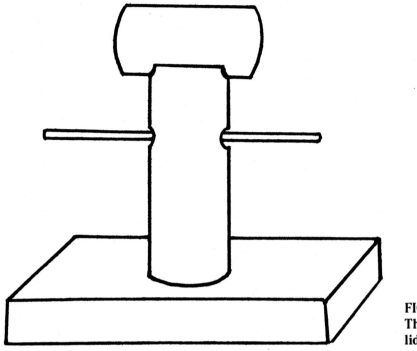

FIGURE 205. Assemble as shown. The base is the optional shoebox lid.

as well as fringe remnants and beads, will enhance the texture of the Kachina dolls. You might want to cut some malleable foil in small circles to replicate Zūni belts and jewelry in scale for your doll. Yarn can be cut ahead of time for hair. Applicator sticks are available in most drug stores and are excellent for use as accessories, such as bows and arrows.

Shoebox lids will provide fine bases for stabilizing dolls, although bases are not always necessary if dolls are well balanced.

Reference materials on the arts and crafts of the Southwest American Indians should aid students with design elements. Pictures of various kinds of Kachinas will demonstrate the differences in the dolls' appearances.

DIRECTIONS

1. Discuss the customs that surround Kachina spirits. Compare the styles and expressions of the dolls.

2. Distribute all materials. If necessary, cut cardboard tubes to desired lengths. Notch the bottom of the roll to represent feet if desired. Cut a section from the opposite end to provide for the doll's head. Also, notch the tube's top. (See Figures 203, 204, and 205.)

3. Cut holes in the sides of the tube for arms, which will be constructed from one piece of rolled paper. Insert pipe cleaner or a wire core through the holes like a crossbar, then build by wrapping paper around it. (Paper may be wrapped around wire beforehand, then fed through holes).

4. Paint the face and body with strong, simple geometric designs. Also, decorate the box lid. Let dry.

5. Clothing, such as skirts, ponchos, headdresses, pouches for arrows, and papooses, may be constructed independently, then attached to the doll with glue or staples. Ornamental details, like beads, necklaces, and conch belts in the Zuñi style, may be added.

6. Glue or staple the Kachina to the base. Your doll may or may not bring the rain, but it will surely draw favorable comments.

ACTIVITY 82
Ghost Dance Shirts

COSTUME: Design, Drawing

The art of the Plains Indian is filled with stories, symbols, and pictures. But you will not find these images painted on a canvas. Rather, it was animal hides—used also for shelter and clothing—on which Indians illustrated their hopes and dreams. The designs on tepees, shields, and clothing often held meanings that went far beyond their artistic significance. Some patterns were actually a kind of record keeping, or they might have been calendars of the cycles of the moon and sun. Among its intended uses, Ghost Dance shirts were made to recount important events and to bring protection to the wearers. The shirt was regarded as a source of power and strength.

FIGURE 206. Ghost Dance shirt by Danika, age 10.

MATERIALS

- Brown butcher wrap (see Teacher Preparation)
- Scissors
- Crayons
- Markers (optional)
- Glue
- Feathers (See Teacher Preparation)

TEACHER PREPARATION

Cut the brown butcher wrap ahead of time to allow one "shirt" for each student, keeping close to life-size in scale. You may want to cut the shirt shapes in advance of class. Several shirts can be cut at the same time. (See Figures 208 and 209.)

Feathers will enhance the shirts and lend authenticity to them. Turkey feathers (known as "fluffs") dyed in bright colors are ideal. However, you may substitute feathers with construction paper shaped and folded to resemble feathers. Other embellishments, such as beads, fabric scraps, and fringe may be incorporated as well. Reference materials on the customs and crafts of Plains Indians would be useful. Look for books on Indian picture language in particular.

DIRECTIONS

1. Discuss the artistry of the Plains Indians using reference materials to illustrate some examples. Students will want to share some of their perceptions.
2. Using the chalkboard, the teacher will draw several Indian pictorial symbols. Figure 207 shows a few basic concepts. Do not label them. Ask students to identify their meanings.

3. Distribute all materials. Students will use the shirt to tell a story in pictures, or relate a dream, or even give a weather report! Design motifs should be considered; strategic placement of decorative elements, such as feathers, should be planned for in advance.

4. Use scissors as creatively as your drawing tools. Fringe effects, as well as paper cuts, will add greatly to the appearance of your shirt. Color should be applied with attention to detail. Be sure to incorporate earth tones, such as tan, orange, brown, yellow, and so on.

5. Consider both front and back of the shirt. Designs should carry over, but do not necessarily have to be repeated. A large mythical animal—a thunderbird, for instance—is quite suitable for the back of the shirt.

6. Finished shirts make intriguing displays. They may be hung in a "clothesline" exhibit where both sides can be properly seen.

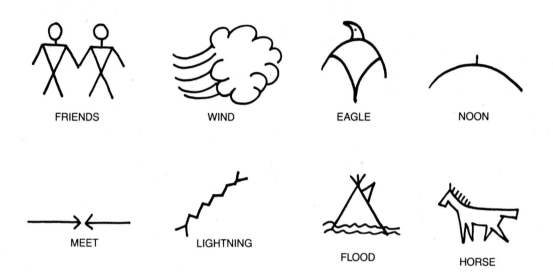

FIGURE 207. Examples of Indian picture language.

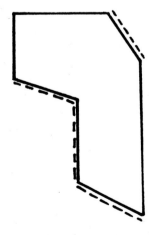

FIGURE 208. Step one: Fold brown butcher wrap paper and cut as shown.

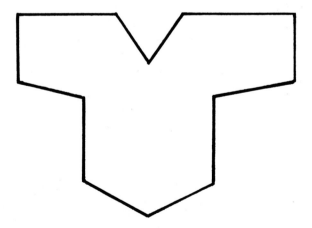

FIGURE 209. Step two: Open. You now have an Indian shirt.

SUGGESTIONS FOR FURTHER DEVELOPMENT

Another paper "artifact" that is simple to facilitate is the Indian shield. Oversized construction paper cut into ovals will do it. This quick activity will please children of all ages. Its design and decorative appeal is quite similar to "Ghost Dance Shirts." The same or similar motifs may be applied to shields as directed above.

ACTIVITY 83
Teddy Bear Totems

PAPER CONSTRUCTIONS: Drawing

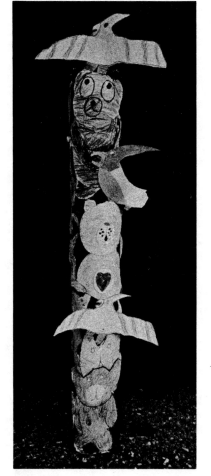

The Indians of the Northwest Coast are famous for the fierce faces they carved onto poles. Totems frequently represented animals—both real and fanciful. The hawks, eagles, beavers, and other animals that surround totem poles are thought to be linked with the formation of particular tribes, and thereby have an ancestral connection. Totem poles might mark the home of a chief or tell of a noble deed. One thing for sure, totems spelled importance. And among the most popular of all animals featured on these impressive poles was the great brown bear!

FIGURE 210. Feelings for students' own beloved animals are translated into a very friendly totem pole!

MATERIALS

- Manila paper
- White drawing paper
- Oil pastels
- Crayons
- Paints (optional)
- Paintbrushes (optional)
- Scissors
- Corrugated paper in rolls (see Teacher Preparation)
- Stuffed toys (see Teacher Preparation)
- Staple gun
- Glue (optional)

TEACHER PREPARATION

This is an irresistible excuse for younger students to bring their beloved stuffed animals to school. Have students bring their favorite soft toy animals to school the day the lesson is scheduled.

You will need a cardboard version of a totem pole on which the teddy bears and whatever else will be mounted. Should you have an appropriately-sized cardboard cylinder, by all means use it! Otherwise, corrugated paper from a roll may be wrapped around a few times to give it some stability; then staple it closed. Try to form a cylindrical pole of approximately twelve inches in diameter for your makeshift totem. You may need a few of these poles for your class.

Reference books on Eskimo art and the arts and crafts of the Northwest Coast Indians will be useful for this activity.

This lesson will require more than one class session.

FIGURE 211. A model totem is made by stacking third-graders' own soft toys that they brought to class just for this purpose.

DIRECTIONS

Part One

1. Students will introduce their stuffed animals to the class to begin the activity. They can give their soft pets' names and how they came by the little critters. Everyone should have a chance to share this information.

2. Collect all teddies and soft toys. Line up several chairs against a wall for support and create totems. Distribute manila paper and crayons.

3. Ask students what they think the animals, vertically displayed, are now supposed to resemble. Establishing the answer, the teacher will offer reference material and other significant points about totem poles. Were they not based on the important animals in the life of the artist?

4. Students will hold paper vertically, select a "soft" totem pole for a model—perhaps the one that contains their animal—and sketch it. The top-to-bottom drawing should assist in the understanding of the nature of totem design principles.

Part Two

5. Distribute white paper, crayons, and scissors.

6. Students will use the entire page for a selected animal. Two animals may be drawn together and on top of each other and should appear as one. The outside contour shape of the animal must be large and *simple*. Animals may be shown holding other animals, like a koala holding a rabbit, or they may be grasping an object, like an ice cream cone.

7. Remember expression! Even a little line that represents a teddy bear mouth can look awfully sad when pointing down, but very friendly as can be when slanted up! Position animals so they will stack when cut out.

8. Cut out along animals' outside shapes. Bring the corrugated paper totem pole(s) forward. Students may attach their paper tigers and not-so-ferocious bears either with glue or with the assistance of the teacher using a staple gun.

9. Paint may be used to enhance the totem's appearance.

10. Teddy bear totems may be installed to mark an important entrance or the home of a great leader. How about outside the principal's office? And, of course, at the door of the art room!

ACTIVITY 84
South of the Border: A Mexican Yarn

YARN PAINTING: Mirrors, Frames

The crafts of Mexico and Guatemala are as bright and sunny as the countries themselves. The regional arts of Mexico are unparalleled, both for their brilliance and distinctiveness of design. The brightly colored wall weavings, known as God's Eyes, have come to us through the Huichols. These Mexican artisans are also responsible for the *nierka,* the source of magical yarn painting. Electric, mystical imagery is described through yarn in flashy colors. It is arresting to the eye, intensely festive, and, above all, very Mexican.

FIGURE 212. Bright ideas from our Southern neighbors—yarn painting makes a crafty frame!

MATERIALS

- Cardboard (see Teacher Preparation)
- Yarn in bright, assorted colors
- Glue
- Scissors
- Pencils
- Practice paper
- Mat knife for teacher's use only (optional; see Teacher Preparation)
- Mirrors (see Teacher Preparation)
- Picture mounts (optional)

TEACHER PREPARATION

Each student will require a square of corrugated cardboard on which to mount mirrors. This will also serve as their frames. You may want to cut the corrugated cardboard ahead of time into eight-inch to ten-inch squares with a mat knife or sharp scissors.

Mirrors may be acquired as mirrored tiles from home center or decorating stores. The glass can be precut with a glass cutting tool to about six-inches. The place of purchase may do this for you. Teachers *only* should do the glass cutting. Handle mirrors with extreme care. Metal mirrors may be substituted for glass ones when feasible. Photographs or favorite pictures may be considered as an alternative if mirrors are completely unavailable.

NOTE: Positioning mirrors with glue on cardboard in advance and allowing glue to have setup time will help avoid the shifting of the mirror while students work with yarn. Yarn may also be precut in lengths.

Materials that illustrate the arts of Mexico and the dominant motifs are suggested. An excellent reference is

Crafts of Mexico, Chloe Sayer, Aldus Books, London, 1977

This lesson will require several sessions.

DIRECTIONS

1. Look over references. Name some popular patterns in Mexican arts. Birds, flowers, butterflies, and themes from nature are good subjects. Describe the Mexican arts—cheerful and full of life.

2. Distribute practice paper, pencils, and crayons. Try out some patterns and color schemes. When ready, make mirror/frames available.

3. Transfer pattern ideas in pencil to frame. Distribute yarn. Squeeze glue outline; lay in the yarn. Do not disturb it. Fill in *after* it sets up, work in *sections*. Simply follow the yarn contours.

4. Use bright, contrasting colors. Continue with overall design in yarn.

5. All areas must be filled in before yarn painting is finished. Darker yarn around the edges makes an effective border and will provide a finished look. Be careful around the edges of the mirror.

6. Now you have a Hall of Mirrors. Muy bonitas! (NOTE: Picture frame mounts, available in hardware stores, may be used according to package directions. Otherwise, stands for mirrors can be created from cardboard, as shown in Activity 19, Figure 52.)

SUGGESTIONS FOR FURTHER DEVELOPMENT

Pottery, tin craft, bright textiles, painted enamel chests—the crafts from south of the border are worth exploring with your students. A good reference book (see Teacher Preparation) will supply visuals; interpretation should come easily and enthusiastically!

ART OF THE MIDDLE AND FAR EAST

China. Japan. Arabia. India. The very names conjure up colorful, exotic images of distant lands. Although we may have never experienced these places firsthand, we probably have our notions about them just the same. In fact, much of our perception may have come to us by way of their art. We may know of Chinese watercolor painting and the art of the Japanese woodblock print. Indian temple sculpture is internationally reknowned as are the splendid carpets and Islamic tiles of the Orient—meaning, in this sense, the Middle East. Design motifs and patterns from the folk arts of these countries have long been assimilated by Western culture.

It's just as important to remember, too, that each of these countries has an art history all its own with periods and stages of art—sometimes even of dynasties—that are equal in breadth to their Western counterparts. There is a sensibility in each of these art forms—a way of seeing and expressing—that is wholly singular and unique. The delicacy of Chinese painting, for example, is in particular contrast to the direct and uncomprising imagery of Japanese woodblock art. You'll find that traditional Persian and Indian picture space are similarly depicted, but Indian subject matter is literally another story. The often surprising manifestations of Indian gods and goddesses and their ongoing involvement with the society on Earth make Indian art quite recognizable on its own. The mosque shapes, specific dress, and customs of the Middle East are clearly painted into their art as well. Yet these otherwise faraway countries are, in different ways, brought even a little closer to home through European art.

When the Japanese print was discovered by the French Impressionists and Post-Impressionists, it became an immediate source of fascination. The shapes and linear quality found in Japanese art was quickly absorbed by the likes of Degas, Lautrec, Cassatt, and Van Gogh. Individual artists pulled from other outside influences too, and have been doing so since travel and trade began. Even the innovative work of Matisse, for instance, drew heavily on the patterns of Moroccan fabric—his compositions on the tilted picture plane and "layer cake" space of Middle Eastern Painting—and his figures on the full volumes of Indian female sculptural form.

All this adds up to the fact that there is much cross-breeding in all of the arts. From the appearance of traditional Chinese porcelain designs in the Dutch-style tiles on our kitchen walls—to the symmetrical patterns of the carpets on our floors—influences are felt everywhere. When you stop to consider, these foreign places may not be so faraway after all!

ACTIVITY 85
Magic Carpets

"Rugs": Wet Chalk Painting with "Fringe" Benefits

Oriental rugs of the Middle East have been with us since Biblical days. Their sumptuous qualities have always drawn admiration and appreciation. Artists depicted oriental rugs in their visual subject selection since painting began. Persian rugs have endured. The variety within their woven patterns, their unsurpassed symmetry, and their sensuousness of texture accounts for their timeless appeal.

FIGURE 213. Come fly with me! There is magic in a carpet such as this one.

MATERIALS

- Colored chalks
- Practice paper
- Pencils
- Extra-large colored construction paper
- Watercolor cups or shallow containers for wet chalk painting
- White glue
- Scissors
- Oriental area rugs (see Teacher Preparation)
- Oil pastels (optional)

TEACHER PREPARATION

The best way to introduce Magic Carpets is to bring a real oriental rug to class. Small-area throw rugs will be close in size to actual construction paper format, so students should be able to transfer their ideas quite easily. The textural woven quality of the rugs is a sensory experience that also interests students. (Oriental-style carpets are acceptable, but the difference between machine-made and hand-woven should be indicated.)

Guidebooks to buying Oriental rugs are readily available in bookstores and libraries. These guides clearly outline specific designs of carpets and their motifs, along with maps and information about the geographical locations that the styles represent. Students will enjoy the color illustrations they contain, too.

Fabric and sewing shops sell fringe from a roll. Sometimes remnant pieces and odd lots can be purchased inexpensively. Be sure to tell store owners that supplies are for school and students. "Magic Carpets" can be accomplished without real fringe, but it definitely adds the finishing touch!

DIRECTIONS

1. Show oriental rugs and illustrations of them to students. Discuss basic design types—medallion with a border; all-over patterns; and so on. Note the names of the carpets and their relationship to the places where they are produced. The hand-woven appearance of rugs should also be examined.

2. Practice designs and motifs on sketch paper.

3. Establish dominant symmetrical format by folding paper—first in half vertically, then horizontally. Open. Cross folds will provide central grid.

4. Students may want to choose a specific rug design (Shiraz, Bokhara, etc.) to replicate, or they may wish to recreate work based on a combination of reference materials and their own imaginations. Encourage incorporation of traditional patterns and motifs, such as arabesques, minaret shapes, Islamic tile patterns—even selections from Middle Eastern calligraphic alphabets.

5. Materials should be distributed: filled water cups and chalks. Dip one end of chalk in the water and draw designs. Wet chalk produces a rich, wooly surface that actually resembles a rug's texture. Students may start with a central pattern, using the folded cross as reference lines.

6. Students might do the border outlines next to establish visual boundaries. The more patterning that occurs overall, the more convincing the rugs look. Oil pastels may be used to enhance surface.

7. When rugs are complete, cut fring to fit the two vertical ends. Glue fringe on to the rug and let dry.

8. Exhibit rugs as wall hangings. Attach information on carpet name and origins, or test students' observation skills by asking them to identify styles. Your carpets in full display should recall all the magic of Ali Baba and a thousand and one Arabian nights!

ACTIVITY 86
Little Gems

PAINTING: "Miniatures"

When it comes to the intricacy of patterns, the art of the Persian miniature has no match. These tiny paintings pack in the elaborate arabesques of Islamic tiles and oriental rugs, as well as selections from the alphabet of the Koran, while carefully depicting several lively vignettes. Because of the unique perspective of early Middle Eastern painting, many events and design elements may be viewed at once. One could easily peek into a desert tent, see inside a minaret, and catch the interaction of people, both on the inside and the outside of a garden wall. There is a fairytale quality to the compartmental Persian miniature, a multi-layered style of painting that wastes no space!

FIGURE 214. Tiny paintings, filled with patterns, pack a wallop! Note the telltale signs of contemporary culture above and below.

MATERIALS

- 8″ × 10″ white drawing paper
- Pencils
- Fine tipped markers (optional)
- Rulers
- Watercolors, including gold if available
- Small paintbrushes
- Photo albums (see step 8 under Directions)

TEACHER PREPARATION

Examples of Persian miniatures may be found in books on the art and architecture of Islam and the Middle East. You may also wish to bring in the same reference materials used for Activity 85 (oriental throw rugs). Students may bring in favorite patterns from wrapping paper, fabric, and so on, as well.

You will need reproductions of Persian miniatures that use space in the manner typical of that style.

This lesson will require several class sessions to complete.

DIRECTIONS

1. Review the patterns found in Persian art. Describe them. Are the tiles symmetrical? Which geometrics can you identify? How about the floral patterns, are they loose and free, or controlled and organized?

2. Consider the composition of Persian miniatures in the reproduction(s). Notice how the space is divided into sections. It is much like a layer cake—everything is stacked up and titled forward on one flat plane. Distribute pencils, paper, and rulers.

3. Hold paper vertically. Using the reproductions as a guide, lightly pencil in *compartments*. A ruler may help. Leave room for arches, curves, and *scenes*! Including a border.

4. What will your subject be? Perhaps a weekend at home with Dad in the garden with his power mower. Mom on the exercise bike, brother listening to his radio, you on the phone, the next-door neighbors having a barbecue—you get the picture!

5. Pencil in your ideas. Try to use the style of Persian miniatures. Your own patterns may be mixed in with Middle Eastern tradition. Use the pattern samples you brought in or simply recreate favorites, like plaids, fragmented geometrics, stripes, and so forth. Be decorative.

6. Distribute watercolors and accompanying paint supplies. Pencil outlines of figures may be retained. Paint into your composition. Use bright, vivid colors, do not thin them extensively with water. Add gold in areas for accents.

7. Take you time. Miniatures are a labor of love. Pencils or fine tipped markers may be incorporated for hard-to-define elements, like facial expressions, and tiny details. Small brushes will be appreciated here, but line work may be used to outline and emphasize selected areas.

8. Has every inch been attended? Finished paintings may be displayed. If there's further opportunity for showing off, slip miniatures into the plastic pages of a photo album. This makes a stunning manuscript. Good things sure do come in small packages!

ACTIVITY 87
Hebrew Manuscripts: A Living Art

PARCHMENT CALLIGRAPHY: Alphabet Art

Trace language back to Biblical times and you will uncover an alphabet that is still in use today: Hebrew! This ancient Semitic language, while closely aligned with Phoenician and early Egyptian, is quite alive and well. Etymology—the study of alphabets and language—reveals Hebrew to be at the very roots of our civilization. Like may other writing systems—Sanskrit, Chinese, and Arabic—Hebrew is not only interesting to the ear, but lovely to look at, too.

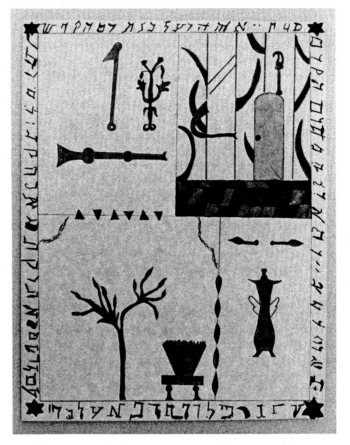

FIGURE 215. The subjects for your manuscript art may be based on stories or proverbs found in the ancient Hebrew manuscripts. Or your illumination might take an archaeological turn—uncovering artifacts of the Hebrew culture, such as menorahs, chalices, ceremonial vessels, and more. Research on these objects and their purposes is rewarding, as the artful example shown here suggests.

MATERIALS

- Felt-tip black pens in assorted sizes, including calligraphy tip (see Teacher Preparation)
- Parchment, such as document paper (see Teacher Preparation)
- Practice papers of various types
- Pen (optional)

- Ink (optional)
- Pencils
- Erasers
- Rulers
- Graph paper

TEACHER PREPARATION

This activity is primarily to familiarize children with the letter forms of various alphabets around the world. Hebrew, with its graceful characters, and its familiarity to many Jewish students, is the core alphabet on which we'll concentrate our efforts. Therefore, if you live in a large city and can get a copy of a Jewish newspaper, many examples may be garnered. Books used for Passover, called "Haggadah," will illustrate Hebrew beautifully. Books on Hebrew manuscript illumination are useful as well.

Sources for transliterations are encyclopedias and dictionaries, where you will find complete and handy alphabet tables. A perfect book to use with children is

Alphabet Art written and illustrated
by Leonard Everette Fisher
(New York: Four Winds Press, a division of Scholastic Magazines, Inc., 1978).

Students will be experimenting with alphabet configurations as well as calligraphy and lettering materials. Parchment is available in art supply stores and is not particularly expensive. You may want to cut the parchment paper into 8″ × 10″ rectangles ahead of time. (NOTE: If you want to make notecards or Hanukkah cards, double the amount of parchment required. Simply work on folded paper, open when cover art is complete, then "calligraph" your greeting inside.)

Have a variety of papers on hand, from smooth and glossy to rougher surfaces, if possible. Lettering pens and ink, along with felt-tip calligraphy markers with different shaped points, would be fun for students to use.

This lesson will require several class sessions to complete.

DIRECTIONS

1. Bring out all art and reference materials. Examine the Hebrew letters and their translations. Pay greatest attention to their expressive forms. If they weren't letters at all, but pure design elements, would they still be appealing? Practice some Hebrew letters with the supplies you select. Save the parchment for later.

2. Based on transliterations, you may want to try some words, like your own name. You might need to be inventive if English equivalents seem to be missing. Also, try some letter forms from other alphabets that interest you. Use graph paper to guide your hand.

3. When your confidence grows, take out the parchment paper. Measure a wide border all around in pencil. This will be your manuscript page layout. You will then design an announcement, a certificate, a one-page greeting card, or a scroll—or simply a sampler of beguiling letter forms! The choice is yours; plan your space inside the border accordingly.

4. The border will be an illumination or decoration based on the chosen format and theme for you Hebrew manuscript. It should carry the line quality of the alphabet letters.

5. These things take time. Go back and practice when you need to work out a problem letter. If you should err (it's human, after all), do your best to turn your mistake into a design motif.

6. Your finished manuscript may, in fact, be suitable for framing. In any case, it's fun to experiment and learn about one of the world's oldest alphabets. Display.

SUGGESTIONS FOR FURTHER DEVELOPMENT

This activity may be a gateway lesson into a number of other exciting areas, such as handmaking of paper, bookbinding, marbleizing and dying paper, and using other decorative printing techniques, and, of course, calligraphy in earnest!

ACTIVITY 88
The Floating World of Japanese Kites

STAMP PRINTMAKING: Kites

The *No* theatrical masks, the tiny *Netsuke* carvings, the *inro* seal boxes—even metal sword guards—reflect the mastery of technique and simplicity of design we associate with Japanese art. Again, the elements of nature are of utmost interest in traditional Japanese patterns found in prints, paintings, and crafts. The arts of Japan reflect great skill as witnessed in the important woodblock prints. They are engaging and inventive, these many arts, from the woven mats on the teahouse floor to the kites that stream under the blue-banded Japanese sky.

FIGURE 216. Our kite is a fish that will float through the air. While this lesson will teach the basics in kite construction, you might want to try your hand at other variations. Remember, stability and balance are of great importance for airborne kites! Therefore, tail(s) may need adjustment, such as tying in extra fabric swatches.

MATERIALS

- Newspaper (see Teacher Preparation)
- Rice paper or other lightweight paper
- Glue
- String
- Scissors
- Fabric strips
- Blue and black stamp pads (see Teacher Preparation)
- Painting supplies (optional)

- Corn pads (optional; See Teacher Preparation)
- Erasers (see Teacher Preparation)
- Razor for teacher use only (see Teacher Preparation)
- Jar lids (small wood blocks are excellent, too)
- Practice paper
- Pencils
- Looseleaf reinforcements

TEACHER PREPARATION

This is both a basic introductory printmaking lesson and a kite construction activity. To assemble kites, newspaper will be needed. The stays of the kite will be made from rolled newspapers. Streamers for kites may be precut into strips. Precutting lengths of paper to estimated sizes of kites is suggested.

Stamp printmaking will require well-inked pads. Erasers can be cut into geometrical shapes by you prior to the lesson. A single-edged razor (to be used by the teacher only) should be inserted at an angle into the erasers to carve out shapes. Corn pads may be applied directly to jar lids by students to create other patterns. Other footcare adhesivebacked products may be used as well and cut to form more elaborate patterns for printing.

Reference materials on basic Japanese design motifs should be made available. Stencils and lacquered trays will provide good examples of basic design elements—you may even find gift wrap in better paper goods stores or museum book shops to be of value (see Activity 91). Strong and simply stated design elements to be sought for kite decoration are the signs of Japanese family crests. Much like Western heraldry, these symbolic images offer ideal shapes for direct prints. Books on basic kite shapes and assembly are recommended.

This lesson will require several sessions to complete and has two parts.

DIRECTIONS

Part One: Printing the Kite Paper

1. Study the elements of Japanese design as suggested in Teacher Preparation.

2. Distribute lengths of paper to be used for the kites as well as all printmaking materials.

3. Cut the various patterns from footcare products. Attach these to the outside of jar lids and/or woodblocks. The teacher should use a razor to execute designs in erasers as directed by the students who can draw them on the eraser surface in pencil. (See Figure 217.)

4. Press printmaking blocks into stamp pads. Print. Students should try it on practice paper first.

5. Print the kite paper. Put aside the paper to dry until the frame is constructed. (Paint may be added later to surface if design suggests it.)

FIGURE 217. Who would think that the humble corn pad could be the source of such delightful design? Other objects for printmaking include erasers, oil-based clay, vegetables (such as onions, potatoes, oranges, etc.) and—yes!—even the actual fish itself!

FIGURE 218. The crests of Japanese heraldry offer ideal motifs for direct prints.

FIGURE 219. A sample Japanese crest.

FIGURE 220. A sample Japanese crest.

Part Two: The Kite

1. Distribute the kite-making materials.
2. Create the rods and crossbars for the kite as shown in Figures 221 and 222.
3. Hold newspaper diagonally and roll tightly. Glue end as shown in Figure 221. Make one length for the "backbone" of your kite; a second rod may be divided to provide crossbars and reel bar for your handline. The size recommended for serious kite flying is 24" × 34".
4. Attach string to ends of paper rod and glue as shown in Figure 223.
5. Attach the kite paper to the kite frame by folding back borders approximately one inch. Glue around the contour (Figure 224).
6. Turn over completed side, frame down.
7. Piece one hole approximately eight inches down from the top, and another hole approximately eight inches from bottom of tail. Glue looseleaf reinforcements to holes.
8. Cut string to 26 inches. Thread one end of string through one hole (approximately two inches) and tie to frame in back. Repeat with other end.
9. Glue string to frame to hold in place.

10. Tie one or more fabric or crepe paper strips to tail section of frame. Weight needed for flights may be adjusted by adding or reducing tail (it's approximately 12 inches long)—so test your kite!

11. Wrap a *generous* length of string around the reel you fashioned from rolled newspaper. (NOTE: You may want to purchase actual kite string to avoid line breakage. Kite supplies, such as string, reels, etc., are available in hobby shops and may be used for this activity.) Attach string from reel to string on frame.

12. Now go fly a Japanese kite! Use them for displays too.

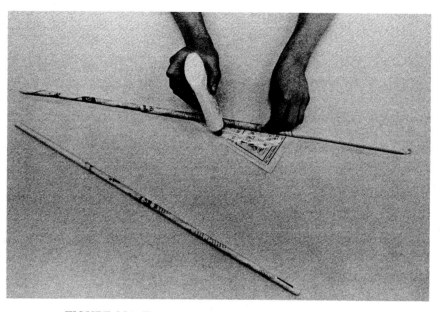

FIGURE 221. The length of your newspaper will establish the dimension of your kite.

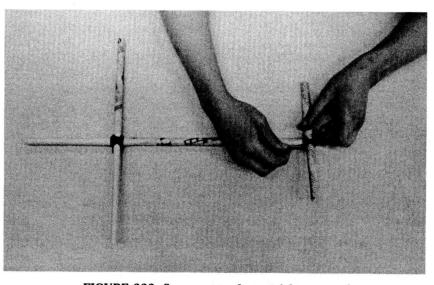

FIGURE 222. Secure crossbars with wrapped string as shown. Glue in place.

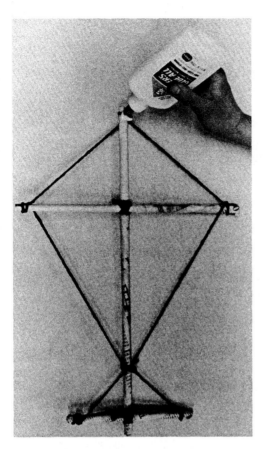

FIGURE 223. The kite frame, constructed as shown. String completes the contour.

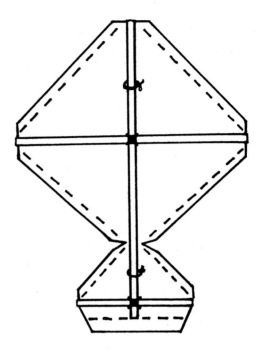

FIGURE 224. Back of kite. (String not shown).

ACTIVITY 89
Chinese Art Unfolds

"ZEN" PAINTING: Chinese Screens

It's not possible to separate Chinese art from its culture, where nature, philosophy, spirituality, and art are intertwined. In accordance with Chinese thought, painting is at one with all these forces—even to include the art of literature and poetry. The subjects found in Chinese painting are as specific as the seasons they may represent, for there is particular symbolic meaning to this oriental art form. Like the bamboo, which signifies resilience, Chinese art finds strength in its quiet expressiveness and continues to survive.

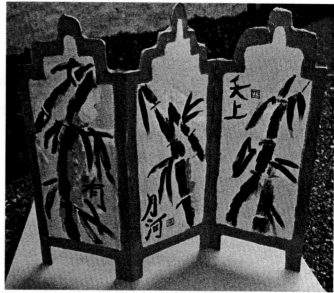

FIGURE 225. Bamboo is the symbol of resilience. It is a most appropriate choice for this calligraphic screen.

MATERIALS

- Bristol board
- Acrylic paints
- Paintbrushes in a variety of types
- Plasticine (see Teacher Preparation)
- Applicator sticks (see Teacher Preparation)
- Clay tools for scooping out plasticine
- Scissors
- Rulers (or yardsticks)
- Ink
- Stamp pads (optional—See Teacher Preparation)

TEACHER PREPARATION

This lesson has several parts and possibilities although it is relatively simple to do. First, we'll make a three-fold paper screen. Paper may be scored by you ahead of time for greater ease of folding. (See Activity 10, Figure 27.) You need nothing more than a three-part fold to fashion your Chinese screen. Basic Chinese screens are simple affairs, usually just rectangles. However, some contemporary furniture catalogs and department store displays that include Oriental furnishings may yield further design concepts for your folding screens. These screens are sometimes referred to as *coramandels*, and are popular as decorative accessories. You may, of course, create screen shapes in accordance with your own artistic ideas.

Chinese calligraphy and painting always have been closely aligned. Therefore, for your reference materials, include books on Chinese painting as well as Chinese calligraphy and watercolor techniques. If you wish to teach a bit more about the culture behind the art, review the texts of these books—they are likely to explain Chinese symbolism often reflected in Zen philosophy and thought. Other than the library, art supply stores are a good source for books on Chinese painting techniques, particularly ink brushwork. It truly is a worthwhile subject, so you might want to leave room for project expansion. (See the suggestions at the end of this activity.)

Plasticine will be used for the production of personal seals or colophons. It's not necessary to do this part of the activity, but it's a great deal of fun and quite simple. Be sure plasticine is malleable. Place in on a sunny windowsill or a covered radiator well in advance of class presentation—the warmth should soften it. Applicator sticks, along with clay tools, are excellent for inscribing seals. They are available in most drugstores. Stamp pads (instead of acrylic print or ink) may be used to make prints.

FIGURE 226. Chinese landscapes are particularly introspective and serene. Stamp prints appear in upper right of last panel.

DIRECTIONS

Part One: The Screen Painting

1. Study the pictorial references of Chinese painting. You will notice that landscapes are a dominant subject filled with great misty mountains and cascading falls. Perhaps there are bridges and rivers, or snowy footpaths. Describe what you see.

2. Shut your eyes and picture a faraway landscape like the ones you just saw. Picture the season and the trees. Is it a soft and peaceful place? Open your eyes. (NOTE: "Guided imagery" is the name given to "talking a student through" an imagination exercise of the kind described here. Because Chinese landscapes often exist in the mind of the artist and are of a spiritual, mystical nature, it is appropriate that students draw upon inner senses, fantasy, and memory. Soothing music may be used to enhance this experience. Soft Oriental music is most suitable!)

3. Distribute drawing and painting materials. If screens have not yet been cut and scored, see Teacher Preparation. Using the visual (and imaginary) references, paint an atmospheric landscape on the screen. Plan for space to accommodate calligraphy. (See Part Three, Steps 3 and 4.)

4. Experiment with painting methods. Use acrylic wash (water added to paint) to create mist and vapors. Work "wet" into rivers and streams.

5. Don't be afraid to add little Chinese temples or fishermen and their boats, but remember that the grand scale of the mountains will be established by size of other present objects. You may also want to add a monkey or a fawn. Let dry.

Part Two: The Seal

1. Divide plasticine into portions the size of a plum. Distribute along with clay tools.

2. Bring out books on calligraphy and symbology. Study various signs and their meanings.

3. Students will carve an emblem which represents their name in Chinese-style characters. Roll plasticine into cylinder or other functional shape and inscribe on the business end. Top may hold a figure or personal trademark, and the sides may contain further inscriptions about the student/artist. Make as many seals as you wish. REMEMBER: Letters print in reverse, so all initials and names must be inscribed *backwards!*

4. Distribute acrylic paint (or poster paint) in a few colors, such as red, black, and green, and distribute paintbrushes. Return the painted screens to the students. Apply small amount of acrylic paint to the working end of the seal. A stamp pad may be used here as well. Press gently into the flat screen to identify your work. More than one seal print may be made. Seals may be kept for future artists' "signatures."

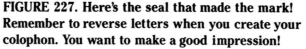

FIGURE 227. Here's the seal that made the mark! Remember to reverse letters when you create your colophon. You want to make a good impression!

Part Three: Calligraphy

1. Distribute soft brushes and ink (use with care) Make calligraphic reference materials available. Return screens.

2. Try your hand at calligraphy. First paint some Chinese characters on the back of the screen in ink. Stand screen up and let dry (be sure lettering isn't too wet, or it will run).

3. Study your landscape. You may compose a short poem based on your reflection of your work. Simple words and descriptions can be quite poetic.

4. As best you can, write your poem in ink and brush onto your paintings. Pick a good spot compositionally. Use Chinese calligraphy as much as you can. Even Chinese-style brushstrokes will be effective. You can "mix and match" scripts. Work flat.

5. Let dry.

6. What a charming display these Chinese screens will make when standing side by side. Long showcase shelves would be ideal for displaying them.

SUGGESTIONS FOR FURTHER DEVELOPMENT

The art of Chinese painting is an intriguing area for study. The tools are quite special (inkstick and stone, beautiful brushes, pans, and saucers). These materials are available in most well-stocked art supply stores, and are not complicated to handle. You might want to check books on the topic. The methods of grinding the stone, and so forth, may be demonstrated to students and shared by them to create their own paintings. Sumi-e (pronounced sue-me-eh), the art of Japanese ink painting, might also be explored. Try different shapes—scrolls and album leafs, too!

Also, the various painting techniques for natural elements, such as leaves and foliage, are translatable for future works. Children love learning them—and all about Chinese art.

NOTE: There are many fine reference materials on the topic of Oriental painting techniques: *The How and Why of Chinese Painting* by Diana Kan (New York: Van Nostrand Reinhold, 1974), *Sacred Calligraphy of the East* by John Stevens (Boulder, CO: Shambala Publications, Inc., 1981), and particularly, *The Mustard Seed Garden Manual of Painting*, edited by Mai-Mai Sze (New York: Bollingen Foundation, Inc./Princeton Press, 1978).

ACTIVITY 90
India: The Fabric of Fantasy

FABRIC DESIGN: T-Shirt "batik"

India is a land with as many faces and forms as the all-pervasive Shiva himself. It is a country of abundance—brilliant bazaars, fantastic temples, and sprawling cities. Bengal tigers, elephants, and peacocks abound. Also, there are enchanting goddesses, mystical and powerful gods, and intense religious devotion. The sights and sounds of India provoke and delight. The arts of India are at once vivid and entirely irresistible.

FIGURE 228. Designs like these should suit you to a tee!

MATERIALS

- Fabric crayons (optional; see Teach Preparation)
- Crayons in a variety of sizes (see Teacher Preparation)
- Practice paper
- Cotton T-shirt (see Teacher Preparation)
- Cold water dyes (see Teacher Preparation)
- Disposable surgical gloves (see Teacher Preparation)
- Large plastic pan for dying fabric
- Cardboard
- Scissors
- Iron

TEACHER PREPARATION

This is a mock batik in the sense that our resist method is crayon and dye, rather than hot wax. This is for the sake of classroom safety and to allow direct control over imagery. You will need enough cold water dye to accommodate your students. A few boxes should do it; check the recommendations on the pack. If you will be using a dry powder, be sure that it is carefully mixed without inhalation. The teacher *only* should do this step. Follow directions on the package.

If students will be dipping their fabric into a dye bath, plastic gloves are available in quantity in tissue-box type dispensers from the medical supply counter of well-stocked pharmacies. Otherwise, use standard rubber gloves.

Students will want to bring a clean white (or light pastel colored) cotton T-shirt in for dying.

You can supply examples of Indian design (see Figure 229). Books on India will likely offer additional reference, as well photographs of elements that inspire Indian art: lotus leaves, peacocks, conch shells, and elephants. If you have any Indian fabrics or paintings, bring them, too.

Finally, crayons that are used and broken will do just fine. Stumpy crayons are worthwhile, too. Place crayons in a sunny spot in advance of lesson so they are good and waxy. Fabric crayons are, of course, idea. They're available in art supply stores. Instructions for their use appear on the package; otherwise, follow directions as outlined in the activity.

This lesson will require the same setup suggested for a painting activity. If may take a few sessions.

DIRECTIONS

Part One: The T-Shirt Design

1. Review reference materials to identify India design motifs. What are the recurring elements? How about the familiar paisley? It is among the favored curvilinear designs of Indian tradition.

FIGURE 229. Examples of Indian design motifs.

2. Practice some design ideas with crayons on scratch paper. When you reach the point where you're ready, retrieve the T-shirt and crayons. Drawn directly onto the T-shirt. You may cut cardboard to fit inside the T-shirt to make it easier to draw upon.

3. Use a variety of repeated patterns. Apply dots and smaller motifs generously. Feel free to include animal and figurative imagery. Borrow details from Indian habitats, such as the "eye" of the peacock feather.

4. Finish the front of the shirt. If drawing on the back is desired, be sure to protect *both* sides from transfer as described in step 6.

Part Two: The "Batik" Dye

5. Get out the T-shirts and supplies for fabric dying as listed in the materials and described in Teacher Preparation. Follow box directions as indicated. Use gloves and care!

6. Dry the T-shirt. You may heat-set the dye and crayon by ironing the shirts. Place plain paper or cloth between the iron and "batik" dyed fabric and between the ironing board cover and fabric, too. The crayon will transfer in this procedure.

7. You may wear your art! However, a word of advice: frequent washing will fade color as will direct sunlight. Also realize that T-shirts will run (particularly at first wash), so separate in the laundering. Handwashing is strongly suggested.

8. Not so fast! Before you wisk these T-shirts away to your wardrobe, share them! They look positively smashing when displayed on dowels (slip dowels through arms, hang by tying ribbon on ends). Hangers may also be used.

SUGGESTIONS FOR FURTHER DEVELOPMENT

Indian mask faces or portrait heads may be drawn on bristol board, cut out, and made to serve as hangers to show off the T-shirts. They're dazzling!

FIGURE 230. Here is a hanger with as much style as the clothing it holds! Paper portrait hangers fashioned from posterboard may be reinforced by taping ordinary flat plastic hangers behind them. The T-shirt is pretty impressive, too!

ACTIVITY 91
Kimonos Are Tops!

ORIGAMI: Costume, Japanese Prints

Silk kimonos are a delight to the senses, right down to their *obi* sashes! Japanese artists have a way with materials, even with one as common as paper. Origami, the art of paper folding, is an example of Japanese resourcefulness—an ordinary square of paper can be transformed into a whooping crane!

The colored woodblock print is perhaps the best known and most influential Japanese art form to be embraced by Western culture. In these technically outstanding prints, stylized images reflect customary pattern and design qualities, as well as offer charming scenes. They invite the viewer backstage to see an actor applying his stage make-up or onto a balcony where women hang their wash out to dry. A direct and open statement is found in the Japanese print—one which understands clarity in design and celebrates life!

FIGURE 231. How lucky can you get? Sometimes, pretty lucky if you find wrapping paper printed with antique silk kimono designs! Japanese motifs are not as hard to find as you might think. The art of the Japanese print meets the ancient art of paper folding in this delightful composition called "Wash Day." The kimonos are hanging out to dry.

**SLIDE #39:   WOMEN WASHING AND
                STARCHING LINEN**

MATERIALS

- Variety of papers in assorted colors and sizes (see Teacher Preparation)
- 12″ × 15″ white drawing paper
- Manila paper for cutting shapes

- Crayons
- Markers
- Scissors
- Glue

TEACHER PREPARATION

Books on origami and similar paper-folding techniques are generally plentiful; have several on hand for your class presentation. It's also a safe bet to first try a few selections yourself, then later offer these samples as demonstration pieces.

You'll also want books and reproductions on Japanese prints. Some of the more distinguished artists—Utamaro and Hiroshige, for instance—will provide a host of pictorial and design ideas to students. Books on traditional Japanese customs, as well as on crafts and design motifs, would be of interest.

A variety of papers may be gathered for origami production. There are special papers for this express purpose sold in hobby shops and art supply stores, but they're not required for this activity. Lighter weight papers do work well for paper folding. Gift wrap remnants are fine; so are some paper wrappers from cosmetic and bath products. Foil, typewriter bond papers, and a host of others will do as well. Experiment! You may want to precut larger pieces into manageable squares. Keep "extras" of mixed types handy. Precut manila into squares for pictorial elements.

DIRECTIONS

1. Study the examples of traditional Japanese prints. What strikes you? The patterns? The costumes? The activities of the people and their settings? Explain your reactions. Describe design elements in your own straightforward terms.

2. Bring examples of origami forward along with illustrative materials. Pass paper-fold samples around so students may examine constructions. Distribute all materials.

3. Students will experiment with paper folding. They may start their pictures on the white drawing paper at any point. Plan a scene that will logically include the origami kimonos. For instance, clothes in a dressing room or on a clothesline. Think about other objects that might be folded, like room-dividing screen, fan, umbrella, etc. Base your scene on the subjects of Japanese prints.

4. Try your own adaptations of origami. Combine and invent paper-folding techniques. Also cut out flat figures and objects. Use compositional planning.

5. Draw Japanese patterns wherever feasible. If you are using plain white paper for origami, for example, design it first. Include details from Japanese life in your pictures, such as tea service sets, masks on the walls, rolled mats, bonsai trees, and so forth.

6. Do you have a "signature" seal? (See Activity 89, Figure 227.) Make your mark on your finished work and display.

TO MAKE A KIMONO...

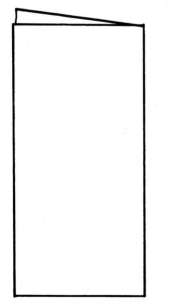

FIGURE 232. Fold 10″ × 14″ sheet of paper in half.

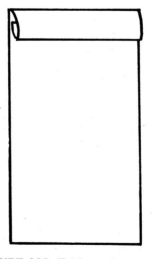

FIGURE 233. Fold top down twice about one-sixth of width.

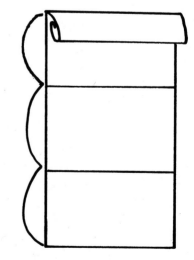

FIGURE 234. Fold bottom up two thirds.

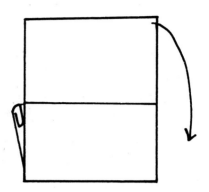

FIGURE 235. Fold top down.

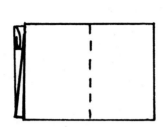

FIGURE 236. Fold in half and unfold. Turn over.

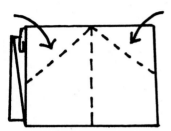

FIGURE 237. Fold top corners into center.

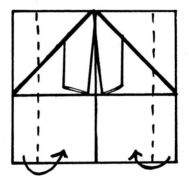

FIGURE 238. Fold sides in.

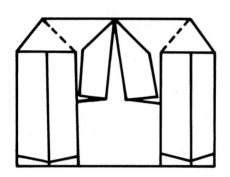

FIGURE 239. Press open sides with fingertips. Flatten tops.

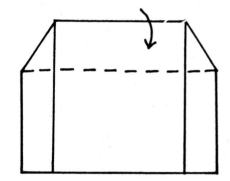

FIGURE 240. Turn over, fold over top, and turn paper over again.

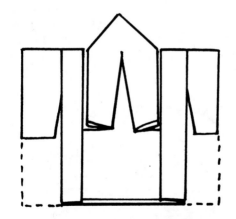

FIGURE 241. Cut away sleeves for a girl's kimono. Do not cut away for a boy's kimono.

ART OF AFRICA

The art of Africa is like a great river that runs far, wide and deep. Deep, because the art is an ancient one, closely tied in with ceremony, tradition, and tribal custom. Far and wide, because the art of Africa is found in its many different forms in the divergent regions of this vast continent. Some areas that have produced the art are quite remote; others are more accessible. Nonetheless, African art reaches out and connects with other major art forms of many nations—and the impact has been enormous.

At one time, the art of Africa was quite shocking to Westerners. Even though there has always been an intrigue between Europe and Africa, the sculptural forms are entirely foreign to the Western standards of beauty. Classical art causes the eye to follow curvy, flowing lines, while African art surprises the viewer with unexpected juts and displacements! African art was poorly understood by the Westerners who rejected it. The reasons cited were usually hung on its being ritualistic in nature and therefore not worthy of serious artistic merit, or it was simply judged as much too primitive. The forceful shapes and rhythms of African sculpture baffled the Europeans. That is, until Picasso stepped in.

Picasso must be credited for familiarizing Westerners with the aesthetics of African sculpture. He was evidently able to read the African use and purpose of distortion—an important element, present in all art—and could aptly translate it into his painting. The principles of African art were then applied to European painting and sculpture and the outcome was Cubism, a radical development in Western art history.

African art, with its many faces, was not only a major influence for Picasso and Braque's Cubism; it dramatically affected many other formidable painters and sculptors, too. The African mask was of particular interest to the painter and sculptor Modigliani who culled from it his graceful elongated figures and original portrait heads. Many whimsical paintings of Paul Klee can be directly traced to specific African works as well. The achievements of African art are many, and may be appreciated for their own artistry as well as for the fresh direction they brought to the world of art.

ACTIVITY 92
Ashanti Treasure Chest

CRAFTS: Jewelry Box

Without the arts of Africa, it would be impossible to imagine Modern Art as it exists today. African art encompasses a full range of sculpture, painting, and crafts. The natural world is favored in Africa's folk arts. Jungle animals, lizards, snakes, and birds are often represented, entwined with dynamic design motifs. The strong shapes and linear expressive qualities of African decorative arts are responsible for its distinctive appearance.

FIGURE 242. The jewelry box not only contains valuables, it also displays a treasured art.

MATERIALS

- Practice paper (optional; see step 3 of the Directions)
- Pencils (optional)
- Cigar boxes (shoeboxes may be substituted; see Teacher Preparation)
- Poster or acrylic paints
- Paintbrushes
- Gesso (see Teacher Preparation)

TEACHER PREPARATION

You will need to gather cigar boxes—tobacco stores are the preferred source. Sometimes students have a cigar smoker in their families who can contribute to the cause. Wooden boxes are great, but the others are fine, too. If cigar boxes are not available, try the next best or most available item—shoeboxes.

You may want to apply one or two coats of gesso well in advance of class. Gesso is a must for undercoating and preparing these surfaces. Its drying time is about 20 minutes per coat, depending on the humidity. Please note this in the event you prefer to do the gesso painting step with the students.

Have examples of African design motifs on hand. (see Figures 243-245.)

DIRECTIONS

1. Introduce African patterns through examples you have on hand. Discuss subjects and the manner in which they are represented. (See the suggestions at the end of this activity for more information.)

2. Distribute painting materials and boxes.

3. Students will paint bold designs directly onto the surfaces of the boxes.
   NOTE: If you and your students are more comfortable doing practice sketches before painting, this is not unreasonable. But the beauty of this art form is in its direct and bold application, so avoid being too concerned about control of line.

4. Let painted boxes dry. Prop lids up with appropriate objects to prevent tops and bottoms from drying shut.

5. Finished! Your jewelry box may also be used for collectibles or anything else you treasure!

SUGGESTIONS FOR FURTHER DEVELOPMENT

There is great wisdom behind the signs and symbols of African folk art. The patterns have meanings. Your students may find their designs even more interesting if introduced to the stories behind them. For example, see Figure 243.

FIGURE 243. Two crocodiles with one stomach.

Other patterns may signify faithfulness, such as the moon and star (see Figure 244); or patience and endurance, as in the sign of the hearts (see Figure 245).

FIGURE 244. A sign of faithfulness.

FIGURE 245. A sign of patience and endurance.

Two resources you might check are *Made in West Africa* by Christine Price (New York: Sutton, 1975), and *Africa's Living Arts* by Anthony D. Marshall (New York: Franklin Watts, 1970).

ACTIVITY 93
The African Mask: Forces of Man and Nature

NATURAL MATERIALS ASSEMBLAGE: Masks

The role of the mask in African culture is an established one. Masks provide ancestral links and are indispensable objects in dance, ceremony, and ritual. Moreover, African masks draw upon immediate natural resources, utilizing available materials in the most imaginative ways. The diversity in style, design quality, and the unique ornamentation of these masks account for their importance in African art. In addition, the sculpture of this country, the masks in particular, are the acknowledged driving force behind Western Modern Art!

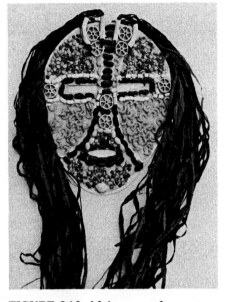

FIGURE 246. African masks vary greatly in design, depending on their region of origin. This one has been locally produced in the artroom! Notice how our ingenious mask-maker has threaded raffia through tubular pasta, adding a crowning touch.

SLIDE #40:   AFRICAN MASK

MATERIALS

- Cardboard (see Teacher Preparation)
- Dried seeds, beans, and pasta (see Teacher Preparation)
- Glue
- Paints
- Paintbrushes
- Shells (optional; see Teacher Preparation)
- Raffia (optional; see Teacher Preparation)
- Practice paper
- Pencils (thick, drawing-type suggested)
- Scissors (see Teacher Preparation)

TEACHER PREPARATION

Before students design their masks, they should be made aware of the stylistic differences within African tribal arts. The dance masks of the Bushonga, for instance, lend more toward this activity because of their decorative and ornamental qualities. However, it is worthwhile to become familiar with the art of other art-producing regions, such as the Ivory Coast and Gabun, for contrast and overall knowledge. Therefore, reproductions and books displaying an array of representative African masks are recommended.

Materials you'll need for this lesson include dry seeds and beans, which are easily purchased in the food market. Also, select various pastas—wheels, shells, macaroni, etc. Any other natural items you or your students might want to add, such as seashells, raffia, small rocks, or minerals, will be fine.

As presented in this activity, masks will be mounted on corrugated cardboard, which may be precut into student-sized sections. This will provide a flat surface for the mask. Scraps may be used for features and other parts. If a more sculptural, convex mask is desired, you may find that paper party goods, like platters will suffice. Students may cut their own mask contours with scissors in good working order.

This lesson may take several sessions to complete.

DIRECTIONS

1. Study the examples of African masks. Notice how most masks reduce features to lines and geometrics? Eyes may be slits and noses shown as triangles and lips as dissected diamond shapes. Pay particular attention to masks that integrate materials, such as beads, shells, and straw.

2. Distribute all supplies. Begin with practice paper and drawing pencils. Try making some mask faces using the reference material to guide you.

3. Ready to start your mask? Switch over to the corrugated cardboard paper. Decide where painted or drawn patterns will be and outline them. Include space for the placement of selected pastas, seeds, etc., in your plan.

4. Materials may be applied in any order that suits the individual design. Just keep in mind that seeds and beans will need adequate time to "set up" after they are glued, so be careful not to jar or move them before the glue is dry. Be generous with the glue.

5. Three-dimensional parts, such as noses and lips, may be added, as well as headdresses, earrings, and other jewelry made from our own available materials. Let dry.

6. You don't have to mask your feelings—you're proud, and you should be! It's only natural. Display.

ACTIVITY 94
Art Charms: African Fetish and Sculpture

MIXED MEDIA CLAY: Animal Sculpture

The history of Western art is chiefly recounted through its painting traditions. African art history, on the other hand, is defined by its sculpture. There are numerous forms of sculpture—carved in wood, cast in bronze and gold, and hewn from stone. The wealth of material and the evocative styling of these works fulfill both artistic and ceremonial purposes. Fetishes exemplify both. They are much like good luck charms believed to hold magical powers. Should they fail to bring results to the bearer, there may indeed be some displeasure. But when their artistry is considered, fetishes (also called power objects) do not disappoint!

FIGURE 247. Watch out! A nail-headed hedgehog goes toe-to-toe with a thumbtack armadillo as the tacky game behind them growls. It's rough out there in the bush!

MATERIALS

- Modeling clay (see Teacher Preparation)
- Clay tools
- Hardware odds and ends (see Teacher Preparation)
- Textural objects (see Teacher Preparation)
- Feathers (optional)
- Toothpicks (optional)
- Fabric scraps (optional)

TEACHER PREPARATION

The animals your students decide to make will determine the supplies needed. This lesson will encourage the imaginative mix of metal, fabric, and other materials with clay to represent the characteristic appearance of animals. Therefore, if the student's choice is a porcupine, toothpicks and brads may be in order. A rhino's skin would be enhanced by the application of small flat metal plates, so check the nail and staple department at the hardware store. Screws, rivets, paper fasteners, etc., may be inserted into the clay to resemble various animals' skins—think about hedgehogs, tortoises, and so on. Feathers will make your birds fly! Materials themselves will suggest ideas. Textural tools, such as meat hammers, can add to expression in clay.

Modeling clay, or plasticine, should be made available. If wet clay is used, be sure to follow the procedure for adequate drying. Prepare the clay as outlined in "The Clay Studio" in Section One. Do *not* kiln fire these pieces.

Plasticine should be malleable. Placing it in small bundles in a warm spot beforehand (such as a sunny windowsill) should accomplish this.

Reference materials may include pictures of appropriate animals, such as pachyderms and others with textural hides. Reproductions of African sculpture and power objects that artistically combine materials would be helpful.

DIRECTIONS

1. Who are the animals with the thick, prickly, or armoured hides? Name and describe them. What other animals have textural coats or skins? Share reference materials.

2. Distribute the clay and all other available supplies. (Reminder: Do *not* kiln fire the pieces in this project. It will melt down the metal, and is *not* suited to the other recommended materials such as fabric and feathers. You may want to use self-hardening clay, provided that you are assured of its safe ingredients. It would be a workable choice, if readily available.)

3. Experiment. Try several animals and various textural effects. The beauty of clay is that it will allow the freedom of play.

4. Do you want to do several different species? How about a mother and her babies? Fabricate your selections. Be imaginative and daring.

5. Finished pieces may be displayed as animal groups. You may even wish to create natural habitat dioramas to offset the sculptures. Tags describing the animal species, its "care and feeding," may be included. On occasion, a "Beware!" sign might be prudent, too!

**FIGURE 248. An unidentified
species grazes with its offspring!**

SECTION FOUR

ART SMART CHART OF EXEMPLARY ARTISTS AND THEIR TIMES

Where in the World?	When?	Who Were the Artists?	What Subjects Did They Paint?	How to Recognize Their Paintings	Names Sometimes Used for the Period of Art
Florence, Italy	1300	Giotto c.1266-1337	Religious stories	Early use of perspective; colorful; frescoes; unusual compositions	Pre-Renaissance—Early Italian Renaissance
	1400	Masaccio 1401-c.1428	Realistic interiors; religious subjects	Dramatic perspective	Early Renaissance
		Uccello 1397-1475	Horses and other animals; battles	Decorative style; linear perspective	Early Renaissance
	1450	Botticelli 1445-1510	Youthful maidens; allegories; portraits	Linear profiles (Birth of Venus)	Early Renaissance—High Renaissance
	1500	Raphael 1483-1520	Madonnas; naturalistic settings	Dark and light modeling	High Renaissance
		da Vinci 1452-1519	Madonnas; portraits; sketchbook inventions	Soft modeling (Mona Lisa)	High Renaissance
		Michelangelo 1475-1564	Biblical figures; religious subjects	Sculptural; anatomical (the ceiling of the Sistine Chapel)	High Renaissance—Late Renaissance
Venice, Italy		(Giovanni) Bellini c.1430-1516	Religious; mythical; portraits	Organized; sharp compositions	High Renaissance
		Giorgione 1477-1510	Landscapes with people; portraits	Warm "Venetian" glowing color	High Renaissance
	1550	Tintoretto 1518-1594	Biblical; portraits	Curvy, swirly lines; dramatic light	Late Renaissance

ART SMART CHART OF
EXEMPLARY ARTISTS AND THEIR TIMES

Where in the World?	When?	Who Were the Artists?	What Subjects Did They Paint?	How to Recognize Their Paintings	Names Sometimes Used for the Period of Art
		Titian 1485-1576	Portraits; nobility	Rich textures of costumes; naturalistic figures	Late Renaissance
		Veronese 1528-1588	Biblical; allegories; portraits	"Pinwheel" compositions	Late Renaissance
Northern Europe	1450–1500	Jan Van Eyck c. 1390-1441 *Flemish*	Refined portraits; groups	Panel paintings with smooth surfaces; alterpieces	Late Gothic—Early Renaissance
		Dürer 1471-1528 *German*	Medieval scenes; portraits	Details and line work important	Late Gothic—Renaissance
		(Hans) Holbein "The Younger" 1497-1543 *German*	Portraits	Many worldly goods are shown	Late Gothic—Renaissance
		(Pieter) Bruegel c.1522-1569 *Flemish*	Feasts and everyday work scenes; people's "weaknesses"	Large space; small brushstrokes	Late Gothic—Renaissance
		Bosch c.1450-1516 *Flemish*	"Garden of Delights"; human folly	Fiery lighting; fine brushwork	Renaissance in the north
Spain		El Greco 1541-1614	Landscapes; noble class; religious	Multi-level composition; mysterious; "lightning" light; long, pointy people; ghostly look	Baroque (after the Renaissance, 1500–1800) *Also…Mannerism*

Region	Date	Artist	Subject	Characteristics	Style/School
Northern Europe	1600	Velázquez 1599-1660	Court portraits; figure groups; genre	Simplification of brushstrokes; harmony of light and color	Baroque
		Rubens 1577–1640 *Flemish*	Active figure groups; dramatic stories told; portraits	Curvy people; curvy compositions; grand scale	Flemish…Dutch Masters
		Hals 1580–1666 *Flemish*	Middle- to upper-class portraits; figure groups; peasants	Loose brushstrokes	Dutch Masters *Also…Genre*
	1650	Vermeer 1632-1675	Domestic scenes; interiors	Light from window; jewel-like paintings	Dutch Masters Genre
		Rembrandt 1606-1669	Biblical scenes; "real" people often in costume; life of his time	Deep expression; use of light; dramatic	Dutch Masters
Northern Europe (Dutch)	1600–1650	Many painters, such as Clara Peeters	Popular subject of still life	Very real objects	Dutch Still Life
France	1600	Poussin 1594-1665	Landscapes; battle scenes; allegories	Calm/active; open spaces; classical	French
		Lorrain 1600-1682	Landscapes	Soft; open spaces	French
	1700	Watteau 1684–1721	Carefree upper-class people; playfulness	Curvy; fluffy	Rococo
	1750	Fragonard 1732–1806	Carefree upper-class people; playfulness	Curvy, fluffy	Rococo
	1700	Chardin 1699–1779	Domestic scenes; kitchen tools (pots, pans, etc.); working people	Dutch-like interest in detail; earthy; Genre	French

ART SMART CHART OF
EXEMPLARY ARTISTS AND THEIR TIMES

Where in the World?	When?	Who Were the Artists?	What Subjects Did They Paint?	How to Recognize Their Paintings	Names Sometimes Used for the Period of Art
	1775–1800	David 1748-1825	Greek revival; heroes; political; elegant people	Frozen; posed; cool; stopped action	Neoclassical
		Ingres 1780-1867	Greek revival; heroes; political; elegant people	Frozen; posed; cool; stopped action	Neoclassical
Spain	1800	Goya 1746-1828	Royalty; political; social commentary; "majas"	Jewel-like detail; black and white	Spanish School (Pre-Realism)
France	1800	Gericault 1791-1824	Exotic faraway; adventure; heroics	Action; movement	Romantic
		Delacroix 1798-1863	Adventure; heroics; exotic people/places	Action; movement; loose brushwork	Romantic
England	1700–1800	Hogarth 1697-1764	Country and city scenes; satire	"Tableaux"; curvy; loose	* * *
		Gainsborough 1727–1788	Portraits; families; children	Sentimental; sweet; idealization of subjects	English Portrait Painting
		Reynolds 1723–1792	Portraits of society; historical military subjects	Sentimental; sweet	English Portrait Painting
		Turner 1775–1851	Outdoor scenes	Loose; explosive light	Pre-Impressionism
		Constable 1776-1837	English countryside	Quite pastoral scenes	Pre-Impressionism
France	1800	Corot 1796-1875	Outdoors; country landscapes	Silvery light; fluffy trees	Barbizon School

	Artist	Subject	Characteristics	Style
	Courbet 1819-1877	Peasants	Blackish-green foliage	Barbizon School and Realism
	Millet 1814-1875	Working people	Realistic; story telling	Realism
1850	Manet 1832-1883	Real-life situations and people; theatrical	Black and white; "sheet plane" background; loose brushstrokes	Early Impressionism
	Daumier 1808-1879	Political; circus; humorous subjects	Darks and lights; loose line work	* * *
	Rodin 1840-1917	Sculpture; people with strong emotions	Stretched poses; sensuous	* * *
	Monet 1840-1926	Waterscapes; gardens; flowers; outdoors	Pastel colors; strong brushstrokes	Beginning of Impressionism
	Gauguin 1848-1903	Island people of Tahiti; exotic interests; French peasants	Strong color combinations; wavy lines	Art Nouveau also Post Impressionism
Holland 1850	Van Gogh 1853-1890	Working people; outdoors; flowers	Swirling paint; powerful, colorful brushstrokes	Expressionism also Post Impressionism
France 1850	Renoir 1841-1919	Women grooming; casual figure groups and children outdoors	Soft edges; pearly skin tones; small brushstrokes; patches of light; curvy	Impressionism
	Cézanne 1839-1906	Still life; mountains; landscapes; portraits and figure groups	Choppy brushstrokes; unusual balance in composition; rocklike qualities; rich blues; tan and green landscape	Post Impressionism

ART SMART CHART OF EXEMPLARY ARTISTS AND THEIR TIMES

Where in the World?	When?	Who Were the Artists?	What Subjects Did They Paint?	How to Recognize Their Paintings	Names Sometimes Used for the Period of Art
	1875–1900	Degas 1834-1917	Ballet dancers; races, theaters; bath scenes; domestic scenes	Photographic quality; soft pastels; candid poses	Impressionism
		Toulouse-Lautrec 1864-1901	Restaurant, circus, and theater scenes	Posters; plastic line; shapes of colors	Post Impressionism
		Seurat 1859–1891	Parks; circus; outdoors	Dots of pastel colors; influenced by mosaics	Pointillism *Also...Impressionism*
		Utrillo 1883–1955	Buildings and streets in Paris	Paint with textured surface; quiet colors	* * *
		Soutine 1894–1943	Animals in the grocer's shop; people; outdoors	Swirling, slashing paint; thick paint quality	Expressionism
		Pascin 1885–1930	Women; interiors; tropical scenes	Pencil line with paint soft, shimmery colors	* * *
Italy		De Chirico 1888–1978	Empty streets; Greek statues; horses; dream settings	Long shadows; yellow and tan colors; empty dream quality	Surrealism
Spain and France		Dali 1904–	Strange combinations of things	Photographic realism	Surrealism
		Picasso 1883–1973	Cafés; street scenes; harlequins	Monochromatic; sensitive line; large, classical figures	Rose and Blue Periods
			Musical instruments; people; masks	Broken up shapes; African influences; many different views of object	Cubism

Region	Date	Artist	Subject	Style	Period
		Modigliani 1884–1920	Portraits; women; figures; sculpture	Long, stretched bodies; African influence; sensitive line	* * *
	1900	Rouault 1871–1958	Circus; clowns; Biblical	Looks like stained glass; thick paint; wide black lines	Modern Art
		Matisse 1869–1954	Balcony scenes on the Riviera; women; interiors	Flat, bold, bright color; loose line; Persian art influence; raised picture plane; decorative	Fauvism
	1900	Miró 1893–1983	Animal "creatures"; fantasy	Like puzzle pieces; lots of shapes; not the real world	Modern *also..Surrealism*
	1900	Rousseau 1844–1910	Jungle and village scenes; military scenes	Things seen singularly; special world of adventure; primitive style; "naive"	* * *
America (and England)	1700	Benjamin West 1738–1820	Historical	"Academic"	Early American
		James Whistler 1834–1903	People (his mother); parks	Flat color	Early American
		John Copley 1738–1815	Romantic; adventurous portraits	"Academic"	Early American
	1800	Edward Hicks 1780–1849	Animals; forests; allegory	"Primitive"	Early American
		Winslow Homer 1836–1901	rural life; outdoors; seascapes; portraits	illustrative portrayal of subject; dramatic use of light	American painting

ART SMART CHART OF
EXEMPLARY ARTISTS AND THEIR TIMES

Where in the World?	When?	Who Were the Artists?	What Subjects Did They Paint?	How to Recognize Their Paintings	Names Sometimes Used for the Period of Art
		Thomas Eakins 1844–1916	Boxers; sports; medicine	Flat color; anatomical interest	American Painting
	1850	Mary Cassatt 1845–1926	Mothers and children; flowers; women dressing	Pastel colors; some Japanese influence	Impressionism
	1900–Present	Man Ray 1890–1976	"Crazy" subjects (things that don't normally go together)	Photographic; irreverent witty	"Dada"/Surrealism
		Glackens 1870–1938	American scenes (soda fountains, streets, beaches); portraits	Illustrative; somewhat Impressionistic	Ash Can School
		Prendergast 1859–1924	Parks; outdoors	Dots; "parade" compositions; almost pointillism; pastel colors	American painting
		Pippin 1888–1946	Country folk; country scenes; war	American primitive	American painting
		O'Keeffe 1887–1986	American southwest; bones; flowers and nature	Oversized "zoomed-in" composition; economy of color	***
		Pollock 1912–1956	Designs of drips	Drips of paint covering the canvas	Abstract Art also...Action Painting
		Kline 1910–1962	Designs of lines	Slashes of paint; limited color	Abstract Art
		Lichtenstein 1923–	Comic book characters; Satire	Graphic art; "screen" of dots	Pop/Op Art

*** Not necessarily identified with a characteristic period style or "ism."

SLIDE CREDITS

1. *Bison*, Room of Bison, Altamira Grotto in Northern Spain. 15,000–10,000 B.C. Art Resource, NY.
2. *Mummy Case*, Egyptian sarcophagus, 12th Dynasty, Vatican Museum. Art Resource, NY.
3. *Hieroglyphs with Egyptian Wall Painting*, Tomb, ancient Egypt. Borromeo/Art Resource, NY.
4. *The Parthenon*, Acropolis East, Athens, Greece c.450 B.C. Art Resource, NY.
5. *Olive Gathering*, Black figured Amphora painted by the Antimenes painter c. 520 B.C. British Museum, London. Art Resource, NY.
6. *Victory*, Paeonius, Female Greek statue, 425 B.C. Olympia Museum. Art Resource, NY.
7. *Rose Window*, Stained glass in Notre Dame, Paris. c. 1200. Art Resource, NY.
8. *Gargoyles*, South side, North tower of Notre Dame, Paris. Art Resource, NY.
9. *The Lady and the Unicorn*, Tapestry, 3.78m high × 4.66m wide, end of 15th century, Cluny Museum, Paris. SCALA New York/Florence. Art Resource, NY.
10. *November* (acorn harvest) from Les Très Riches Heures du Duc de Berry. Limbourg Brothers, Giraudon. c.1400. Condé Museum, Chantilly. Art Resource, NY.
11. *Mona Lisa*, da Vinci, 1503–1505. 30¼″ × 21″, Louvre, Paris. SCALA New York/Florence. Art Resource, NY.
12. *Ranuccio Farnese*, Titian, 1542. 35¼″ × 29″, National Gallery of Art, Washington, D.C. Samuel H. Kress Collection. Art Resource, NY.
13. *Marriage of the Virgin*, Raphael, 1504. 67″ × 46½″, Brena Gallery, Milan. Art Resource, NY.
14. *A Princess of the d'Este Family (Ginerva d'Este)*, Pisanello, c.1440. 16⅞″ × 11¾″, Louvre, Paris. SCALA New York/Florence. Art Resource, NY.
15. *Sistine Chapel Ceiling*, Michelangelo, 1508–1512. Art Resource, NY.
16. *Portrait of the Artist at His Easel*, Rembrandt, 1660, 111 cm × 90 cm, Louvre, Paris. Art Resource, NY.
17. *Lady Reading at an Open Window*, Vermeer, c.1658, 33¾″ × 25⅜″, Dresden Gallery. Art Resource, NY.
18. *Still Life With Crabs and Fruit*, Van Beyeren, c.1655, 98 cm × 76 cm, The Hague, Mauritshuis. Art Resource, NY.
19. *The Artist and His Family*, Jordaens, 1593, 71¼″ × 72¾″, Prado, Madrid. SCALA New York/Florence. Art Resource, NY.
20. *Back from the Market (or The Provider)*, Chardin, 1739, 18½″ × 14¾″, Louvre, Paris. Art Resource, NY.
21. *The Swing*, Fragonard, c.1765, 85″ × 73″, National Gallery of Art, Washington, D.C. Samuel H. Kress Collection.
22. *The Ford (or Il Guado)*, Lorrain. (date and dimensions not available). Louvre, Paris. Art Resource, NY.
23. *Majas on a Balcony*, Goya, c.1810, 76¾″ × 49½″, The Metropolitan Museum of Art, Bequest of Mrs. H. O. Havemeyer, 1929. The H. O. Havemeyer Collection.
24. *View of Toledo*, El Greco, c.1597, 47¾″ × 42¾″, The Metropolitan Museum of Art, Bequest of Mrs. H. O. Havemeyer, 1929. The H. O. Havemeyer Collection.
25. *Koelman Heaving in Coals by Moonlight*, Turner, c.1835, 36½″ × 48¼″, National Gallery of Art. Widener Collection. Art Resource, NY.
26. *The Gleaners*, Millet, 1857, 33″ × 44″, Louvre, Paris. Art Resource, NY.
27. *Georges Clémenceau*, Manet, 1879–1880, 37″ × 29¼″, Jeu de Paume Museum, Paris. Art Resource, NY.
28. *The Cathedral of Rouen in Full Sunlight*, Monet, 1894, 107 m × 73 cm, Jeu de Paume Museum, Paris. Art Resource, NY.
29. *At the Grenouillère*, Renoi, 1879, 73 cm × 93 cm, Jeu de Paume Museum, Paris. Art Resource, NY.
30. *Seascape at Port-En-Bessin, Normandy*, Seurat 1888, 25⅝″ × 31⅞″, National Gallery of Art, Washington, D.C. Gifts of the W. Averell Harriman Foundation in memory of Marie N. Harriman.
31. *Moulin Rouge*, Toulouse-Lautrec, 1891, 67″ × 47¼″ (poster). JOSEPH MARTIN/SCALA. Art Resource, NY.
32. *The Starry Night*, Van Gogh, 1889, 29″ × 36¼″, Collection, The Museum of Modern Art, New York. Acquired through the Lillie P. Bliss bequest.
33. *Still Life with Peppermint Bottle*, Cèzanne 1890–1894, 25⅞″ × 32¼″. Art Resource, NY.
34. *The Equatorial Jungle*, Roussean, 1909, 55¼″ × 51″, National Gallery of Art, Washington, D.C. Chester Dale Collection.
35. *Beasts of the Sea*, Matisse, (19)50, 116⅜″ × 60⅝″, National Gallery of Art, Washington. Ailsa Mellon Bruce.
36. *Women of Tahiti (or On the Beach)*, Gauguin, 1891, 27″ × 35½″, Jeu de Paume Museum, Paris. SCALA/Art Resource, NY.
37. *Still Life with Chair Caning*, Picasso, 1911–1912, 10½″ × 13¾″, Private Collection. SCALA/Art Resource, NY.
38. *New York City*, Mondrian, 1940–1941, 57″ × 45″, Lyme, Connecticut, Harry Holtzman Collection. Giraudon/Art Resource, NY.
39. *Japanese Ukiyo-e Woodblock Print*, Edo era (1615–1867). Daily activities, Japan. Art Resource, NY.
40. *African Mask*, Mossi plank mask. Art Resource, NY.